# Monastic Daoism Transformed

## The Fate of the Thunder Drum Lineage

by

Karine Martin

Three Pines Press                          EU Representation
St Petersburg, FL 33713                    R. Vencu
www.threepinespress.com                    Negoi 58b, Sibiu, RO-550275
threepinespress@gmail.com                  richard.vencu@gmail.com

© 2025 by Karine Martin

All rights reserved. No part of this book may be reproduced in any form or by any means, electronic or mechanical, including photocopying, recording, or by any information storage and retrieval system, without permission in writing from the publisher.

9    8 7 6 5 4 3 2 1

First Three Pines Edition, 2021
Printed in the United States of America
⊗ This edition is printed on acid-free paper that meets
the American National Standard Institute Z39.48 Standard.
Distributed in the United States by Three Pines Press.

Photographs by the author.
Cover art: Feng Xingzhao at Leigutai. Photograph by the author.

<u>Library of Congress Cataloging-in-Publication Data</u>

Names: Martin, Karine, 1974- author.
Title: Monastic Daoism transformed : the revival of the Leigutai lineage / by Karine Martin.
Other titles: Contemporary monastic Taoism
Description: First. | St Petersburg, FL : Three Pines Press, [2025] | Revised version of the author's thesis (doctoral)--Hong Kong, 2015 under the title: Contemporary monastic Taoism: process of revival of the Leigutai lineage. | Includes bibliographical references and index.
Identifiers: LCCN 2024041337 | ISBN 9781931483780 (paperback)
Subjects: LCSH: Quan zhen jiao--China--Ziyang Xian (Shaanxi Sheng)--History--20th century. | Taoist monasticism and religious orders--China--Ziyang Xian (Shaanxi Sheng)--History--20th century. | Quan zhen jiao--China--Ziyang Xian (Shaanxi Sheng)--History--21st century. | Taoist monasticism and religious orders--China--Ziyang Xian (Shaanxi Sheng)--History--21st century.
Classification: LCC BL1943.C55 M36 2025 | DDC 299.5/14657095143--dc23/eng/20240928
LC record available at https://lccn.loc.gov/2024041337

This book is dedicated to all the courageous,
innovating, and indomitable Daoists of China
who are giving their lives to this
marvelous, fascinating, and incomparable tradition,
making sure that it survives and flourishes
under all different circumstances.

Most dear to me among them
and most sincerely thanked are
Feng Xingzhao
Huang Shizhen
Liu Shitian
plus
all my teachers, friends,
and fellow students.

# Contents

| | |
|---|---|
| Acknowledgments | |
| Introduction: Reconstructing Daoism | 1 |
| 1. Political and Legal Context | 12 |
| 2. Issues of Transmission | 24 |
| 3. Temple Reconstruction | 55 |
| 4. Lineage Diffusion | 77 |
| 5. From Religion to Culture | 91 |
| 6. Social Relevance | 103 |
| 7. The Third International Daoist Forum | 115 |
| 8. From Revival to Survival | 125 |
| Conclusion: A Tradition Transformed | 135 |
| Appendix 1: The Lineage | 140 |
| Appendix 2: Timeline | 142 |
| Appendix 2: Maps of Temple Locations | 145 |
| Bibliography | 147 |
| Index | 169 |

# Acknowledgments

This book is the revised version of my Ph. D. dissertation, submitted to the Department of Religious Studies of the Chinese University of Hong Kong in 2015. It would not have been possible without the support of the faculty members at the Department. I am particularly grateful to my supervisor, Professor Lai Chitim, who offered wonderful encouragement and pertinent advice. The work would not have been created or grown without his incredible guidance. My gratitude also goes to the professors who sat on my Qualifying Examination Committee when this work was submitted as a dissertation.

Beyond that, I wish to thank Professor Vincent Goossaert who suggested that I pursue a Ph. D. at the Chinese University and whose research was a great inspiration.

In terms of material support, I am most grateful to the Chinese University, in particular its Centre for Studies of Daoist Culture, for providing continuous help, accommodation, and financial resources; and to the Shaanxi Academy of Social Sciences, especially Professors Li Jiwu and Fan Guangchun from the Department of Religious Studies, for providing invaluable support for my field work in Shaanxi province.

I wish also to extend my deep gratitude to the employees and directors of the Fungying Seenkoon temple: they provided unfailing support of my work from the moment I first arrived in Hong Kong.

Last, but certainly not least, I feel deeply indebted to all the Daoist masters who served as my guides of the Way during my many years in China and to Livia Kohn for editing the work and Three Pines Press for making it accessible to a wider audience.

# Introduction

# Reconstructing Daoism

"When I was young, my life was totally carefree; when I reached middle age, I was also carefree; now that I am nearly seventy, I am so busy! How amusing!" Thus said Feng Xingzhao 馮興釗 (冯兴钊, 1945-2023) on 5 October 2015, as he turned off his cell phone and headed toward his small bedroom to catch up with his meditation practice. He had spent the morning and the early afternoon answering the phone and receiving various local government leaders, juggling to provide solutions for the renovation and development of the various temples he managed in Ziyang 紫陽 county, Shaanxi.

During the Cultural Revolution (1966-1976), Master Feng witnessed his temple home being damaged and closed down. He himself was expelled and forced to return to his village to work and renounce his beliefs. Thirty years later, at age 69, he had become a well-known figure in the same county, respected by both locals and government officials for his contribution to the redevelopment of Daoism in the area.

Master Feng is a monk of the main monastic school of Daoism, the Quanzhen 全真 (Complete Perfection) order, founded under the Jin dynasty by Wang Chongyang 王重陽 (1113-1170). More specifically, he belongs to its dominant branch, called Longmen 龍門 (Dragon Gate) and named after a cave where Wang's leading disciple and succeessor patriarch Qiu Chuji 丘處機, aka Changchun 長春 (1143-1227), meditated and attained immortality. Having flourished for 900 years, the Quanzhen order with all its many branches ceased to function in 1966 when the Cultural Revolution led to the stoppage of all religious activities, the closure of temples and monasteries, the defrocking of monks and nuns, and the dispersal of congregations.

2 / Introduction

Religious activities legally resumed in 1979. In 1983, Daoism officially restarted with the registration of twenty-one key monasteries (Huang 2007). Thirty years later, there were 30,000 Daoist temples and 100,000 priests, including 30,000 Quanzhen clerics. Twenty-six provinces had Daoist associations as did 300 cities and counties.[1] Such an impressive resurgence did not happen without a supportive political, legal, and cultural context involving the central government and the Chinese Daoist Association (CDA) but also local and often unknown priests who shifted their practice focus from internal to external, from meditation to temple building (State Council 1997; Guojia 2008).

This book explores the various processes that allowed the redevelopment of monastic Daoism. It begins with the hypothesis that the revival required significant modifications at the structural and doctrinal level of the Quanzhen order. Only in this way could the organization adapt to the new social, political, and legal context. To document the development in detail, I present particularly the activities of clerics involved with a temple (daoyuan 道院) known as Leigutai 雷鼓台 (Terrace of the Thunder Drum), located on an isolated peak of the Qinling 秦岭 mountain range in Ziyang county, Shaanxi. It was named after the heroic feat of the legendary general Zhuge Liang during the Three Kingdoms period who led his troops to victory by sounding a big drum from this mountain. The work focuses on the period from 1979 through 2015 and centers on three aspects:

1) the process of the internal transmission of doctrines and practices of internal alchemy, following particularly the methods applied by a young nun named Jingyi 景一;

2) the rebuilding of temples and the revitalization of community, especially examining the activities of two masters, Feng Xingzhao and Liu Shitian 劉世天, who represent different approaches in their views and methods;

3) and the construction of a public image according to the new political context, as represented by the work of Liu Shitian and his attendance of the Third International Daoist Forum in 2014, a major event organized jointly by Daoists and the government.

My main approach is to define a broad general context of the revival process by observing a small section. The activities of Thunder Drum members, especially those of Liu Shitian, present a representative sample to identify the trends of development set up by the CDA and the government.

---

[1] The web page in Lin, Xie, and Li 2011 describes the press conference during the second international forum held in Nanyue by Master Lin Zhou 林舟, vice chairman of the CDA, who provided information on the situation of the development of Daoism at the time.

## Materials and Methodology

The work draws on three main sources of reference material: personal field observations, written materials used by contemporary Quanzhen clerics, and websites of the Daoist community as well as the government, including the CDA, to communicate both internally and with the world at large.

As regards field observations, I was a "participant observer" of Daoist monastic life for ten years, myself ordained as a ritual master of the Thunder Drum lineage. In this role, I was able to gather a great deal of information on religious and spiritual training within a close master-disciple relationship as well as in more formal training, such as the three-months-long advanced workshop for ritual masters organized in 2008 by Ren Zongquan 仁宗全 at the Dadao guan 大道觀 (Monastery of the Great Dao) in Wuhan 武漢, Hubei.

In addition, I also undertook the traditional practice of "cloud wandering" (*yunyou* 雲游), that is, moving through the country and staying at numerous different temples. Doing so, I was able to participate in the life of many institutions, both small hereditary temples (*zisun miao* 子孫廟), such as the one shown below, and major public monasteries (*shifang congli* 十方聰林; see Herrou 2005; 2013; Goossaert 2007).

In terms of contemporary print publications, I relied heavily on the journal of the CDA, *Zhongguo daojiao* 中国國道 (Chinese Daoism), distributed free to all Daoist temples in China. Within this journal, I focused mainly on articles published by Quanzhen priests as they provide a glimpse of the way they understand their doctrine today. In addition, I also made

# 4 / Introduction

use of websites run by Quanzhen masters or local Daoist associations, which provided articles or comments on their day-to-day realization and interpretation (*ganwu* 感悟) of the teachings.

Third, numerous websites have sprung up in the Daoist community. Most Daoist associations have their own, updating them regularly, as for example that run by the Shaanxi Daoist Association (Shaanxi sheng daojiao xiehui 2015). They provide information on current events, but also explain their ways of interpreting history and tradition. Beyond that, individual Quanzhen masters have their own blogs, such as the Thunder Drum cleric Liu Shitian (2008a; 2008c; 2009b) and the vice chairman of the CDA at the time, Huang Xinyang 黄信陽 (2008).

Two other types of websites provide a wider range of information. One is *Daojiao zhiyin* 道教之音 (The Voice of Daoism), which still covers most Daoist events and is updated regularly. Be it the latest opening ceremony of a temple, the renovation of a mountain hermitage, or the agenda and participants of a national meeting, this site has it all. It also provides videos of contemporary Daoists, talks and conferences, and a large selection of portraits of the most influential masters. However, it is always good to verify the information provided by comparing it to other sources and personally contacting their authors—masters, representatives, and journalists.

More online resources that present legal and administrative matters on the official level appear in the website of the State Administration of Religious Affairs (SARA) (see Guojia 2008; SARA 2014) and that of the law faculty of Peking University (Beida 2014). Beyond these, I carefully chose sites that officially represent one or the other local association or temple and always cross-examined the information they provided with personal knowledge and observations.

So far, studies of Daoism have rarely utilized internet-based references, but they are not to be neglected and are really essential in order to understand the trends of the current situation.

## Ethnography

Over the last twenty years, the ethnographic study of Quanzhen Daoism has emerged as a new academic field in China, with its own research centers, often established by temples of the order. The first to set up such a center was the Qingsong guan 青松觀 (Green Pines Temple) in Hong Kong in 2000. Since then, it has regularly sponsored publications and conferences as well as provided financial support for the creation of a similar institution at Huazhong Normal University in Wuhan and one at Shandong Normal University in Jinan 濟南.

Research on the Quanzhen order, including many studies in Chinese, Japanese, and Western languages, so far has focused mostly on its early unfolding. Works tend to explore the doctrinal and self-cultivation writings of the early patriarchs and examine the political and social history of the school (e.g., Eskildsen 2004; Komjathy 2007; Goossaert 1997; 2001; 2007). There are only few studies of its contemporary situation in China, most notably two books published by Li Yangzheng 李養正 (1993a; 2003), which provide information on the history of the CDA and the Quanzhen headquarters during and after the Cultural Revolution.

In Western academia, scholars have highlighted the paradigm of gradual modernization and secularization through the late imperial, Republican, and Communist periods. This paradigm describes the processes through which Daoist clerics, temples, texts, and practices moved into secularized institutions (Palmer and Liu 2012). The book *Quanzhen Daoists in Chinese Society and Culture, 1500-2010* (Goossaert and Liu 2013) was the first to focus on modern Daoism and its transformation in Chinese society and culture.

It contains one article specifically on monastic practice after the Cultural Revolution (Palmer 2013), which reconstructs American encounters with contemporary Quanzhen clerics and examines their self-cultivation regimens and techniques. David Palmer shows that the interest American practitioners take in pilgrimages to centers on Mount Hua 華, stimulates inspiration yest can also be a source of tension and even humiliation for the Daoists. This is because the encounter takes place in a context where Daoists pursue their long-standing efforts to reshape and yet maintain their religious identity, working under conditions of pervasive devastation of the tradition as well as restrictive central and local regulations.

The only thorough study on contemporary monastic Daoism is by the French ethnographer Adeline Herrou (2005; 2013). Her work explains how Quanzhen Daoists construct their identity through discourse, attitude, vestments, and ritual. Based on field work in a temple in southern Shaanxi, it offers a general depiction of life in a Daoist monastery, including the initiation process, by which aspirants to the priesthood leave ordinary life and enter the religious order. It also identifies the unique characteristic of their world, focusing particularly on their break with the kin-based organization of lay society and the establishment of an alternative set of pseudo-kinship relationships, designed to transcend gender divisions (see also Palmer 2006).

The aim of my work in this context is to study the process of revival over the past thirty years, utilizing both ethnographic and textual sources. It differs from Adeline Herrou's focus on identity construction within the order by looking more specifically at the social, political, and legal context of Daoism in China today.

6 / Introduction

# Textual Resources

Quanzhen texts go back far in history. According to Daoist doctrine, they began even before creation when, as the *Wuliang duren miaojing* 無量度人 妙经經 (Wondrous Scripture of Limitless Salvation, DZ 1;[2] trl. Bokenkamp 1997) says, "even nothingness was not yet." At that time, "during the ancestral eons of primordial beginning, in the highest heaven of Grand Network (Daluo tian 大羅天), in the midst of the inaugural azure realm," the Celestial Worthy of Primordial Beginning (Yuanshi tianzun 元始天 尊; shown on the left) revealed the *Wondrous Scripture*. Specified in the Qing-dynasty manual *Quanzhen bidu* 全真必讀 (What Quanzhen [Clerics] Must Read) as one of five major texts to recite during daily services, this work still features in the regular morning liturgy (see Paynter et al. 2020), which begins with a poem from it.

Another text recited frequently is the *Daode jing* 道德經 (Book of Dao and Its Virtue), dated to the 5th century BCE and associated with the sage Laozi 老子 who allegedly transmitted it during his emigration to the west. Riding his water buffalo, he was stopped by the border guard Yin Xi 尹喜 at the Hangu Pass 函谷關 west of Mount Hua and there dictated the scripture in 5,000 words. Under the influence of a descendant of Yin Xi, in the 5th century CE, this location was transferred into the foothills of the Zhongnan 终南 range. Later it became the site of the major monastery Louguantai 樓觀台 (Observation Tower), still active today.

Other important texts, as specified by the Quanzhen founder Wang Chongyang, are the *Qingjing jing* 清静經 (Scripture of Clarity and Stillness, DZ 620; trl. Kohn 1993; Wong 1995) and the *Yinfu jing* 陰符經 (Scripture of Hidden Correspondences, DZ 31; trl. Komjathy 2008), both of Tang origin, as well as the Buddhist *Xinjing* 心經 (*Heart Sūtra*; T 250-57)[3] and *Jin'gang jing* 金剛經 (*Vajracchedikā Sūtra; Diamond Sūtra*; T 235-37, 273; both trl. Conze 2001).

---

[2] "DZ" stands for *Daozang*, the Daoist Canon of 1445. Numbers refer to the annotated catalog in Schipper and Verellen 2004.

[3] "T" stands for *Taishō daizōkyō* (Great Canon of the Taishō Era), the standard edition of the Buddhist canon, published in Tokyo in the early 20th century.

In 1167, moreover, Wang Chongyang received secret transmissions from the immortals Zhongli Quan 鐘離權 and Lü Dongbin 呂洞濱, leading to the incorporation of ideas and texts of the Zhong-Lü tradition of internal alchemy into the Quanzhen system (see Kohn 2020). In their wake, a plethora of texts emerged, so that about sixty early works are still contained in the Daoist Canon of the Ming dynasty (Schipper and Verellen 2004, 412-21). They include poetry collections, discourses, recorded sayings, literary anthologies, hagiographies, and commentaries as well as monastic manuals, such as the *Quanzhen qinggui* 全真清規 (Pure Rules of Complete Perfection, DZ 1235).

Further anthologies and collections followed, until the 19th century, when Jiang Yupu 蔣予蒲 (1756-1819) received more teachings of Lü Dongbin through spirit-writing, and his disciple Liu Shouyuan 柳守元 compiled the *Daozang jiyao* 道藏輯要 (Collected Essentials of the Daoist Canon; see Esposito 2009; Lai 2021). To the present day, moreover, Quanzhen groups in Hong Kong worship Patriarch Lü and still receive texts through spirit-writing.

Scholars have worked hard to define Quanzhen on the basis of this extensive textual corpus, but the process has been arduous. They have identified about thirty-two texts works written or edited by the first generation of masters in the Song and Yuan dynasties. Especially Louis Komjathy has examined this set of works, using textual analysis along with methods from comparative religion, mysticism, and psychology. He says:

[This research is] from the perspective of comparative religious studies, specifically in terms of conceptions of self, religious practice, and comparative mysticism. Utilizing classical Chinese source materials from the early Quanzhen textual corpus, this study gives particular attention to textual, interpretative, and terminological issues. Here I examine Quanzhen views and practices in terms of conceptions of self, consciousness studies, psychology, embodiment issues, meditation, and mysticism. (2007, 2)

This contributes to our understanding of the tradition but does not resolve the issue of lineage construction and identity. As Vincent Goossaert notes,

Our lack of a fundamental text defining a Quanzhen identity is not an effect of faulty transmission. There was indeed no such thing as a specific Quanzhen scriptural tradition, because there is no Quanzhen revealed scripture. Of course, Wang Chongyang, later Quanzhen masters, as well as a number contemporary religious seekers not belonging to the order met with immortals and received from them poems and oral instructions. These revelations, however, were of a personal nature and were not meant to be the basis of a written tradition. . . .

8 / Introduction

The ultimate authority within the early Quanzhen order was not a fundamental text but the action and speech of the patriarchs and masters. . . .

The huge majority of Quanzhen literature is either performative or narrative: it proposes a detailed pedagogy in action, by exhorting adepts and telling the exemplary story of the order's patriarchs and former masters. It aims at convincing auditors and readers to join the order and imitate its patriarchs. As such, this literature can be considered a huge repertory of fragments of contextualized teachings that together form a Quanzhen lore. (2001, 120-21)

Kristofer Schipper echoes this:

The major problem with Quanzhen writings lies in their unsystematic nature. Quanzhen is not a revelation, and there is no founding scripture on which the whole tradition can be said to rest. The fact that the school produced no classic was considered a blemish by the early Ming theoretician Zhao Yizhen [d. 1382]. For a school with a deep sense of its unity and mission, the corpus left by Quanzhen is dispersed and heterogeneous. (in Schipper and Verellen 2004, 1130)

One text, though, the *Chongyang lijiao shiwu lun* 重陽立教十五論 ([Wang] Chongyang's Fifteen Discourses on Establishing the Teaching; DZ 1233; trl. Kohn 2003; 2004b; Komjathy 2008), has been considered a representative expression of the early movement, often cited as a general introduction to its key practices.

Another relevant text is the *Chongyang zhenren jinguan yusuo jue* 重陽真人金關玉鎖訣 (Master Chongyang's Instructions on the Golden Gate and Jade Lock, DZ 1156; trl. Komjathy 2007). It presents a technical discussion of early Quanzhen practice principles, training regimens, and models of attainment and is one of the most representative of its doctrine.

A further group of twenty-two texts, translated by Louis Komjathy (2013), form the backbone of slightly later Quanzhen doctrine, outlining "early Quanzhen as a twelfth-century Daoist religious movement in terms of its own beliefs, practices, goals, and ideals" (2013, 19).

A key scripture of the Qing dynasty is a work on monastic rules by the patriarch Wang Changyue 王常月 (1622-1680). The *Chuzhen jie* 初真戒 (Precepts of Initial Perfection, *Daozang jiyao* 278, 292; trl. Hackmann 1920; Kohn 2004a) begins by requiring ordinands to take refuge in the Dao, the scriptures, and the masters, then swear to obey sets of five and ten precepts. The latter specify, among others, that they should not "be lascivious or lose perfection, defile or insult the numinous *qi*." They should also avoid "ruining others to create gain for themselves and instead stay with their own flesh and blood," as well as abstain from "drinking wine beyond measure or eating meat in violation of the prohibitions."

A complementary work, the *Qinggui xuanmiao* 清規玄妙 (Pure Rules, Mysterious and Marvelous, *Zangwai daoshu* 361), similarly prohibits the consumption of wine and fancy foods, such as luscious mushrooms and meat, and punishes violations of this rule by caning and expulsion (see Yoshioka 1979; Kohn 2003).

Further texts of rules, including also the *Zhongji jie* 中極戒 (Precepts of Medium Ultimate, *Daozang jiyao* 293; trl. Hackmann 1931; Kohn 2004b) and *Tianxian dajie* 天仙大戒 (Great Precepts for Celestial Immortals, *Daozang jiyao* 291), are the subject of Monica Esposito's work (2014; 2016). She analyses the origin of each section in great detail and demonstrates that the more initial parts are strongly influenced by regulations of the Tang dynasty while the *Tianxian dajie* is a pure product of the lay spirit-writing tradition under Quanzhen auspices in the Ming. The latter in particular, as Livia Kohn points out, does not contain a list of rules. Instead, it gives general encouragements to develop wisdom, selflessness, and compassion. It also presents the text of the *Qingjing jing* as well as passages from the *Daode jing* and a number of other medieval texts, together with various holy verses (*gāthas*) and hymns of praise (2004a, 111).

Most Western studies, therefore, approach Quanzhen from historical, sociological, or comparative studies and describing its doctrines and practices in the light of transmitted scriptures. Only few studies have focused on its organization and role after the Cultural Revolution.

## This Book

This book remedies this. It examines how exactly the eradication of temples, the disappearance of old masters and scriptures, as well as the condemnation of religious practices as superstitious has impacted the order, how Quanzhen clerics have rallied after the official reopening of religious activities, and how they fare today. It divides into eight chapters.

The first presents the political and legal context of the revival process of monastic Daoism. It outlines the various national organizations involved, examines the specific regulations applied, and provides a legal definition of what a Quanzhen master is. It highlights just how the current legal doctrine of "freedom of religious belief" contributes to the revival of monastic Daoism, while the SARA exerts strict control on all religious activities.

Chapter two centers on the way alchemical knowledge is transmitted today, examining the training of a young Thunder Drum nun. During her years of cloud wandering, she not only received various textual materials but also encountered two hermits from the Zhongnan range who became her practice teachers. Examining her career, the chapter shows how the transmission of the doctrines and practices of internal alchemy, one of the

10 / Introduction

most important dimensions of monastic Daoism, embodies both continuity and change.

The third chapter concentrates on temple building. It analyzes how Quanzhen masters, traditionally recluses practicing internal alchemy in remote mountains, under current conditions came to redirected their efforts to rebuild the physical sites and institutional structures that were destroyed during the Cultural Revolution. It focuses particularly on the Thunder Drum lineage and the activities of Master Feng Xingzhao.

Following this, chapter four on "Diffusion Abroad" shows the impact of rebuilding in a wider context, focusing on the life and work of Master Huang Shizhen 黄世真 who first spread the tradition abroad and contributed to the founding of the British Daoist Association and other Western groups. It also outlines the temples rebuilt by Liu Shitian at the provincial level, presenting his biography and describing how he came to realize his projects.

The chapter concludes with a comparison of the two modes of rebuilding and revitalizing temples used by the old master Feng Xingzhao and the new master Liu Shitian. It shows a shift in the function of temples. Feng placed priority on developing temples as dwellings for the immortals and places of worship, while Liu put all his efforts into developing temples as centers of transmission of traditional Chinese culture and the development of tourism.

Chapter five discusses the various strategies of rebranding Quanzhen ideology and activities in order to adapt to modern society and the new political context. It highlights how Quanzhen clerics shifted their discourse from the religious to the cultural realm, changing their image from intermediaries of the gods toward transmitters of Chinese culture. It presents especially the activities of Liu Shitian, comparing them to those of the CDA and the SARA.

Chapter six, entitled "Social Relevance," outlines various activities Daoists have undertaken to make a positive contribution to modern society. They revived orchestras of Daoist music at various temples, making this expression of Chinese culture accessible to wider audiences to great acclaim. They engaged in charitable activities and donations, supporting the poorer segments of society. In addition, they came to support and spread methods of nourishing life—an important aspect of traditional practice—helping people recover and maintain their health. Beyond that, Daoists also engaged in ecological efforts, raising environmental awareness in accordance with their inherent honoring of natural processes. Plus, they established an online presence, fitting temples with Wi-Fi, constructing websites, and participating in social media.

Chapter seven focuses on the Third International Daoist Forum, held in 2014 on Mount Longhu 龍虎. I show that the revival processes described in the previous chapters at the particular level of a small lineage are a reflection of a general trend within Daoism at large, moving from the description of specific cases to more general observations. The Forum provides a window into the rebranding process of Daoism presented to the world by the CDA, the government, and the academia. Analyzing the content of the event is a way of understanding just how monastic Daoism was redefined as a tool toward the attainment of the China Dream, Xi Jinping's 习近平 dominant political agenda at the time.

Chapter eight, written in June 2024, adds supplementary information about the state of monastic Daoism in China today. It outlines the new policy of "sinicization," a government priority since 2016 that aims to make places of worship and religious teachings better reflect the ideals of Han Chinese culture and the Chinese Communist Party (CCP). Affecting all religions and executed with particular severity in Tibet and the Muslim region of Xinjiang, it involves restructuring doctrines and practices to tow the Party line while making many religious activities suspect and subject to persecution. Daoists as much as Buddhists try hard to comply, but the effects of the policy are nothing short of devastating, causing clerics to leave, temples to decline or close, and activities to cease.

# Chapter One

# Political and Legal Context

Since 1912, China has officially recognized five religions: Daoism, Buddhism, Catholicism, Protestantism, and Islam (Kim 2015, 27; Goossaert and Palmer 2011, 58). According to a 2007 Ministry of Education survey, there are 300 million Chinese believers: 200 million Buddhists, Daoists, and followers of traditional folk religion plus 40 million Protestants and Catholics. 62 percent of believers are between the ages of 16 and 39, and many live in the economically advanced coastal areas (Wu 2007; Kim 2015, 27). According to a study in 2012, the number of adherents of folk religion numbered around 578 million, that is, half the population (Yang and Hu 2012, 514).

## The Role of Religion

Religion in China has been the subject of various ideological debates, held by government organizations as well as academic institutions. For example, the Institute of World Religions of the Chinese Academy of Social Sciences expresses the government's position in its study of religion. Its director, Zhuo Xinping 卓新平, represents the mainstream interpretation of the role of religion in society today. In November of 2014, at the conference on "Religion in China Today: Resurgence and Challenge," organized by the Center on Contemporary China at Fudan University in Shanghai, he said that there are currently five major ongoing debates (Zhuo 2014).

The first debate is whether contemporary China needs religion at all, given its historical background and socialist reality. Many argue that "China is a secular state historically and culturally and does not need religion at all." Anti-religion movements in the early 20th century and during the Cultural Revolution smashed traditions and created doubt whether there was a place for religion in modern Chinese society. This led to the rise of several sets of dialogues in the 1960s, asking whether religions are merely superstition and, in the 1980s, questioning whether religion is a pervasive cultural phenomenon or just an "opiate for the masses," as described by Karl Marx.

The second debate focuses on religious culture versus cultural wisdom. Is the re-emergence of religion a sign of going backwards or of regaining cultural wisdom? Some argue that religious culture should be limited to religious sites only; others believe that religion is an intangible part of society's cultural heritage and, therefore, forms the foundation of the state.

The third debate centers on the complicated relationship between religion and politics. In the Chinese tradition, the relationship has always been one of "state dominated and religion subordinated." In contrast, Western societies promote a clear separation between church and state.

The fourth debate is on the significance of religion as an ideology or as a value system. This discourse is based on the ideological conflicts between religion and Communism. Religious philosophy revolves around theism and idealism, whereas communist ideology centers on atheism, materialism, and Marxism. Zhuo believes that there is tension between religion and a harmonious society. Some religious groups in China use the slogan: "Love the country, love the party, and love the religion."

The fifth debate deals with the relationship between religion and "hostile forces," "extremism," and "terrorist ideas." This discourse is connected to Christianity, understood in China as part of Western ideology and as challenging Chinese society and cultural heritage.

Zhuo thinks that the wave of "rediscovering the values of Chinese traditional culture brings hope to religions." It goes well with Xi Jinping's China Dream, as it rediscovers traditional values, belief systems, and ways of teaching and spiritual cultivation. Together they may bring a new perspective to bear on religion. Zhuo hopes that Chinese religions "may enjoy an objective and fairer view through the realization of the China Dream in social, cultural and political harmony," because the "expression of cultural beliefs brings understanding and tolerance of religions."

This suggests that the government attempts to reconcile two contradictory positions and thereby give an answer to the question of how, as representatives of a communist government, leaders can allow religious activities to flourish although their predecessors condemned them as useless and dangerous superstition. How can religion be useful to the development of socialism with Chinese characteristics despite having been considered an impediment just a few years earlier?

The result in an ongoing dance, in which each side tries to find an adequate position. On the one hand, religious groups present themselves as useful for the development of socialist society, matching government criteria of "usefulness." On the other hand, the government presents itself as a tolerant leader, allowing the presence of various religious groups by investigating the usefulness of their activities. They use religious organizations as venues to maintain "a harmonious society," that is, political stability.

14 / Chapter One

# Freedom of Belief

Until 2018, Daoism was regulated through ordinances handed down by the SARA (Guojia zongjiao shiwu ju 國家宗教事务務局), which even then worked closely with the Communist Party's United Front Work Department, under which it was later subsumed. The basic legal framework, described in terms of "freedom of religious belief," is outlined in detail in "The Situation of the Freedom of Religious Belief in China" (Zhongguo de zongjiao xinyang ziyou zhuangkuang 中國的宗教信仰自由狀況), a manfesto published by the State Council Information Office (Guowu yuan xinwen bangong shi 國務院新聞辦公室) in October 1997.

According to this, the religious beliefs of all Chinese citizens are protected by the constitution, and freedom of religious belief is considered a basic right to be enjoyed by all. The document further states that that no citizen may be compelled to believe or fail to believe by any particular institution or individual (State Council 1997).

The constitution says the same. In Article 36, it stipulates, "Citizens of the People's Republic of China enjoy freedom of religious belief," then goes on to say,

> No state organ, public organization or individual may compel citizens to believe in, or not to believe in, any religion; nor may they discriminate against citizens who believe in, or do not believe in, any religion.

It further assures that "the state protects normal religious activities" and emphasizes that "no person may make use of religion to engage in activities that disrupt the public order, impair the health of citizens, or interfere with the educational system of the state." In addition, it makes a strong point that "religious bodies and religious affairs must not be subject to any foreign domination."

Other legal agencies, be they concerned with regional autonomy, civil society, education, labor, elections, village committees, media, and more, similarly stipulate that all citizens, regardless of religious beliefs, have the right to vote and stand for election. They also assert that the legitimate property of all religious bodies is subject to legal protection, that education is separate from religion, and that all citizens—regardless of their religious beliefs—are to enjoy equal educational opportunities. They insist that the people of all ethnic groups should respect each other's languages, customs, and religious beliefs. In addition, the law protects citizens from discrimination in their employment because of different religious beliefs, and states that "no advertisements or trademarks shall include discriminatory contents against any ethnic group or religion" (State Council 1997).

## State Regulation

Within this framework, the SARA created a blueprint for all religious activities known as the Regulations of Religious Affairs (*Zongjiao shiwu tiaolie* 宗教事務條例). Each temple, church, mosque, and monastery must post it prominently on a wall near the entrance, visible to all visitors as shown below.

The Regulations consist of ten sections that cover the legal definition and implementation of various religious activities, including publications, education, center building, appointment of leaders, legal liability, etc. Headings are:

> General Provisions (Zongze 总總則)
> Religious Groups (Zongjioa tuanti 宗教團體)
> Personnel of Religious Instruction (Zongjioa jiaoshi renyuan 宗教教識人員)
> Sites of Religious Activities (Zongjiao huodong changsuo 宗教活動場所)
> Religious Activities (Zongjiao huodong 宗教活動)
> Religious Academies (Zongjioa yuanjiao 宗教院校)
> Religious Properties (Zongjiao cachan 宗教財產)
> Religious Foreign Relations (Zongjiao shewai wuju 宗教涉外務局)
> Legal Liabilities (Falü mairen 法律買任)
> Supplementary Provisions (Fuze 附則). (Guojia 2014e)

A recent copy from Shaanxi reads as follows:

16 / Chapter One

The term "religion" in these Regulations shall refer to Buddhism, Daoism, Islam, Catholicism, and [Protestant] Christianity.

Citizens enjoy the freedom of religious belief. Any organization or individual shall not enforce citizens to believe in or not to believe in any religion, nor discriminate against the citizens who believe in or those who do not believe in religions.

Their lawful rights and interests and normal religious activities shall be protected by law.

The people's governments at or above county levels shall uphold under law the lawful rights and interests of religious groups, religious activity sites, religion instructing personnel and citizens believing in religion, hear the opinions from religious groups, religious activity sites, religion instructing personnel and citizens believing in religion, coordinate the administrative work of religious affairs and lead the religion to adapt to socialist society.

Certain articles, moreover, are of particular relevance. Thus, Article 9 deals with congregations and activities in relation to the state. It says,

Religious groups shall conform to the respective articles of association to organize their religious activities, to deal with their religious affairs, to carry out their religious culture and academic research and exchange, to expand their foreign friendly religious communication, and to provide the education of patriotism, socialism and legal system for their religion instructing personnel and the citizens believing in religion.

Article 10 specifies the particulars of censorship and control of publications.

The internal data publications to be compiled and printed by religious groups and religious activity sites shall be subject to the approval by the administrative department of religious affairs of Shaanxi Province and shall obtain the printing permit to be issued by the administrative department of the press and publication of Shaanxi Province.

Publication of publicly released the newspapers, periodicals, books, audiovisual products, and electronic publications of religious kind shall go through the procedures according to the provisions specified by the state publication administration.

All personnel of religious instruction shall be granted a qualification certificate of religion instructing personnel by religious groups after the aforesaid cognizance and recording.

Article 12, moreover, keeps a tight lid on all activities and engagements that may take practitioners out of their home institution. It states,

When a person of religious instruction is invited to host or participate in religious activities outside his or her own region, but within Shaanxi province, the group or activity site to which he or she belongs, as well as the group or activity site located at the hosting place, shall report the general planning of the activities to local administrative department responsible for religious affairs of the cities with districts for record keeping fifteen days abbot to initiating the religion activity. (Guojia 2014e).

In other words, while officially religious activities are permitted, their scope and practical application are extremely limited and kept under tight state control.

This control also requires that any individual's belief must fit into the classification of the five officially recognized religions. In addition, to be legally recognized, all religious organizations must fulfill three criteria.

1) They must limit themselves to performing "normal activities," which allows the government to determine what is classified as "superstitious" and therefore illegal.

2) They must refrain from disrupting public order, impair the health of citizens, or interfere with the educational system of the state, which again gives the government leeway to curb religious activities.

3) They must be free of "foreign domination," which puts limits especially on Catholicism and can lead to possible charges of treason (State Council 1997).

According to the Regulations, moreover, all publications and journalistic endeavors must first be approved by local and provincial authorities, in some cases even the national SARA. All events open to the public are subject to official review, and religious leaders of high standing can only travel after receiving formal permission. Nor can they participate in events outside their district of residence unless they have received proper authorization.

The main agency, then, that communicates general guidelines and specific directives from the state and enforces them on the local level is the CDA (Zhongguo daojiao xiehui 中國道教協會).

## The CDA

The first Daoist association was created in 1912 in Beijing as part of governmental administration by the Baiyun guan 白雲觀 (White Cloud Monastery) abbot Chen Yukun 陳毓坤 (1854-1936), also involving supportive and influential lay followers (Daobei 2000). It followed an administrative model established by the founder of the Ming dynasty, Emperor Taizu (r. 1368–1399), who made all religious affairs subject to approval and control by the Ministry of Rites. Within this institution, all Daoist affairs were supervised by the Bureau of Daoist Registration, which had branch offices in each province (Bureaus of Daoist Institutions), each prefecture (Bureaus of Daoist Supervision), and each district (Bureaus of Daoist

Assemblies). In this way, even the most remote Daoist activity occurring in the empire could be monitored and controlled by an arm of the central government (Kohn 2001, 173).

The Republican successor organization was called Daoist Association of the Republic of China (Zhonghua minguo daojiao xiehui 中華民國道教協會) and represented first and foremost the Quanzhen order. Soon after, the Zhengyi 正一 (Orthodox Unity) or Tianshi 天師 (Celestial Masters) school created its own national institution in Shanghai under the direction of the 62nd Celestial Master Zhang Yuanxu 张元旭 (1862-1925). This was called Comprehensive Daoist Assembly of the Republic of China (Zhonghua minguo daojiao zhonghui 中華民國道教總會).

In 1957, they were replaced by the CDA that represented both schools and was formally established under government auspices and under communist guidance at the Baiyun guan in Beijing. Its first chairman was Yue Chongdai 岳崇岱 (1888-1956), a 26th-generation Longmen master from the Taiqing gong 太清宮 (Palace of Great Clarity) in Qingdao 青岛 (Fungying Seenkoon 2014b).

Over the years, Association members met regularly in Beijing, gathering as many as 324 representatives from all fifty-two provinces and electing two administrative organs: a Board Committee constituted of fifty-five to over 165 members, plus a smaller group of about twelve so-called executive members, one of whom would be elected chairman and another who would serve as secretary.

By 2015, nine meetings of national representatives had been held. The first occurred in 1957, when they established the institution. The second occurred in 1961, seeing the election of Chen Yingning 陳櫻寧 (1881-1969), a 19th-generation Longmen master from Shanghai (Fungying Seenkoon 2014a; Liu 1999).

During the Cultural Revolution, all religious activities stopped, and the CDA ceased to exist from 1967 to 1979. Its third meeting occurred under government guidance on 7-13 May 1980, convening a mere fifty-two representatives. Still, it was a milestone in the resurgence of Daoism, since it was the first meeting held after the reopening of religious activities.

At the time, Daoists gave priorities to the repair and reconstruction of temples, the preservation and reprinting of scriptures, the support of research centers, the training of new Daoist leaders, and the modification of regulations. They elected Li Yuhang 黎遇航 (1906-2002) as chairman, a Zhengyi master from Mount Mao 茅 near Nanjing, Jiangsu (see Yuan 2000).

Following this meeting, a Daoist College with a two-year training program with strong political content was established at the Baiyun guan in Beijing to ensure that the new generation of monks would receive proper education in both Daoist and official state matters. It ran its first class in 1982 and has continued since, leading also to the establishment of another similar training center for monks on Mount Qingcheng 青城 in Sichuan in the 1990s.

The fourth meeting was held in September 1986, bringing together ninety-seven representatives. It was the first to be organized within the walls of the Baiyun guan, following the temple's legal authorization to act as a religious center, granted two years earlier (17 March 1984). The meeting was an important turning point in the development of Daoism: for the first time, the CDA considered Daoist groups beyond their usual territory, proposing to create a relationship with Daoists from places such as Hong Kong, Macau, and various foreign countries (Li 1993b).

Representatives also for the first time discussed the establishment of a training course for nuns (Chen 1988). They described this as a first in modern history, one that could only have taken place thanks to the new society led by communist ideology and its active support of gender equality (Li 1993b). Sixty-two nuns from twelve provinces and twenty-two temples participated in the first training, held at the Baiyun guan in Beijing. A few years later, this led to the founding of the Kundao Academy at the foot of Nanyue 南岳, the sacred peak of the south, near Changsha 長沙, Hunan (see the photo below).[1]

---

[1] Courtesy of Robin Wang (2009).

At the fifth meeting, in 1992, Fu Yuantian 傅元天 (1925-1997) was elected chairman, a Quanzhen master from Mount Qingcheng. He was succeeded, at the sixth meeting in 1997, by Min Zhiting 閔智亭 (1924-2004) from the Baxian gong 八仙宮 (Palace of the Eight Immortals) in Xi'an 西安.

In 2005, at the seventh meeting, representatives elected Ren Farong 任法融 (1936-2021), a Longmen master from Louguantai in Shaanxi, then reelected him in 2010, at the eighth meeting (Huang 2006). The ninth meeting convened in 2015 and elected Li Guangfu 李光富 (b. 1955), a Longmen master from Mount Wudang 武當 in Hunan, who has held the leadership position since.

## Becoming a Daoist

The legal definition of a professional Quanzhen Daoist is based on the traditional liturgical definition of the term *daoshi* 道士 (Daoist priest). As Min Zhiting points out (1990), only after having gone through formal initiation, a ritual described as "taking the cap" (*guanjin* 冠巾), shown below in a picture of the Mingsheng gong 明聖宮 (Palace of Enlightened Sages) on Mount Li 驪, can an adept be called a Daoist priest.

This ritual is usually performed after a minimum of three years of training at a small hereditary temple. Adepts start out by choosing a place and a master for their training and attend a ritual called "bowing to a master" (*baishi* 拜師). This makes them formally disciples, so they can start learning the basic teachings in a close master-disciple relationship. After three years, they can undergo an initiation ceremony, during which the master brushes their hair into a topknot, presents them with cap and gown, and bestows a formal Daoist name upon them.

After this, they can either stay locally and serve a temple or enter a larger public monastery to increase their knowledge and learn the scriptures, rules, and rituals of other lineages. Initiations performed in hereditary temples are a prerequisite for all further training (Min 1990, 43-44), and public monasteries cannot take disciples who have not passed through the rite.

However, these larger institutions have the power to organize ordination ceremonies that involve the transmission of the three sets of formal precepts described earlier and make adepts into Daoists of higher rank. Taking precepts in formal ordination marks the highest level of attainment in the Quanzhen order.

The liturgical elevation of a person to "Daoist priest" through undergoing initiation forms the basis of the legal definition of a professional Quanzhen Daoist, accepted by all relevant government institutions involved in the regulation of religious affairs. The main document in this context is entitled "Specification of Daoist Professionals;" it was adopted on 20 September 2007 during the second board meeting of the seventh session of the CDA and promulgated on 4 March 2008 (CDA 2008). It clearly mentions that only a Daoist who has undergone a formal initiation ritual and obtained the appropriate "Certificate of Taking the Cap" (Changchun 2012) can be legally recognized as a professional Quanzhen Daoist. The equivalent in the Zhengyi school is the ritual of "Receiving the Registers" (*shoulu* 受籙).

Once the official regulation was in place, local temples all over the country organized initiation ceremonies. Many clerics, although they had worked in temples for years, had not passed through such a ceremony and were suddenly in danger of potentially being considered outlaws. To rectify this, both local Daoist associations as well as major public monasteries got actively involved in the process. In many places they set up large-scale initiations to legitimize the greatest number of clerics in the shortest possible time. Until 2018, similar ceremonies were performed regularly by various Daoist associations and in some public monasteries, but they have since been subject to greater restrictions.

For example, one of the most famous Quanzhen monasteries, the Changchun guan 長春觀 (Temple of Eternal Spring) in Wuhan, held an initiation on 18 May 2012 (Changchun 2012). The Baiyun guan in Lanzhou 蘭州, a major city in the far northwest, organized one on 1 August 2012 (Daojiao zhiyin 2012). Monasteries on sacred mountains similarly followed this trend so that, for example, the temple on Mount Song 嵩, the sacred peak of the center, organized them on an annual basis (Songshan 2013). Not to be left out, the Yuquan yuan 玉泉院 (Jade Spring Monastery) at the foot of Mount Hua, the sacred peak of the west, held a ceremony on 10 June 2011 (Ren 2011).

Typically, a master of "high merit" (*gaogong* 高功) of the temple would perform the initiation in the presence of the novice's main teacher. Having trained the candidate for at least three years and selected his or her Daoist name, he or she served as formal "ordination master" (*dushi* 度師).

The ritual itself began with the adept taking refuge in the Three Treasures of Dao, scriptures, and masters.

> With my body, I take refuge in the all-highest great Dao of non-differentiation.
> With my spirit, I take refuge in the venerable scriptures in thirty-six sections.
> With my life-destiny, I take refuge in the great masters of the mysterious center.[2]

He then would vow to honor the gods and take a set of five precepts: to abstain from killing any living being, consuming impure foods or intoxicants, lying, stealing, and engaging in perversion and depravity (Komjathy 2013).

---

2 身皈依太上無極大道. 神皈依三十六部尊經. 命皈依玄中大法師.

After that, the main body of the ritual consisted of an audience rite with the gods, during which a memorial was sent to the celestial administration to register the name of the novice. The master would brush his or her hair into a topknot, held in place by a wooden or jade pin, and places the Daoist cap on his head, most commonly using one of a design called Chaos Prime (*hunyuan jin* 混元巾; Herrou 2015, 51), and garb him in a long dark-blue robe. The novice then would pay homage and bow to all the deities of the temple as well as to his teacher, the various masters present, and his or her new Daoist brothers and sisters. The day concluded with the evening performance of a ritual for the salvation of the new cleric's ancestors as well as all orphaned souls.

According to Quanzhen lore, the tradition of this ritual initiation began with Qiu Chuji, the founder of the Longmen branch. It is still the only way to enter the monastic life (Min 1990; Ren 2006; Huang 2007b). The ceremony serves to from an alliance between the gods and the clerics. Humans swear to follow the precepts, while the gods commit to supporting and protecting them. All good deeds are rewarded, while bad deeds are punished by the celestial administration. In addition, the ritual cleanses the novice of his past and eradicates all sins, even those from before this lifetime.

All this is accomplished by the memorial or petition sent to the heavens that enters the novice's name into the registers of the Three Officials (*sanguan* 三官) of Heaven, Earth, and Water. Beyond that, he of she receives eternal protection from Wang Linguan 王靈官, the protective deity of all Quanzhen temples and clerics. Only after passing through this ritual may a person wear the Daoist outfit, be called a Daoist master, and will no longer pass through the hells after death (Goossaert 2007, 2).

# Chapter Two

# Issues of Transmission

Self-cultivation practice forms the backbone of Quanzhen Daoism, and particularly the system of internal alchemy (*neidan* 內丹). From the beginning, it has been shrouded in secrecy, its techniques communicated only to sincere disciples who, after severe tests and years of training, have reached a high level of ethical awareness and religious understanding.

As already pointed out by the Yuan-dynasty master Qin Zhi'an 秦志安, aka Shuli 樗櫟 (1188-1244), in his *Jinlian zhengzong ji* 金蓮正宗記 (Record of the Correct Lineage of the Golden Lotus, DZ 173, 2.2b-3b), the master imparts the secret way of perceiving the inner workings of creation and the transformations of the universe, then explains how they can be contained and developed within the adept's own body. This transfer of knowledge takes the form of "mind-to-mind transmission" (*xinzhuan* 心傳), also described as "mouth-to-mouth transmission" (*koukou xiangzhuan* 口口相傳). The overarching rule in all cases is that "the methods must not be transmitted among six ears" (*fa buzhuang liuer* 法不傳六耳), that is, remain limited to two people.

## Personal Connection

The prime Quanzhen text in this regard is the *Dadan zhizhi* 大丹直指 (Pointers to the Great Elixir, DZ 244; trl. Komjathy 2013, 115-68). In content, it inherits a great deal of early Zhong-Lü materials, using much of the same terminology and presenting similar stages and practices. It is attributed to the Longmen founder Qiu Chuji, but more likely dates from the late 13th century (Eskildsen 2004, 61).

The text emphasizes that the yin spirit, the rudimentary basis of the person, is useless for cultivation and methods associated with its development are not effective. The latter include particularly holding on to stillness and emptiness, associated with Buddhist meditation. Such techniques focus too much on the mind and neglect the body. Instead, practitioners should cultivate their yang spirit, working in close relation with all major forces of the person: physical reality or "life-destiny" (*ming* 命) as well as the various psychological dimensions, here called "innate nature" (*xing* 性). This is known as "dual cultivation of innate nature and life-destiny (*xingming shuangxiu* 性命雙修). The text says,

24

Through the above-mentioned practice of refining spirit to unite with Dao, of casting off the husk to ascend to immortality, accomplishment is reached naturally. For Buddhists, this involves entering *samadhi* in order to attain transformation through meditation. For Daoists, it means entering stillness in order to send out the yin spirit.

Both, however, become ghosts of the clear void; they do not become immortals of pure yang. Murky, unclear, and without manifestation, they accomplish nothing in the end. How can students commit such mistakes? They do not know [the alchemical process].

After refining vital essence to become the elixir, the pure yang *qi* is generated. After refining *qi* to become pure spirit, the perfect numen of spirit immortality transcends the mundane and enters the sacred. One casts off the husk and ascends. This is called "transcendence through casting off." Throughout endless generations, the methods for becoming a spirit immortal have not changed.[1] (2.8b-9a; Huang 2006; Komjathy 2013)

A similar system, combined with great emphasis on receiving proper oral transmission from a master, also appears in the *Weisheng shengli xue mingzhi* 衛生生理學明指 (Clear Explanations of Hygiene and Physiology ; trl. Despeux 1979), by Zhao Bichen 趙避塵 (1860-1942 ; portrayed on the right). He was the 11th master of the Wu-Liu branch 伍柳派 of Quanzhen, beginning around 1644 on the basis of Longmen background. He was also the founder of a subsect of this line, known as Heaven of the Immortals of a Thousand Peaks (Qianfeng xiantian pai 千峰仙天派).

According to him, internal alchemy centers on creating an immortal embryo and nourishing it carefully into maturity for three years. During this phase, one should avoid letting it exit the body through the Heavenly Gate (*tianguan* 天關) at the top of the head, since it would still be too weak, being mostly a yin spirit. Resting in the upper elixir field (*shang dantian* 上丹田) or Niwan Palace 泥丸宮 in the center of the head, it would take three years for the yin energy to transform fully into yang.

In other words, nourishing the embryo means strengthening the yang spirit. It is possible to allow it to exit from the body for short periods of time

---

[1] 右件鍊神合道, 棄殼昇仙, 功到自然. 此僧人入定, 以來坐化, 道士入靜, 以出陰神, 皆為清虛之鬼, 非為純陽之仙. 窅冥無像, 終無所歸, 學人何其誤耶. 殊不知鍊精為丹, 而後純陽氣生, 鍊氣成神, 而後真靈神仙, 超凡入聖, 棄殼昇仙, 而日超脫萬萬世, 神仙, 不易之法也.

## 26 / Chapter Two

and limit its excursions to short distances. As a result, it grows gradually stronger and eventually merges with emptiness or the void, that is, the ultimate pre-creation potency of pure Dao. Zhao describes the yang spirit as consisting of golden light, in overall appearance resembling the body of the adept. A miniature representation or alter ego of the Daoist, it can be seen by others. However, if the adept feels that a formless body leaves his corporal presence and cannot be seen by others, he or she is dealing with the yin spirit and is in a trance that is not unlike the dream state (Despeux 1989, 80-81).

Another major text in this context is the *Xingming guizhi* 性命圭旨 (Imperative Pointers to Innate Nature and Life-Destiny, *Daozang jinghua* 5; dat. 1615; see Darga 1999), which Zhao Bichen cites frequently. It notes,

> The yin spirit has a shadow but no body: it is what people call a ghost immortal. The yang spirit has both a shadow and a body: this people call a celestial immortal.[2] (4.19)

When the embryo leaves the body while still containing some yin, it is weak and can easily be attacked or destroyed by demons. Many texts warn against this danger and the illusions or psychotic illness it may cause (Kohn 2020, 63-64). Zhao Bichen specifically mentions that any advance can only happen through the secret transmission from master to disciple. He says,

> After ten months, the numinous embryo shines and suddenly exits, as the spirit is focused: the yang spirit ascends. However, the true formula for the exit of the embryo must be transmitted by a master. During oral transmission, the disciple's mind is filled with a mantra of six words.
>
> Then, from the ancestral cavity, the yang spirit can exit through the Heavenly Gate. As soon as it exists, one must bring it back quickly, so that external demons do not cause it any harm. One must work carefully for three years, then meditate in deep trance for nine years, and only then one can become a celestial immortal. (Despeux 1989, 135)

Zhao also wrote another text, the *Xingming fajue mingzhi* 性命法訣明指 (Clear Instructions to the Prescripts for Innate Nature and Destiny, *Zangwai daoshu* 26), where he explains the difference between the yin and yang spirits and outlines just how essential the support of a true master is.

> We have dealt with the creation of the yin and yang spirits as taught by competent masters. The yang spirit is firmly visible to people, while the yin spirit appears only as a shadow. When a practitioner reaches a high stage, if he has not received authentic instruction, he can only produce a yin spirit and will start to see the plane of ghosts and specters.

---

[2] 神則有影無形, 世所謂鬼仙是也.

Issues of Transmission / 27

If and when he creates a yang spirit, he can open of the temple gate [at the top of the head]. As long as this is closed, only the yin spirit can manifest. The opening of the temple gate, therefore, also ensures the realization of the six supernatural powers, the permanence of radiant heart-nature and the bright light of wisdom. . . .

From antiquity to today, it has been transmitted in person from patriarch to master by word of mouth. Never pass it on it lightly to others![3] (ch. 15-16; Lu 1970, 160, 162)

In other words, the practice of internal alchemy is intimately linked with the direct transmission from master to disciple or divinity to human, a great mystical event of divine potency.

## Divine Encounters

Early Quanzhen sources show that disciples can acquire knowledge of internal alchemy by one of four means: secret transmission in divine encounters, oral or mind-to-mind teachings from a master, textual studies, and personal experience. Whichever mode is applied, however, the transmission is always shrouded in secrecy and also closely connected to the idea of intense and hard trials as a prerequisite.

More specifically, the secret transmission through divine encounters often involves dreams of immortals or other divinities who explain methods and share their knowledge. Still common today, this goes back far in history. For example, as the *Miyu wupian* 秘語五篇 (Secret Teaching in Five Sections, DZ 173) points out, the Quanzhen school owes its inception to the 1159 conversion of Wang Chongyang through a mystical encounter with the immortal Lü Dongbin (see the picture below), followed in 1160 by his transmission of a secret formula in five sections (2.2b-3b).

These events were followed by numerous further secret transmissions throughout Quanzhen history (Eskildsen 2004, 102; Komjathy 2013, 33-63). A key figure in this context is the patriarch Wang Chongyang himself, who continued to appear to his disciples after his death to encourage and instruct. Yin Zhiping 尹志平, aka Qinghe 清和 (1169-1251), the leading disciple and patriarchal successor of Qiu Chuji, relates the following event in his *Qinghe zhenren beiyou yulu* 清和真人北遊語錄 (Recorded Sayings during the Northern Journey of the Perfected of Clear Harmony, DZ 1310):

---

3. 煉陽神陰神, 在師點傳耳. 陽神者人能見, 陰神者能人. 若修至此, 無真師傳授, 准煉陰神為鬼仙也. 煉者廟門開也. 若閉廟門陰神出也. 廟門開是六通. 心性常明, 輝輝不昧出慧光 [...] 由古至今, 祖師口口親傳, 不可輕傳於人.

One evening in my surroundings, I saw the Patriarch-Master [Wang Chongyang, who had passed away several years prior to this] with a child approximately a hundred days old seated on his knee. When I woke up, my mind had enlightenment; I realized that my Dao nature was still shallow.

Half a year later, I again saw surroundings similar to the previous ones. The child had already reached about two years in age. I awoke with the realization that my Dao nature was gradually growing, and later became aware that I no longer had any evil thoughts.

One year later, I saw the same surroundings again. The child was now three or four years old and was able to walk and stand by himself. After this, I no longer saw this. Thereby I realized that aid had come directly to me and that I myself had the means by which I could stand on my own.[4] (4.5ab; see Eskildsen 2004, 99)

Such mystical encounters are both a recognized and needed aspect of Longmen practice, typically seen as the result of self-cultivation sincere enough to move the sages. As the text insists, "What you hear in your ears and what you see in your eyes, to none of this you must become attached.

---

[4] 忽一夕夢境中, 見祖師膝上坐一嬰兒, 約百日許. 覺則有悟於心, 知吾之道性尚淺也. 半年復見如前境, 其兒已及二歲許. 覺則悟吾道性漸長, 在後自覺無惡念. 一年又如前境, 其兒三四歲許, 自能行立. 後不復見, 乃知提挈, 直至自有所立而後已.

Issues of Transmission / 29

If you train conscientiously the holy sages will aid you from the dark," i.e., without directly manifesting themselves (Eskildsen 2004, 102). The *Dadan zhizhi* in its concluding verse similarly emphasizes,

> When ordinary people try to speak about the Celestial Pivot,
> It can only be reckless speech because they are unable to know this.
> Sentient beings in the mundane world will not have clear apprehension
> Unless they meet Perfected who will explain what the Dao is and is not.[5]
> (Komjathy 2013)

Typically, the process involves an absorptive trance, deep meditation, or other state of mental receptivity, during which the adept is open to receive messages from the beyond. The encounters then commonly lead to new insights, a conversion toward a new level of identity. They also come with specific instructions and the revelation of knowledge. As Louis Komjathy notes,

> Adepts must recognize mystical encounters with immortals and other anomalous experiences for what they are: triggers for a conversion process, inspiration for greater commitment, guidance for deeper understanding and practice, and/or confirmation of successful training. . . .
> Mystical encounters with immortals thus were often triggers for a conversion process. It is also clear that the early adepts participated in the deification of their fellow practitioners and their incorporation into a Quanzhen cult of the immortals.
> In addition, the central importance of mystical encounters with immortals and anomalous experiences established models for the second- and third-generation adepts. In the lives of early Quanzhen adepts, such experiences provided spiritual guidance and support as well as signs of successful training. (2013, 227)

## Karmic Retribution

Whatever the means used for the transmission, be it mystical or in flesh, it always takes place in secret and must not be shared or transmitted widely. In a religion with the expressly stated goal to "save all living beings" (*pudu zhongsheng* 普度眾生)—a phrase commonly displayed in Daoist temples and found frequently in the literature—the question arises: Why keep the methods of salvation secret?

According to the early Quanzhen masters, one reason for this is the risk of accumulating bad karma for oneself and one's ancestors if sacred knowledge is transmitted to an unsuitable person. The *Dadan zhizhi*

---

5 凡流開口論天機, 只能狂說不能知. 世上眾生無鑑識, 及至逢真說道非.

repeatedly warns disciples of dreadful calamities if this taboo is broken, including repercussions for ancestors up to nine generations. It says,

> From ancient times to the present, there have been those among the highest perfected who carelessly transmitted the instructions, failing to keep them secret. Their ancestors up to nine generations forever suffer in the depth of the hells![6] (2.10b; trl. Komjathy 2013)

The degree of punishment, moreover, differs according to the level of potency of the methods wrongly transmitted. They divide generally in three levels—of lesser, intermediate, and highest completion—the latter two carrying the most violent forms of retribution.

Lesser completion involves various techniques that prepare adepts before they reach the refinement stage of the alchemical ingredients with its complex fire phasing. While the *Dadan zhizhi* hardly mentions them, other early texts, notably of the Zhong-Lü corpus, indicate that they support the accumulation and replenishment of the three internal treasures of the body—essence, energy, and spirit—the key constitutent forces of internal alchemy (Kohn 2020). Although working with more physical methods and leading only to a minor accomplishment, this level still brings joy, happiness, and longevity to the adept. As the *Dadan zhizhi* says,

> Not practicing according to the firing times and not engaging in internal refinement are methods of lesser completion. Through them, one can gain peace, joy, and longevity.[7] (2.11b)

Specific threats of retribution appear from the intermediate level onward, where adepts refine their vital cosmic energy ($qi$ 气) by guiding it through the so-called Three Passes along the spine and learn to circulate the five phases through the five organs in the torso, reconstituting themselves in subtler form (as shown below).

---

[6] 古今上真有輕傳而不秘者, 九祖永受地獄.
[7] 如不行火候, 不內鍊, 係小成法, 安樂延年.

Eventually this practice leads to the attainment of the status of an earth immortal, that is, someone who can live on this planet as long as he likes and then ascends at will into the heavenly realms. If an adept reveals the relevant techniques to unworthy people, he or she receives punishments that also apply to their ancestors.

> When the Three Passes along the back are connected, this is the reversion of the three elixir fields. When the five phases in the Central Palace [torso] are circulated and applied, we refer to this as their inversion. Doing this, you gradually reach intermediate completion, the way of eternal life and freedom from death. Once you reach this, we may speak of spirit immortals who traverse the earth. If you transmit this to unworthy people, the transgression will extend to nine generations. Be careful! Be very careful![8] (1.11b; Huang 2006)

The text clearly mentions that the methods of intermediate completion bring immortality but must under no circumstances be revealed to outsiders, not even to one's family members. In this context, the *Dadan zhizhi* presents a "Diagram with Instructions on the Five *Qi* Meeting the Origin and Refining Form into Greater Yang," and says,

> This relates to a method of intermediate completion that affords extending life and not dying. This method is extremely intimate, it may not be transmitted even between father and son. If you lightly disseminate it and allow distant relatives to look at it, you will meet with calamities and grave retribution. Be careful about this![9] (1. 18b; Komathy 2013)

The methods of highest completion, too, are transmitted only under strict rules of secrecy and should never even be mentioned in the presence of "inferior people." Attaining this level, adepts are able to leave their body in the form of the immortal embryo and attain full ascension to immortality. Here the *Dadan zhizhi* has a diagram on refining the spirit to a high level and notes,

> This is a method of highest completion, which involves casting off the husk and ascending to immortality. If it is discussed with inferior people, there will surely be obstruction and calamity. It is best to be attentive when speaking.[10] (2.1a)

---

8 背後三關通, 曰三田返復. 中宮五行運用, 曰五行顛倒. 漸入中成長生不死之道, 乃曰陸地神仙. 如傳非人, 罪及九祖. 慎之, 慎之!
9 係中成法, 長生不死. 此法至親, 父子不傳. 如輕泄及與契義觀者, 定主災橫及重危. 戒慎之.
10 大成法, 棄殼升仙. 如與小人說者, 定有橫災, 宜自謹言.

32 / Chapter Two

This highest level also involves some methods that bypass more elementary techniques and lead directly to immortality, which makes them particularly potent and even more hazardous to transmit.

> Make sure your perfect *qi* accords with the times as you circulate it. Carefully investigate the days and examine the hours as you undertake its cultivation. In one hundred days, *qi* becomes abundant and spirit manifests. [This indicates] that you will soon ascend to immortality, without stopping on [the level of] eternal life and freedom from death.[11] (2.2a)

To find the right kind of disciple, moreover, someone who is "worthy" as opposed to "inferior," Quanzhen masters designed a particular process of selection, examining potential candidates in various ways and testing their sincerity and authenticity. Several hagiographical records tell how the founder Wang Chongyang excluded the unworthy. As Li Daoqian 李道謙, aka Hefu 和甫 (1219-1296,) records in his *Ganshui xianyuan lu* 甘水仙源錄 (Record of the Immortal Stream of Ganshui, DZ 973),

> Because he frequently manifested extraordinary and divine features [*shenyi* 神異], people of the east [Shandong] came to follow him. He forged and purified those who were authentic and reliable, and excluded and purged those who were hollow and false. Refining them a hundred times, he punished and angrily insulted them. The unworthy fled.[12] (1.10b; Komjathy 2013, 45)

When the text speaks of "forge and purify," it means that the masters put prospective disciples through highly strenuous tests and selected only those worthy to receive their knowledge. This is a feature contemporary clerics are reminded of every day as they perform the morning and evening services, where they chant related materials (see Min 2000). Among early works, the *Zhong-Lü erxian biandan yi* 鐘呂二仙變誕儀 (Formalities of the Transformative Rebirth of the Two Immortals Zhongli and Lü, DZ 1070, *Daozang jiyao* 209) mentions that even the great immortal Lü Dongbin had to undergo ten trials before Zhongli Quan would accept him as his disciple (3.42b-3.59b). It says,

> He walked about in the Lu Mountains, where he encountered old man Zhongli, who taught him the sword techniques of the celestial immortals. After ten trials, he attained the great Dao of the golden elixir. Subsequently, he obtained the secret instructions on fire phasing from the Perfected Cui as documented in

---

[11] 當真氣隨時運轉, 當審日察時, 鍊之百日, 氣足神現, 將欲升仙, 非止長生不死.
[12] 亟顯神異, 東人畢從. 陶汰真實, 杜絕虛假, 鍛鍊百端, 捶楚怒罵, 餘鄙解散.

the *Ruyao jing* [Mirror of All-Penetrating Medicine,] and practiced self-cultivation to attain Dao.¹³ (Hudson 2007, 143)

## Activated Presence

Quanzhen liturgies frequently contain references to secret transmissions, mystical encounters, aptitude trials, and personal qualities that adepts should develop along the path. They are particularly found in the "precious invocations" (*baogao* 寶誥) of the patriarchs, recited daily as part of the morning and evening services, and here appear in the form of "allusions" (*diangu* 典故). Cryptic to outsiders, they are yet quite clear to the clerics as they represent stories frequently transmitted in oral tales, through paintings on temple walls, or in parallel verses (*duilian* 對聯) on boards and gate posts. In addition, the allusions are explained in commentaries to the daily liturgy (Min 2000).

But they are not simple. A single allusion may well relate to many stories that sometimes cover a patriarch's entire life time. In the case of the daily liturgy that contains precious invocations of the five ancestral patriarchs, the perfected of the north, and the five masters of the south, the clerics are reminded daily of the efforts it takes to cultivate oneself successfully. Thus, the *Lüzu baogao* 呂祖寶誥 (Precious Invocation of Patriarch Lü; Min 2000) contains the expression "awakening through the yellow millet dream" (*huangliang mengjue* 黃梁夢覺).

---

¹³ 縱步遊廬山,遇鍾離翁,授天仙劍法,又十試而授金丹大道,續得崔眞人入藥,鏡火候秘旨修行成道.

This refers to Lü's first meeting with Zhongli Quan, whom he encountered in an inn when returning from a failed attempt at the imperial examination (see the image above). While the millet was cooking, he dreamt his entire official career, awakening not only to his evening meal but also to the realization that worldly attainments were fleeting and short-lived. He fully appreciated the emptiness of all ambition and duly abandoned his official aspirations to follow his new master into the mountains and toward cultivation of Dao.

In the case of the Longmen patriarch Qiu Chuji, the "Qizhen Baogao" 七眞寶誥 (Precious Invocation of the Seven Perfected; Min 2000), contained in the *Taishang xuanmen gongke jing* 太上玄門功課經 (Highest Scripture of Official Services of the Gate to the Mystery, *Daozang jiyao* 263; trl. Paynter et al. 2020), contains the expression "six years in Panxi and seven years in Longmen" (*Panxi liunian Longmen qizai* 磻溪六年龍門七載, 1.11b). This refers to the fact that Qiu undertook six years of intense training on Mount Panxi and seven years of self-cultivation in the Longmen cave. In other words, a mere eight Chinese characters tell of significant experiences of a lifetime.

The most famous of stories transmitted liturgically are also available in pictures. The allusion to the yellow millet dream is depicted in most halls devoted to Lü Dongbin, such as, for example, on the walls next to the doors of the main hall in Louguantai, in the headquarters temple of Baiyun guan, and at the famous Yongle gong 永樂宮 (Palace of Eternal Bliss), Lü's major sanctuary. Similarly, allusions to the hardships of Qiu Chuji are visually represented in a temple called Longmen dong 龍門洞 (Dragon Gate Grotto), built below the entrance of the cave where he practiced so assiduously. It also contains a rounded stone that Qiu would push up the mountain over and over again to discipline his mind and improve his perseverance.

All this indicates that, according to the textual corpus of the early Quanzhen masters, and especially the Seven Perfected (shown above), the transmission of knowledge is a secret process that involves mystical encounters with immortals and advanced masters, whether dead or alive. An initial inspiration or first encounter of conversion to Dao usually happens without trials. After that, however, trials take place to verify the aptitude of the student. Only after he or she has demonstrated perfect ethics, a charitable heart, and deep sincerity in the quest can the disciple receive the secret techniques of self-cultivation and internal alchemy. This pattern is safeguarded by the firm conviction that any transmission of esoteric knowledge to an unworthy person causes the accumulation of bad karma for oneself and one's relations, including both ancestors and descendants.

The views formulated in the early corpus are still very much part of the contemporary monastic tradition. Clerics today hold on firmly to the idea that trials are necessary and that secrecy is essential. Thus, the recluse Master Hou on a snowy day in December 2006 transmitted an important aspect of internal alchemy to me after I had climbed the steep mountain in the middle of winter to visit him. Since he had made a vow not to speak, he drew a few characters in the snow to pass on his explanation. As the snow melted, the writing vanished, but the teaching lived on.

The overall reticence toward teaching and the pervasive "culture of warnings," then, are apparent in the textual corpus of the early masters as widely reprinted and distributed. Its spread is easily attested by the contents of the publications of official Quanzhen institutions, such as the Baiyun guan. For example, many contemporary writings including journals such as *Zhongguo daojiao* and relevant websites cite the early classic *Dadan zhishi*. The full version of the text, moreover, is included in the *Xiudao yangsheng zhenjue* (Perfect Instructions of Cultivating Dao and Nourishing Life) by Huang Xinyang (1993), a major contemporary resource by a former Baiyun guan abbot.

The transmission of this culture, shrouded in obscurity and formulated in allusions, also takes place through oral stories, murals, paintings, and parallel verses in the monastic living environment. The most vibrant and most frequently activation is in the regular recitation of the precious invocations of the patriarchs as part of the daily services.

However, there is one major exception to the secrecy rule: the wide and open teaching of concept and practices in regard to methods of "nourishing life" (*yangsheng* 養生).

## Leaving the Mountains

In July 2014, the following electronic poster appeared on my Facebook page:

> Singapore Daoist College Talk on Nourishing Life: 21st generation Quanzhen Longmen master Zhang Zhishun 張至順, over a hundred years old, transmits the secret knowledge of the ancestral patriarchs that he received in mind-to-mind transmission. 14 August 2014. FREE. Book early. Seats are limited."[14]

Zhang Zhishun (1902-2015) was no stranger to me. I had met him briefly during a Daoist event in Hong Kong a few years earlier. He stood out as soon as I entered the room where the celebration lunch was held, mainly because of his demeanor: fully present and vibrant, he yet remained untouched by all the noisy activities. I had no way to guess his age as the twinkle in his eyes showed the liveliness of an eighteen-year-old.

---

[14] https://www.facebook.com/112716535479925/photos/a.112978558787056.26731.1127 1 6535479225 /666612173423689/?type=1&theater

In the 2010s, Zhang Zhi-shun came to do what the Quanzhen order calls "leaving the mountains to spread the Dao" (*chushan xingdao* 出山行道). According to the hermit tradition,[15] one "enters the mountains" (*jinshan* 進山) to develop personal expertise and cosmic wisdom, then leaves them again to transmit this when the world is ready and in need, leading ideally to alternate periods of entering and leaving the mountains.

This certainly holds true for Zhang Zhishun. He left his family to become a Daoist at age eighteen in 1930, residing first in the Biyun'an 碧雲庵 (Hermitage of Azure Clouds) on Mount Banjie 半截 in Huazhou 華州, Shaanxi. There he "entered the mountains" under the tutelage of Liu Mingcang 劉明蒼. In 1955, he left his seclusion to share his knowledge and took the position of guest prefect (*zhike* 知客) at the Baxian gong in Xi'an, the major monastery dedicated to the Eight Immortals.

In the early 1960s, when the political climate changed, he went to hide in the Zhongnan range and stayed out of sight for twenty years. As religious activities reopened, he left the mountains again and, in 1982, came to serve as abbot (*fangzhan* 方丈) at the key institution of Louguantai in the foothills of the Zhongnan mountains, where the *Daode jing* was transmitted. At this time, Zhang contributed to the development of Daoism by rebuilding temples and holding various official positions in the local Daoist association. In 1998, he went into the mountains once more and stayed in seclusion for ten years. He emerged again in 2008 and since them has spent his time between the Zhongnan range and the Yuchan gong 玉蟾宮 (Palace of the Jade Moon) on the island of Hainan 海南 (see Mi 2012; 2013; Zhang 2014).

By 2014, he was widely respected in the Quanzhen community who bestowed numerous honorific titles upon him, not only making him honoorary abbot of the Baxian gong and abbot of the Yuchan gong, but also recognizing him as a "living divine immortal" (*huo shenxian* 活神仙). Resid-

---

[15] For the hermit tradition in Chinese history, see Berkowitz 1989; Vervoorn 1990. For hermits in contemporary China, see Porter 1993. As regards Daoist hermits, I rely on my field work among Quanzhen master I met on various sacred mountains.

38 / Chapter Two

ing mainly on Hainan, he yet frequently visited temples in all sorts of places—including Singapore—to teach seminars to both clerics and lay followers. Many of them became available, free of charge, through video recordings posted on the internet, especially on YouTube. As he and his staff made ample use of modern technology, he reached a very broad audience—as many as 70,000 viewers—more than any other hermit in the Quanzhen tradition, making a major impact during his time in the world.

I first heard the expression "leaving the mountains to spread the Dao" in the Baxian gong in 2007, a few days before the First International Daoist Forum with focus on the *Daode jing*. While spending a day at the temple as I would often do, I was surprised to notice many Daoists who sported long beards and ample robes and were full of rather striking glances. When I asked some of them who they were, they remained enigmatic, just stating that they were from "the heavenly halls" (*tiantang* 天堂), had emerged from "deep within the mountains" (*shanli* 山里), or were "wandering like the clouds all over the four seas" (*yunyou sihai* 雲游四海).

Finally, I turned to one of the resident monks for an answer. He said, "They are hermits who have left the mountains to check if the world is ready for their teachings. They heard of the International Forum on the *Daode jing* and saw it as a good sign."

"But how did they hear of the Forum if they live deep in the mountains?" I asked, astounded.

With a smile, he simply pointed to the white clouds floating by above. Later that day, when I managed to get better acquainted with some of the mystery men, they gave me the same answer.

Among Quanzhen masters who chose to make a public appearance at the time were also two old monks I had known for years. They, too, had decided to leave their quiet mountain refuges to come and check out the current situation: they had not set foot into Xi'an in ten years.

## Spreading the Dao

Zhang Zhishun, too, must have seen promising signs around that time, since he officially started his public activities shortly after the Forum. He taught various techniques under different names, including "secretly transmitted Daoist practices for nourishing life" (*daojia michuan yangsheng gong* 道家秘傳養生功), "diamond practice in eight steps" (*babu jingang gong* 八步金剛功; shown below), and plain old "longevity techniques" (*changshou gong* 長壽功). All these he himself had received in secret instruction from his master.

In the preface to his book on the diamond practice, published under his Daoist honorific Mi Jingzi 米晶子, he provides information on the origin of the method and his motives for spreading it. He says,

The diamond practice of longevity is known to only few people, since it is a method transmitted to one person per generation. Because it was taught through oral transmission with no written records, ordinary people in society do not know it. Even within the Daoist community, it does not circulate.

When I was seventeen, I encountered my master Liu Mingcang on Mount Hua. I left my family and inherited this practice from him. By practicing for eighty-four years without interruption, I have come to deeply appreciate it and have reached an age of well over a hundred.

Through the transmission of this method from my master, I was granted the great favor of heaven to have a strong body and be in good shape. I now use this to develop Daoist culture in my homeland, opening it to the descendants of the Fiery and Yellow Emperors. I hope to enhance the prosperity of all of human civilization, to bring blessing and longevity. In all this, I abide to follow the tradition of the ancestral masters.

On this basis, I have decided to pass on the knowledge from one generation to the next without interruption, to share what was traditionally only bestowed upon one person per generation, a method transmitted in secret. I have dedicated ten years of my experience to compile this work and thereby spread the method to the world. The goal is to support all beings and give to them in charitable deed. I pray that the ancestral masters nod and smile and help me to attain the great Dao.[16] (Mi 2013, preface)

---

[16] 金刚长寿功为历代单传之功法, 知者甚少. 由于历代皆是口传, 無文字留下, 社会上尚無此功法, 即便道友中亦無流传. 吾十七岁于华山遇師刘明苍而出家, 承传此功, 八十四载习练不辍, 获益殊深. 今虽年居百岁有余, 因得師之法, 又承天施大恩, 体格还

In another work, he similarly says,

> The eight forms of the southern lineage also known as diamond practice is a method of nourishing life developed in traditional Chinese Daoism. Each form connects to a profound theory of strengthening the body and enhancing overall health.
>
> It involves reaching harmony between heaven and humanity, working with the dual cultivation of innate nature and life-destiny, and finding a balance of yin and yang. Practicing it will expel disease and increase longevity. Because it was only transmitted to one person per generation orally from master to disciple, very few know of it.[17] (Zhang 2014)

In other words, Master Zhang received originally secret knowledge in the traditional way, then broke the mold and came to transmit it widely by any means available.

As a traditional hermit of the Quanzhen order, he acquired his expertise through mind-to-mind transmission from his master after having spent many years by his side and demonstrating both his commitment and sincerity. He integrated the knowledge transmitted by practicing internal cultivation (*neixiu* 内修) or internal mastery (*neigong* 内功) for over ninety years, many of which he spent isolated in the mountains. Whenever he left his seclusion, he would join the monastic community to develop "external cultivation" (*waixiu* 外修) or external mastery (*waigong* 外功) by rebuilding temples and getting involved in the local Daoist association.

Then, however, when the time came to transmit the knowledge he had originally obtained secretly and personally, he chose to open it to the public, including numerous people he never met or would ever meet. Using the means of modern technology, he transitioned from personal interaction to internet broadcasting. His training sessions usually lasted a week and were open to anyone. Even today, his books are readily available on sites like Amazon, and one of them (Mi 2012) even contains texts on internal alchemy with plain explanations, making its extremely obscure symbolical language accessible to all.

This means that, unlike himself in his early years, people today can acquire esoteric Daoist knowledge without having to demonstrate their commitment, undergoing strenuous trials, leaving society, or being for-

---

算硬朗. 为弘扬祖国道教文化, 为炎黄子孙乃至全人类的文明昌盛、福寿康宁, 遵循祖师"代代传, 不能断"之遗训, 将此单传口授之秘法, 结合自身数十年修炼之心得, 整理成文, 公诸于世, 以期对众生作微薄贡献, 使功德更大圆满. 愿历代祖师颔首微笑, 助我修成大道也. 中国道教全真龍門派第二十一代米晶子.

17 南宗八式即金刚功是中国道教传统养生法, 它每一招每一式都暗含着强身健体的玄机, 以达到天人合一、性命双修、陰阳平衡、祛病健身、延年益寿的目的. 由于历代皆是单传, 师承口授, 故知之甚少.

mally ordained into a religious order. The length of training, too, changed considerably: what took years before is now compressed into weeks or months. In the 21$^{st}$ century, that is to say, the transmission of esoteric Daoist knowledge has morphed from a tight master-disciple relationship to an open, loose connection that does not even require physical presence, but can be established through various distance media, such as print, video, or internet.

## Distinct Modes

During his lifetime, Zhang Zhishun worked with two distinct modes of transmission: the traditional way based on a series of trials, a close personal relationship with a master, and the secret mind-to-mind transmission, limited to one person per generation; plus, the new way of utilizing various means of communication and spreading the teachings to large numbers of people, often with no personal or direct connection. However different the two modes seem, what can they possibly have in common?

Studying Zhang's writings and activities, it appears that for him the goal remained the same and only the modality has changed. The original goal was to protect the continued presence of the knowledge, which in Daoist cultivation was best done by practicing the techniques with dedication and authenticity. This was why the traditional way of transmission was established; is also key to the modernized mode.

However, they go about it differently. Traditionally, the key was to keep things secret in order to protect the knowledge from dilution and keep it pure and correct. The idea was that only a few chosen ones were truly able to understand the deeper meaning of the practices and were thus privileged to have access and receive the authorization to transmit. Today the open and wide transmission is another way of protecting the knowledge, but the focus is on keeping it alive, preventing it from being lost and going extinct. The motive behind this transformation has to do with a change in external circumstances: the holders of secret knowledge almost disappeared completely during the Cultural Revolution. Those few still left today carry the responsibility of passing it on before it is lost forever.

Thus, Zhang Zhishun notes that he feels "pressured to transmit the knowledge widely to avoid its loss" (Mi 2013, preface). He has the urgent sense that time is running out, so that he, a rare centenarian carrier of esoteric knowledge, until the end of his life never tired of teaching, sharing, and transmitting, continuously on the go and incessantly active. This sense of responsibility and emergency is also manifest in his writings, where he insists that "the way of knowledge transmission must shift from passing it on to a single person (*danchuan* 单傳) to passing it on from one generation to the next without interruption" (*daidai chuan buneng duan* 代代傳不能斷).

42 / Chapter Two

This applies most vividly to the methods of nourishing life, but also to the practices of internal alchemy and even to the procedures of Daoist ritual.

The question then arises whether this shift has an impact on the quality and content of the teachings. Recent publications of contemporary Quanzhen leaders as well as by Zhang Zhishun himself tend to place nourishing life and internal alchemy in close proximity—quite contrary to the traditional way. Does this mean that the new mode of transmission comes with a shift in content? Or it is just a shift in vocabulary?

## Nourishing Life

Nourishing life and internal alchemy traditionally are two different types of Daoist cultivation, each with their own specific terminology, practice goals, and sets of techniques. The methods of nourishing life are usually presented as representing a lower level within the sequence of the overall transformation toward immortality, while internal alchemy designates more advanced and specialized methods. Although most definitely not equivalent, they have been increasingly conflated.

One example is a highly popular work, Huang Xinyang's *Xiudao yangsheng jue*. Published in 1993, it contains Daoist texts from the Song to the Qing dynasties. Reprinted numerous times by the Baiyun guan and elsewhere, notably at the Fungying Seenkoon 蓬瀛仙館 temple in Hong Kong, the work is distributed free of charge, making it widely available both within monasteries and among the general public.

In his foreword, Huang mentions that the knowledge Daoists have acquired in the field of enhancing health and nourishing life over the millennia makes an important contribution to the healing and life extension of all human beings (1993, 3). He thus compiled this book "to introduce nourishing life techniques as undertaken by Daoist perfected from different historical periods and to present relevant texts of reference for the study of internal alchemy" (1993, 5).

Although the book claims to focus on nourishing life, as documented in its very title, the term *yangsheng* itself does not appear in any of the texts he presents nor does he include any of the most representative texts of the nourishing life tradition (see Engelhardt 2000; Kohn 2012). None of his selections contain methods typically associated with nourishing life, such as herbal remedies, self-massages, breathing techniques, healing exercises (such as those shown below), stretches, or sexual hygiene.

On the contrary, the works he selects focus on cultivating the "golden elixir" (*jindan* 金丹), a term used over a hundred times, on becoming an immortal (*chengxian* 成仙), an expression found fourteen times, and on "merging with Dao" (*he-dao* 合道), a phrase that appears thirteen times. All these are characteristic of internal alchemy, which traditionally encompasses quite a different set of parameters from nourishing life.

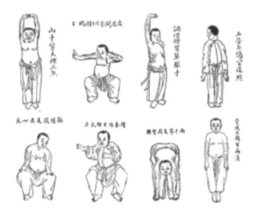

More specifically, nourishing life is defined as strongly rooted in the methods of Chinese medicine. Scholars and practitioners generally agree that it involves a set of specific techniques used mainly to restore and enhance physical well-being. Catherine Despeux in *The Encyclopedia of Taoism* defines it as follows:

> The idea of "nourishing" (yang 養) is prominent in Chinese thought: one can nourish life (yangsheng 養生), innate nature (yangxing 養性), the physical form (yangxing 養形), the whole person (yangshen 養身), the will (yangzhi 養志), and the mind (yangxin 養心).
> The term *yangsheng* designates techniques based on the essence, the inner or outer breath, and the spiritual force (*jing, qi, shen*). These techniques are grounded in physiological, psychological, and behavioral principles and include healing exercises (*daoyin* 導引), massage (*anmo* 按摩), breathing (*fuqi* 服氣), sexual hygiene (*fangzhong* 房中), diets (*bigu* 避穀), healing, meditation and visualization, and rules of daily behavior. (2008, 2:1148-49)

Historically the term *yangsheng* appears first in the *Zhuangzi* 莊子 (Book of Master Zhuang; trl. Watson 1969; Graham 1981) of the early 3rd century BCE, most prominently in the title of chapter 3, "Yangsheng zhu" 養生主 (Mastery of Nourishing Life). The work contrasts nourishing life with nourishing the physical form and maintains that the best way is to "depend on the celestial principle," relegating bodily techniques to a minor level. In chapter 19, the text again notes that methods of nourishing the body are insufficient for attaining immortality. The *Huainanzi* 淮南子 (Book of the Prince of Huainan; trl. Major et al. 2010) from the middle of the 2nd century

44 / Chapter Two

BCE also considers the techniques of nourishing life inferior because they require external support.

Health practices both for rehabilitation and prevention flourished during the Han dynasty, as is most evident from a collection of manuscripts unearthed from a tomb at Mawangdui 馬王堆 near Changsha, Hunan, which was closed in 168 BCE. They emphasize sexual hygiene, dietary methods, the internal guiding of vital energy, and breath control (see Harper 1998). During the Six Dynasties, many new writings appeared in medical, Daoist, and philosophical writings, enhancing the overall culture of caring for body and health and bridging the gap between different segments of the educated elite (see Kohn 2012).

People at the time were aware of the difference between methods for the attainment of immortality, mostly working with operative or external alchemy, and those of nourishing life, centered on internal and immediate physical transformation. The would-be alchemist Ge Hong 葛洪 (283-343), in his well-known *Baopuzi neipian* 抱朴子內篇 (Inner Chapters of the Master Who Embraces Simplicity, DZ 1185; trl. Ware 1966) established a distinction between inferior techniques and those that aid the attainment of immortality. According to him, nourishing life methods are complementary and work in a system of gradation.

In his wake, nourishing life was described as a set of methods to enhance and maintain health. The aim of the methods was prophylactic and therapeutic, as described in one of the most influential works of the 4th century, the *Yansheng yaoji* 養生要集 (Essentials of Nourishing Life; trl. Stein 1999). Later masters also integrated certain Buddhist techniques related to concentration on breathing and yoga-style movements and added greater importance to stillness of mind and meditation.

In the Sui and Tang dynasties, most methods centered on healing exercises and breathing techniques, strongly connected to medical circles as expressed in the works of the famous physician, Daoist, and alchemist Sun Simiao 孫思邈 (fl. 673). Among Daoists, they also revolved on breathing but with a more transcendental goal, as can be seen in Sima Cheng zhen's 司馬承禎 (647-735) *Fuqi jingyi lun* 服氣精義論 (Essay on the Essential Meaning of the Absorption of *Qi*; trl. Engelhardt 1987; Kohn 2012).

# Internal Alchemy

Internal alchemy, on the other hand, was first formulated as a comprehensive system in the Song dynasty, and soon thereafter its terminology and methods began to enter the nourishing life tradition. As more and more literati engaged in these fields, moreover, there was an increased integration, and about twenty books on the subject were published. This trend continued under the following dynasties, with more Confucian and ethical elements being added into the mix, leading to the notion of the integration of the three teachings, that is, the syncretism of Daoist, Buddhist, and Confucian notions (Despeux 2008).

Daoist scholars discriminate clearly between techniques of internal alchemy and those of nourishing life. Thus, Livia Kohn notes that only few works on internal alchemy actually discuss methods for nourishing life. She says,

> Adepts strive to identify, control, modify, and transform subtle energies as they are present in the human body. One effect of this transformation is the attainment of long life, just as basic longevity practices form the foundation of more advanced alchemical practices. While the Daoist Canon contains many scriptures and manuals on internal alchemy, only few of them discuss methods for nourishing vitality or can be connected directly to the nourishing life tradition. (2012, 251)

Isabelle Robinet agrees and defines internal alchemy as a complex system of techniques geared toward reaching the highest level of attainment and sublimation, noting that it leads to "finding illumination by returning to the fundamental order of the cosmos" (1989, 299). She further distinguishes internal alchemy from nourishing life as being based on a different and higher level of intellectual speculation, then warns that texts about it are not the same as those dealing with breathing techniques and healing exercises. "Internal alchemy is, in fact, distinguished quite clearly from those materials in that it gives greater weight to intellectual speculation of an original and unique form" (1989, 300). In addition, she establishes a set of characteristics found in texts that belong to the tradition of internal alchemy.

> One may say that texts belonging to the current of inner alchemy are characterized by 1) a concern for training the mind as much as the body, with the mental aspect usually predominant; 2) a tendency to synthesize various Daoist currents, certain Buddhist speculations and Confucian lines of thoughts; 3) references to the *Yijing* 易經 (Book of Changes); and 4) references to chemical practices. (1989, 301)

Still, she acknowledges that *qi*-related techniques, which form an important aspect of nourishing life, are one of the three roots of internal alchemy.

> Let us point out clearly the three major heritages: alchemy in the sense of proto-chemistry (in turn an heir of pharmacology); the various practices of *qi*; and the cosmological speculations typical for the *Yijing*. In addition, inner alchemy is a direct successor of the masters of magic (1989, 299).

Based on her intensive study of many important alchemical texts, she notes that materials on nourishing life generally present a lower intellectual or analytical level than those dealing with internal alchemy. In terms of practice, too, long life methods are placed beneath or, in the actual cultivation process, prior to the various techniques leading to alchemical transformation. Long-life cultivation works with ordinary bodily aspects, such as essence, energy (*qi*), and spirit, where techniques of internal alchemy modify the person's energies to fundamentally different levels that are more primordial and a great deal subtler.

In general, adepts become aware of those minute components only at the end of the first stage of the alchemical process as they obtain the mysterious first spark of true Yang—written here with a capital letter to distinguish it from ordinary yang. At this point, the real alchemical process begins, and adepts come to gather "the true ingredients." Isabelle Robinet says,

> The first stage, from essence to *qi*, comes to be known as the initial moment when one first gets hold of the spark of eternal Yang . . . believed to be transcendent and impossible to locate. . .

At this point, one becomes conscious of the existence of the three basic constituents of essence, vital energy, and spirit. One realizes that they are but one and fundamentally different from the ordinary human forces known by these same names. The latter are merely materials for external alchemy (*Zhonghe ji* 2.6a), which here refers to the classical respiratory and physiological practices of Daoism. In other words, inner alchemy begins where the various exercises of the gross breath end. (1989, 317-19)

*Qi* in nourishing life and internal alchemy is not entirely the same. Where texts of the former use the term to refer mainly to "grosser energies" and outline various breathing and physical techniques to enhance health, materials presenting the latter work with it more as a cosmic force, not so much based on respiration but more representing the original potency of the universe. Accordingly, "it is essential in alchemical practice to isolate the spark of true eternal Yang and make it return to the ancestral breath. This is different from ordinary respiration; it is the original breath, the primordial breath of the cosmos, the creative force of the universe" (1989, 321).

## The Early Masters

The scholarly analysis of these differences closely matches the Daoist understanding. Thus, the early Quanzhen masters rarely use the term "nourishing life" in their writings. In fact, it appears only in one text, the *Danyang zhenren yulu* 丹陽真人語錄 (Recorded Sayings of the Perfected Danyang, DZ 1057), compiled to record the teachings of Ma Yu 馬鈺, better known by his sobriquet Danyang 丹陽 (1123-1184), one of the Seven Perfected and a direct disciple of the Quanzhen founder.

48 / Chapter Two

The term here is used to explain that Quanzhen adepts can "nourish life" only through ascetic self-denial—a far cry from the traditional understanding of nourishing life that includes mainly breathing techniques, healing exercises, dietary management, and sexual methods. The text says,

> The Master also said: A Daoist must not dislike being poor. Poverty is the root of nourishing life. If hungry, eat one bowl of rice porridge; if tired, spread out a grass mat. Pass your days and nights in tattered garments. This truly is the life of a Daoist. Thus, you must realize that the single matter of clarity and purity cannot be acquired by the wealthy.[18] (10b-11a; Komjathy 2013, 170)

Even more striking, warnings against applying regular nourishing life practices, that is, working with the wrong methods, feature clearly in the early texts as well as in the works compiled by Huang Xinyang—thus contradicting the very title of his book.

For example, he presents a text that specifically warns against misunderstanding the difference between nourishing life and internal alchemy and being misguided into choosing the wrong kind of technique. The *Hao Taigu zhenren yulu* 郝太古真人語錄 (Recorded Sayings of the Perfected Hao Taigu, DZ 1256) records the oral teachings of another early Quanzhen master and member of the Seven Perfected, Hao Datong 郝大通 (1140-1213). He expresses his frustration that students are not following the original methods of the patriarchs but seek inferior methods related to nourishing life, turn into followers of vulgarity, and make it impossible to reach the highest level of returning to Dao. The text says,

> Now, the discourses of the Seven Perfected and Five Patriarchs all expound the principles of innate nature and life-destiny. Despite this, many later students have sought out inferior methods and deviant paths.
>
> Some employ the mind to direct *qi*, while others count breaths to forget the heart-mind. Some circulate water and fire so that they commingle. Still others focus on the dragon and tiger so that they merge.
>
> These myriad doctrines cannot fully contain the principles that have been conveyed by the patriarchs and masters of Complete Perfection. If they become extinguished, they will not appear again.
>
> So, my way takes opening pervasion as the foundation, realizing innate nature as the substance, and nourishing life-destiny as the application. It takes deferential harmony as virtue, withdrawing retreat as practice, and guarding one's endowment as accomplishment.
>
> After a long time of accumulation and development, celestial radiance manifests inwardly. The perfect *qi* infuses and flows forth, while form and spirit are mutually wondrous. Through Dao, one merges with perfection. . .

---

[18] 師又言：道人不厭貧, 貧乃養生之本. 饑則餐一缽粥, 睡來鋪一束草, 繿繿縷縷以度朝夕, 正是道人活計. 故知清淨一事, 豪貴人不能得.

Issues of Transmission / 49

However, once adepts have become followers of vulgarity, they fail to penetrate the meaning of the scriptures. Breathing like oxen and acting like horses, they do not know the principles of Dao. They can make anything seem like its opposite, turning black into white.[19] (1.19a-22b; Huang 1993, 206-07; trl. Komjathy 2013).

Similar distinctions and warnings against methods considered inferior, typically associated with nourishing life practices appear variously in the textual corpus of the early Quanzhen masters and from there have made their way to Huang Xinyang's book. Thus, Ma Yu sees health techniques as part of the gradual path and warns that they should not be confused with the great Dao itself. As intentional exercises, they represent the opposite of the state of nonaction and are accordingly classified as "limited techniques." As the *Danyang zhenren yulu* records,

> The master [Ma Yu] said, "The thirty-six healing exercises and twenty-four reverted elixirs are but gradual gateways for entering Dao. Do not mistake them for the great Dao itself. If you exhaust yourself investigating stove and furnace or obtaining the symbolism of turtle and snake, you are creating issues where there are none and adding falseness to your innate nature. All of this is extremely misleading! Thus, as transmitted within the Daoist tradition, the alchemical classics and texts of various masters, the thousand scriptures and ten thousand treaties may all be covered with a single phrase: clarity and purity."
>
> The master said, "Considering clarity and purity, clarity refers to clarifying the source of the heart- mind, while purity refers to purifying the Ocean of *Qi*. When the source of the heart-mind is clear, external phenomena cannot disturb it. Through this, emotions settle and spiritual illumination emerges. When the ocean of *qi* is pure, deviant desires cannot affect it. Through this, vital essence becomes complete and the abdomen becomes full.
>
> "Thus, you must purify the heart-mind as though purifying water, and nourish qi as though nourishing an infant. When *qi* flourishes, spirit becomes numinous. When spirit becomes numinous, *qi* turns transformational. This is the result of clarity and purity.
>
> "If you practice conscious, deliberate exercises, these are limited techniques. But if you practice the principle of no-mind and nonaction, this is unlimited clear emptiness."[20] (8ab; trl. Komjathy 2013)

---

[19] 夫七真五祖之語, 皆演性命之端的, 後學者多求小法邪徑, 或用心引氣, 或數息忘心, 或運水火交馳, 或究龍虎會合, 萬端不可盡錄, 致使祖師全真之理, 滅而不顯. 夫吾道以開通為基, 以見性為體, 以養命為用, 以謙和為德, 以卑退為行, 以守分為功, 久久積成, 天光內發, 真氣沖融 形神俱妙, 與道合真. [. . .] 不通經義, 呼牛作馬, 不知道理, 轉黑為白. 郝太古真人語, 真仙直指語錄.

[20] 師曰: 三十六道引, 二十四還丹, 此乃入道之漸門, 不可便為. 大道若窮於爐竈, 取象於龜蛇, 乃無事生事, 於性上添偽也. 此皆侯人之甚矣. 故道家留丹經子書, 千經萬論, 可一言以蔽之曰清淨. 師曰: 清淨者, 清為清其心源, 淨為靜其黑海. 心源清則

50 / Chapter Two

# Merging the Traditions

All this suggests that a Quanzhen master deliberately choosing the term "nourishing life" in the title of a book on practices of Daoist cultivation relevant today is a rather interesting phenomenon. In his preface, Huang Xinyang makes no effort to differentiate internal alchemy from nourishing life. On the contrary, he merges them into a single tradition, never intimating that the chosen texts actually contain criticisms of the entire nourishing life complex. To him, the historical development of the tradition occurred as follows:

> The origin of Daoist nourishing life practices are early, starting even before the Qin dynasty (220-207 BCE) and gradually evolving into various fundamental methods, such as guarding the One [concentrative meditation], breathing, stretching, and the like.
>
> In the Han dynasty (207 BCE-25 CE), they incorporated the Huang-Lao notions of clarity, stillness, and nonaction as well as the theory of the oneness of heaven and humanity. At the time, the science of yin-yang and the five phases, the theory of the *Yijing* with its hexagrams, lines, definitions, and numbers all were blended together, so that theory and practice mutually contributed to each other.
>
> In the Eastern Han (25-220 CE), Wei Boyang relied on the doctrines of the traditions of Huang-Lao, *Yijing*, and external alchemy to write the *Cantong qi* (Matching of the Three). Under the Jin dynasty (265-420), Ge Hong used the ideas of the hundred schools to write his *Baopuzi*.
>
> Soon after, the divine immortal Wei Huacun advocated visualization of the body gods to deploy the mysterious application of essence, *qi*, and spirit as she revealed the *Huangting jing* (Yellow Court Scripture). These items constitute the three main branches of Daoist nourishing life practices, which then gradually merged into one![21] (1993, 3-5)

Aware that "books on the elixir number in the thousands and one can reach the same goal by a thousand different routes," Huang therefore made the decision to present the methods of nourishing life as supposedly advo-

---

外物不能撓, 故情定而神明生焉. 黑海淨則邪欲不能干, 故精全而腹實矣. 是以澄心如澄水, 養黑如養兒, 黑秀則神靈, 神靈則黑變, 乃清淨所致也. 若行有心有為之功, 則有盡之術法也. 若行無心無為之理, 乃無盡之清虛也. The first part also appears in *Dadan zhizhi* 2.11b.

[21] 道教养生来源甚早, 自先秦以来, 逐渐奠基, 如宁一、吐纳、导引等. 两汉养生术与黄老清静無为, 天人合一的观点; 陰阳五行学说;易理卦爻象数融合, 理论与实践相互渗透, 东汉魏伯阳依黄老、大易、炉火等《参同契》; 晋葛洪会归百家著《抱朴子》;魏华存元君主张存想自身之神、调配精气神之妙用, 传《黄庭经》, 至此已构成了道家养生的三条支脉, 后渐会归一流. 道家丹鼎修炼方术, 有内丹、外丹两种, 而丹书万卷, 大抵殊途同归.

cated by the Quanzhen patriarchs, inheriting and expanding the three main branches that flourished in history. His work is unique in that it has the term "nourishing life" in the title yet contains mostly works on internal alchemy—something I have not found in any other compilation, whether traditional or modern.

Even during the Qing dynasty, the term "nourishing life" appears rarely in Quanzhen writings. None of the more representative texts of the time have it, such as the instruction manual *Longmen xinfa* 龍門心法 (Essential Methods of the Longmen Branch), the ledger of initial rules *Chuzhen jie* 初真戒 (Precepts of Initial Perfection; see Kohn 2004), or the regulation text *Quanzhen bidu*. Even Liu Yiming 劉一明 (1734-1821), the most famous Qing-dynasty alchemist and Quanzhen master, uses the term only five times in his *Wudao lu* 悟道錄 (Record of Awakening to Dao) and here always in the context of curbing desires. The main Qing collection *Daozang jiyao* has not a single text with "nourishing life" in the title.

This changed in the early 20th century, when masters like Jiang Weiqiao 蔣維喬, aka Master Yinshi 因是先生 (see Kohn 2002), and Chen Yingning, the second chairman of the CDA (Liu 2009) experimented with traditional Daoist methods for health purposes and began to explain them in modern scientific terms and concepts—a tendency that came to great fruition in the development of qigong in the 1950s (Palmer 2007).

In time this led to a more powerful merging of the traditions, most obvious in the works of Xiao Tianshi 蕭天石 (1908-1986), a physician and Daoist scholar who lived in Sichuan after 1939 and moved to Taiwan in 1949. Combining materials on internal alchemy, sexual hygiene, medical recipes, longevity techniques, ethics, and virtues under the generic term "nourishing life," he wrote the well-known *Daojia yangsheng xue gaiyao* 道家養生學概要 (Overview of the Study of Daoist Ways of Nourishing Life). Published in 1963, it demonstrates his endeavor to classify the methods of internal alchemy as nourishing life practices.

Xiao is also the compiler of the major collection, *Daozang jinghua* 道藏精華 (Essential Blossoms of the Daoist Canon), published from 1956 to 1969 by Ziyou Publishing House in Taipei. Its seventeen volumes contain over 600 texts, both traditional and modern, but with a leaning toward later works, especially those dealing with internal alchemy (see Valussi 2008). The most prominent authors in the collection are alchemical masters of the late Ming and Qing, such as Lu Xixing 陸西星 (1520-1601; see Mozias 2020), Wu Shouyang 伍守陽 (1574-1644), Liu Yiming (1734-1821), Fu Jinquan 傅金銓 (1765-1844), and Li Xiyue 李西月 (1806-1856).

He also included works related to the Ming-dynasty immortal Zhang Sanfeng 張三丰, the alleged founder of taijiquan and practitioner of internal alchemy, who revealed extensive instructions in spirit-writing sessions under the Qing.[22] In addition, Xiao himself wrote fourteen works that he placed in the collection, dealing with internal alchemy and self-cultivation.

Overall, forty texts in the *Daozang jinghua* have the term "nourishing life" in the title. Its very first document is a prime example. The *Daojia yangsheng mizhi daolun* 道家養生秘旨導論 (Secret Pointers and Guiding Discourses on Daoist Ways of Nourishing Life) integrates materials on breathing, massages, meditation, and taijiquan with alchemical records such as the *Danyang zhenren yulu*, a text in essence critical of nourishing life practices.

## The Modern Situation

Until recently, Daoist academics and Chinese scholars affiliated with official research institutions and universities continued along the same lines, publishing their own compilations of ancient texts on internal alchemy and health preservation under titles like "Manual on Nourishing Life." One example from 1989 that may have inspired Huang Xinyang is the *Daojiao yangsheng gongfa jiyao* 道家養生功法集要 (Collected Essentials of Daoist Methods of Nourishing Life) by Wang Xiping 王西平, a scholar at the Graduate Science Institute of Shaanxi Province. It follows the dominant academic mode of the 1980s and compiles materials in the fashion originally set up by lay Daoists in the early 20th century.

---

[22] Zhang is a highly controversial figure. For studies and translations of texts associated with him, see DeBruyn 2000; Phillips 2019; Seidel 1970; Wong 1982; Wu and McBride. 2020.

Quanzhen masters also went along with this trend, as exemplified in the *Zhonghua daoxue baiwen* 中華道學百問 (A Hundred Questions on Chinese Daoism) by the Baiyun guan abbot Li Xinjun 李信軍 (2013a). Here the term "nourishing life" appears over 300 times, much more frequently than "internal alchemy," which features only thirty-eight times. Part of this statistic has to do with the fact that political considerations make it prudent to emphasize health over spirituality. Li simply replaces the traditional phrase "master of internal alchemy" (*neidan jia* 内丹家) with "expert on nourishing life" (*yangsheng jia* 養生家). This applies in retrospective even to historical figures so that, for example, Zhang Boduan, one of the top Song alchemists, is presented as follows:

> The author of the *Wuzhen pian* 悟真篇 (On Awakening to Perfection): Zhang Boduan 張伯端, aka Pingshu 平叔, Daoist name Ziyang 紫陽, 987-1082, from Tiantai in Zhejiang. Famous Daoist of the Song dynasty, expert in nourishing life, founder and ancestral patriarch of the Southern School.[23] (Li 2013a, 100)

The same classification applies to the Quanzhen ancestral master Lü Dongbin,[24] the Longmen patriarch Qiu Chuji,[25] as well as some other recognized great writers on internal alchemy such as Liu Yiming,[26] and more. All of them are called "experts on nourishing life," using an appellation created by the 20th-century Quanzhen headquarters at the Baiyun guan. In the same way masters of internal alchemy are presented as specialists of nourishing life, so are all texts on internal alchemy mentioned in Li Xinjun's now classified as "nourishing life texts" (2013a). His definition of nourishing life, moreover, matches that used by academics and texts on nourishing life and Chinese medicine. He mentions that nourishing life focuses strictly on keeping good health and originally includes no terminology or concepts of internal alchemy (2013b, 100).

To conclude, the term "nourishing life" has replaced the term "internal alchemy" in many publications and presentations of 21st-century Quanzhen Daoists. While the concept is ancient and goes back far in Daoist culture, it has seen an increase in usage and more intense conflation with internal alchemy from the late Qing dynasty onward, with a particular upsurge in the early 20th century. Furthermore, since the early 1990s, especially with

---

[23] 悟真篇作者, 张伯端, 字平叔, 道号紫阳, 公元 987-1082 年, 浙江天 台人. 宋代著名道士、养生家、南宗开 山祖师.

[24] Li 2013a, 87. "吕岩, 字洞宾, 号纯阳子, 山西芮城人, 唐末著名道士、诗人, 养生家. 道教八仙之一 . . ."

[25] Li 2013a, 107. "丘处机, 字通密, 号长春子, 公元 1148-1227 年, 栖霞（今山东）人. 金元时 期著名高道, 理论家, 养生家, 龍門派创始人."

[26] Li 2013a, 125.刘一明, 号悟元子, 素朴 散人, 公元 1734-1821 年, 山西曲沃（今山西闻喜县）人. 清代著名道士, 养生家, 医学家."

the publication of relevant works by the Baiyun guan abbots Huang Xinyang and Li Xinjun, the term has become the mode of choice for Quanzhen clerics to describe the tradition and mastery of internal cultivation.

# Chapter Three

# Temple Reconstruction

The Leigutai temple belongs to a lesser branch within the Longmen lineage of the Quanzhen order, as documented in the names of its masters on a stele engraved by Feng Xingzhao (see Appendix 1). It is a hereditary temple, not a big public monastery, and stands in close relationships with other temples. Since the Cultural Revolution, its lineage has increasingly spread through the systematic renovation of various local temples under the guidance of Master Feng. He has also been instrumental in spreading its teachings and practices abroad, while his fellow abbot Liu Shitian has been active in the evolution of Daoism in the county, pursuing ways to help the tradition to return to its roots and give back to the community.

## Temple Functions

According to Quanzhen ideology, the pursuit of Dao is the most important aspect of the Daoist life, and temples or monasteries are the place to do so. Within a cloistered enclave, adepts are free from the obligations of society: they can obtain proper guidance and move quickly toward their goal of merging with Dao through ethical living, focused meditation, and the practices of internal alchemy. When Wang Chongyang established his religious communities, he emphasized that "leaving the family" (*chujia* 出家) and living in a monastic community was the most important aspect of an aspiring cleric. Thus, his *Chongyang lijiao shiwu lun* in the very first regulation says,

> Once you leave family life, you must first join a cloister. A cloister is a kind of residence. It provides your personal body with a foundation. When your personal body has a good foundation, your mind can gradually find peace. Then energy and spirit radiate in harmony, and you can enter perfect Dao.[1] (Kohn 1993, 86; Komjathy 2013, 115)

Temples, monasteries, and cloisters are not only places to find a master for intense training and fully focus on Daoist practices, but also the residences of the gods. As such they present an enclosure where heaven and earth come together. Thus, the earliest formal manual on monastic Daoism,

---

[1] 凡出家者, 先須投庵. 庵者舍也, 一身依倚. 身有依倚, 心漸得安, 氣神和暢, 入真道矣.

dated to the early Tang dynasty, the *Fengdao kejie* 奉道科戒 (Rules and Precepts for Worshiping the Dao, DZ 1125; trl. Kohn 2004c) describes in some detail how to build temples properly. It notes that temples are a place where immortals come to dwell on earth and thus the most suitable place for Daoists to pursue their cultivation practice. To make the celestials comfortable, they should be constructed as replicas of the heavenly palaces above, with plants and beautiful ornaments as, for example, in the courtyard of the Leigutai (shown below). According to the text, in the heavens,

Coagulating *qi* forms towers and pavilions, halls and sanctuaries; in others, accumulating clouds create terraces and kiosks, palaces and chambers. Sometimes [wondrous beings] live among the sun and the moon, the planets and stars; or they reside in interiors formed by misty clouds and rosy vapors. In some cases, the residences emerge from spontaneous transformation; in others, they are produced through divine power. [....]

Inevitably they invite humans and celestials to return to them, while the foolish and the wise gaze at them in wonder. People on earth imitate these structures found in the heavens and set up numinous monasteries over here, creating auspicious places and residences fit for immortals.[2] (1.12b; Kohn 2004c, 87-88)

---

[2] 或結氣為樓閣堂殿, 或聚雲成臺榭宮房, 或處星辰日月之門, 或居煙雲霞霄之內, 或自然化出, 或神力造成. [. . .] 必使人天歸望, 賢愚異域, 所以法彼上天, 置茲靈觀, 既為福地, 即是仙居.

Temple Reconstruction / 57

In other words, buildings should be constructed to allow easy access for immortals and celestials. Terraces, pavilions, and towers should have doors and windows large enough to let the cloudy carriages of the deities come and go as they please.

> On the outside, all buildings should have doors to the four luminants; on the sides, windows should be open to the eight winds. This will allow the carriages of the immortals to freely enter and leave, the steeds of the perfected to easily come and go.[3] (1.17a; 2004c, 93)

Beyond that, all structures should be embellished beautifully and surrounded by well-sculpted gardens, again to invite the divinities to descend and bless them. These amenities allow Daoists to live in closeness to the deities and join the immortals at hand.

> The buildings should be admirable and rare, lofty and spacious, so that practitioners join the immortals hand in hand, cherishing their closeness in their day-today lives and seeing them both morning and evening.[4] (2004c, 93)

Monasteries and their various amenities are essential for Daoist practice: they include a place of worship, a meditation chamber, a place to practice *qi* cultivation, as well as a bathhouse, and a medicine hall. "These [facilities] must all be set up adequately: make sure they lack in nothing" (1.16b). In addition, the rules mention that the institution should have a number of specific buildings to facilitate various esoteric practices, allowing adepts to "to pursue perfection, refine *qi*, pray to the perfected, absorb the luminants' essences, receive the immortals, gather the dew of the nine clarity heavens," and more. The practices in this setting, then, allow practitioners to join the immortals in their own sphere.

> There they soar up in imagination to the highways of the clouds, ascend in sincerity to the roadways of the stars. They wander in their minds outside of all known bounds and send they eyes to the center of the universe. They rise to the provinces of the Eight Luminants and approach the swinging assemblies of the ten kinds of immortals.[5] (1.16b; Kohn 2004c, 93)

Since temples present a replica of heavenly palaces, they are the perfect and most wonderful place for Daoists to quiet the heart and practice cultivation. "Imitating the jasper terraces above and looking like golden

---

3 外啟四景之門, 旁開八風之牖, 令仙軿出入, 真騎往來.
4 可仰可希, 彌高彌廣, 則晉携手常生撫袂, 旦夕可得矣.
5 翹想雲衢, 騰誠星路, 遊心方外, 送目寰中, 冀八景俯臨, 十仙遙集, 既非常事, 理須遐絕.

58 / Chapter Three

towers below, temples are places to elevate the heart, records of a celestial sojourn on earth" (1.19a; 2004c, 97).[6]

Also, because temples are meant to serve numerous generations to come, they must be protected and maintained in good shape. The *Fengdao kejie* says,

> A building or garden can rightfully be named an auspicious place, justly called a pure residence. For eternal kalpas, it can be inhabited in perpetuity, but it must never be allowed to deteriorate or fall into disrepair. [Building and repairing such an enclave] gives good fortune without measure. It is first among all the deeds that generate merit and virtue.[7] (1.14a; 2004c, 90)

For contemporary Quanzhen clerics this gave primary guidance. It was eminently clear that, as soon as religious activities were permitted again, they had first to rebuild the temples and monasteries that had been destroyed and assigned other purposes. The CDA made a formal declaration to this effect during its third national meeting in May 1980. Representatives ordered all local organizations to give priority to rebuilding and repairing temples, collecting and reprinting scriptures, supporting research centers, training new leaders, and establishing appropriate regulations. At the local level, Daoists quickly stepped up to do their part.

## The Leigutai Temple

The Leigutai temple is located at an elevation of 1886 meters on an isolated peak in the Qinling mountain range (see photos opposite). Since 1995, the peak has been part of a nature conservancy, controlled by the forestry administration. For many years there were no roads to it, and only about twenty years ago a paved strip of twenty kilometers was built to connect the mountain to the nearest village, called Hanyin Puxi 漢陰蒲溪. From this, the temple is still seven kilometers of dirt track away (see Fan 1989; 1991; Shaanxi sheng zongjiao shiwu ju 2009).

Administratively Leigutai is located in Ziyang county. This in turn is part of the municipality of Ankang 安康, located in the southern part of Shaanxi near the Sichuan border, about 300 kilometers south of Xi'an. The population of 350,000 is mostly concentrated in the county seat of Ziyang as well in twenty-one villages. The landscape is highly mountainous, with Mount Fenghuang 鳳凰 in the north and the foothills of Mount Daba 大巴 in the south. The highest peak is 2522 meters. The nearest river is the Hanjiang 漢江, a major tributary of the Yangtze. No polluting industries are allowed,

---

[6] 上擬瑤臺, 下圖金關, 契心之所, 是焉棲記.

[7] 稱為福地, 亦曰淨居, 永劫住持, 勿使廢替, 得福無量, 功德第一.

and the GDP is calculated differently from the official economic assessment.

Historically, Ziyang is the only county in China whose name came from the title of a Daoist perfected (Liu X. 2013). According to the local government, it adopted this name in 1512, because the famous immortal Ziyang zhenren 紫陽真人 (Perfected of Purple Yang; image below) attained Dao here. Originally named Zhang Boduan (987-1082), he lived for almost a century during the Song dynasty, trained extensively in internal alchemy, and became the first patriarch of the Southern School.

According to local lore, he came to the area on his way from Zhejiang to Sichuan in 1069 and decided to stay and practice internal cultivation in a cave in the Hanyin mountains above the Hanjiang River. There, in 1075, he wrote his major treatise on internal alchemy, the *Wuzhen pian*, now engraved on stone at his temple (Fan 1991, 22-23; 2010b, 331).

In terms of the physical plant, the Leigutai temple consists of several key structures. Its main sanctuary on top of the peak is the Zhenwu dian 真武殿 (Hall of the Perfect Warrior). It was originally built in 1626, at the end of the Ming dynasty, as a small temple of its own, dedicated to this deity and called Xuantian guan 玄天觀 (Monastery of Dark Heaven) or Zhenwu miao 真武廟 (Temple of the Perfect Warrior). 300 meters below, connected by a steep flight of stone stairs, are the Sanqing dian 三清殿 (Hall of the Three Pure Ones) as well as living quarters and administrative offices.

Historical records and local stone steles show that there were religious activities from the late Ming onward: the temple was an important place of worship for the local population. Data from 1815 show a succession of annual temple festivals held on the birthdays of various deities, such as the Perfect Warrior (shown below), the Goddess of Mercy Guanyin 觀音, the Earth Official (*diguan* 地官), the Mountain God, and more. Today, the most active period of worship is in the summer, from the 1st day of the 6th to the 15th of the 7th lunar months (Fan 1989).

The Leigutai temple can be classified as a hereditary or private temple (Goossart 2007; Kohn 2003), that is, one where disciples are led personally by a single master who will select one of them to succeed him eventually. The temple belongs to a specific lineage or sub-branch of the Quanzhen order, and its teachings and administration is transmitted individually from master to disciple. Only disciples of the particular lineage are allowed to live there.

As a hereditary temple, it is also a place where adepts can enter Dao (*rutao* 入道), bow to a master (*baishi* 拜師), train as novices, and take precepts. These include the three vows of the ceremony of taking refuge (*guiyi shi* 皈依式) and the ten precepts administered during the observance of taking the cap (*guanji ke* 冠巾科). Hereditary temples are unique in these features since they are only Daoist institution that can accept novices.[8] Most Quanzhen temples are hereditary and act as places of worship and practice; beyond that, some may also play an important role in their locality and the development of the order.

---

[8] Public monasteries cannot perform any of them, but they can organize ceremonies of bestowing the "three levels of great precepts" (*santan dajie* 三壇大戒), that is, perform full ordinations.

According to Quanzhen regulations, no matter how important a hereditary temple is, it must never be called "big." As the former Baiyun guan abbot Huang Xinyang says "No matter how big the grounds of a hereditary temple are, it can only be called small temple" (2000).

Leigutai, shown above with its major buildings, took center stage in the rebuilding effort when the local Daoist association was set up on 3 November 2004 and elected Master Feng Xingzhao to serve as its chairman. It is a lesser chapter of the provincial Shaanxi Daoist Association, which was established in 1986. Before this, in 1983, only three active Daoist institutions had been allowed to reopen among a total of twenty-one temples in all of China: Louguantai, Baxian gong, and Yuquan yuan. By 2009, the province had three major public monasteries of historical significance—Louguantai, Baxian gong, and Zhangliang miao 張良廟 (Temple to Zhang Liang)—plus several ancestral shrines of the Quanzhen order.[9]

---

[9] Official statistics published by the local Bureau of Religious Affairs in 2009 show 290, 000 Daoist believers and 736 professional Daoists (547 male and 189 female), practicing in 309 officially registered places of worship under the auspices of eighteen local Daoist associations (Shaanxi sheng zongjiao shiwu ju 2009).

The latter include first of all the Chongyang gong 重陽宮 (Palace of Master Chongyang, shown above) in Hu 戶 county, dedicated to the founder. Then there are the Longmen dong in honor of Qiu Chuji's lineage as well as several temples on Mount Baiyun 白雲, a major early center (Shaanxi sheng zongjiaoshiwu ju 2009). Fang Xingzhao stayed at all these places, most importantly for five years at the Baxian gong (1985-1990) and for two years at the Yuquan yuan on Mount Hua.

The provincial associations in turn are subject to guidance form the CDA with its headquarters at the Baiyun guan in Beijing, which is also the central administration of the Quanzhen order. It is known as "the first public monastery under heaven" and the "first ancestral shrine of the Longmen school." Historically, it was where Qiu Chuji established this lineage and also where he was buried. In addition, the first Quanzhen consecration ceremony was held here, in 1656 under the leadership of the 7th Longmen patriarch Wang Changyue (Huang 2007a). Feng Xingzhao went there in 1989 to participate in the first national consecration ceremony and receive his three sets of precepts.[10]

---

[10] Another Leigutai abbot, Yin Xingshu 尹興鉥, received his precepts in 1995 during the second national consecration ceremony held at the Tianshi dong 天師洞 on Mount Qingcheng in Sichuan.

# The Lineage

Master Feng as well as all Daoists at Leigutai and other Daoist temples in the Ziyang area belong to the Longmen branch, the leading lineage of the Quanzhen order. They venerate Qiu Chuji, one of the Seven Perfected and a direct disciple of the founder Wang Chongyang as their ancestral master (*zushi* 祖師), as well as Qiu's senior disciple Zhao Daojian 趙道堅, as their lineage masters (*zongshi* 宗師).

Beyond that, Thunder Drum clerics identify two masters as their earliest ancestors. One is a 9th-generation master called Tan Zhenren 談真人, originally from a temple called Taizipo 太子坡 (Prince's Hill) on Mount Wudang in Hunan (shown below); the other is a Daoist called Perfected Sun 孫真人 from the Tiantai guan 天台觀 (Heavenly Terrace Monastery) on Mount Yunwu 雲霧 in Shiquan 石泉 county of Shaanxi province.

Founded and inspired by these figures, Leigutai itself was built in 1626. Various records mention religious activities even in the early years, but clear lines of transmission and management are only documented since the beginning of the Republican Period in 1912, when Liu Chenghong 劉誠洪 a 24th-generation master from Tiantai guan, took over the leadership.

A recently carved stele shows all the abbots up to Fang Xingzhao himself (see Appendix 1). It begins with Liu Chenghong's transmission to Xie Xincheng 謝信誠, who moved from Mount Yunwu in 1929 to take up the management of Leigutai., He passed the leadership on to Yang Chongyi 楊崇

義 and Luo Gaolian 羅高連, who left in 1945 to return to Mount Yunwu. They were followed by Huang Sishou 黃嗣壽 and Wu Siliang 吳嗣亮.

In 1948, the 30th-generation master Yang Faxiang 楊法祥 succeeded Wu Siliang. In 1953, he was commandeered to work as a physician in a hygiene and health workers association, and Chen Xinzhong 陳信忠 took over as abbot. In 1957, Yang returned to the temple as second in command; he resumed his full abbacy in 1963 after Chen's death.

During this period, Feng Xingzhao became his disciple[11] Born on 12 December 1945 in the village of Luya 爐埡 in Hanwang 漢王 township of Ziyang county, he was originally called Feng Zhongkun 馮忠坤. In his fifth year of primary school, he got very sick and was unable to continue his schooling. Medicines and treatments remained ineffective. Finally, in 1961, his mother, desperate to find a solution to her son's illness, took him to Leigutai to pray to the god Zhenwu. Through divination, the deity told her that her son was destined to live in the temple and become a Daoist and that this was the only way to restore his health. In this manner, Yang Faxiang became Feng's master and initiated him as a 30th-generation Longmen priest, giving him the Daoist name Feng Xingzhao.

Soon after, the Cultural Revolution began and the temple was closed. Yang Faxiang managed to hide the sacred statues in a cave deep in the nearby mountains before he had to leave to work as kitchen staff in a people's commune. However, he did not stay there long but soon re-turned to Leigutai, where he waited out the decade of upheavals in isolation. There are many stories of villagers sneaking out at night in defiance of official prohibitions to make the six-hour climb up the mountain and bring him various necessities. Feng Xingzhao in the meantime saw a great improve-

---

[11] I collected much information on Feng's life and deeds in personal interviews. Other sources include Ceng 2008a; Fang 2014; Mu 2012; Xu H. 2014; Xu S. 2013.

## 66 / Chapter Three

ment in his health and, in 1966, followed the official command and left the temple to work in civil society.

In late 1979, the temple officially reopened as a religious center and Yang Faxiang once more resumed his role as abbot. He expanded the facilities and trained numerous disciples, including Yin Xingshu 尹興鉢, Chen Xinghui 陳興會, Chen Xinglin 陳興林, Zhang Xingde 張興德, and Liu Xingdi 劉興地.

Feng Xingzhao returned in 1981 and stayed for two years, studying closely with Yang. In 1983, he set out to undertake cloud wandering, traveling mainly in Shaanxi, where he went to Yaowang dian 藥王殿 (Hall to the King of Medicines) in Ankang, Louguantai in the Zhongnan range, and Yuquan yuan at the foot of Mount Hua. In 1985, he settled in the major monastery of Xi'an, the Baxian gong, and stayed for five years. Soon he was drafted into management and became head of the ritual team of the temple as well as an executive manager in the provincial Daoist association. In 1989, he was selected to undergo full ordination at the Baiyun guan in Beijing and there received the three sets of Quanzhen precepts. Ranking third among over a hundred participants, he was also given the honorary title Gexinzi 革新子.

In 1990, having been fully trained, Feng went back to Leigutai, where Yang had reached advanced old age and no longer wished to shoulder the responsibilities of abbot. Feng duly took over and started to train disciples. Soon after, he invited Min Zhiting to teach local clerics. The latter had been his roommate at Yuquan yuan and was then abbot of the Baxian gong as well as an associate dean of the Daoist College in Beijing. The friendship between the two continued even after Min became the chairman of the CDA and relocated to Beijing.

Feng stayed in charge of the Leigutai temple until 1996. When Yang Faxian passed on, he decided to leave the mountain to renovate temples and revitalize Daoism in the greater Ziyang region. At this point, the abbacy went to Yin Xingshu. Originally from the village of Miaohe 苗河 in Ziyang county, he arrived at Leigutai in June 1993 and officially became Yang's disciple. In October 1995, he underwent formal ordination on Mount Qingcheng and took the three sets of Quanzhen precepts. In October 2003, however, his life was cut short: he was brutally murdered by bandits who attacked him near the temple.

At that time, Master Feng was busy renovating temples elsewhere and chose his younger Dao brother Zhang Xingde to take over the management, the only one among Yang's many disciples who still remained at the temple. In 2014, Zhang went back to his native village, Hengkou 恒口 in Ankang, to renovate the local Yaowang miao.

Master Feng duly took on the role of abbot again. However, since he was busy renovating other temples, the actual management came to be in the hands of priests engaged by Liu Shitian. He selected his disciple Li Jingsong 李景松 to serve as central manager and sent helpers from the Chenghuang miao 城隍廟 (City God Temple) in Xi'an and the Mingsheng gong on Mount Li (shown below) to take care of the daily activities.

The lineage, in other words, works like a family, where everybody is either a disciple (*tudi* 徒弟), an uncle (*shishu* 師叔), or a grand-disciple (*tusun* 徒孫). During my last visit, five priests were actually living at Leigutai, all closely affiliated with Yang Faxiang in one way or another, as direct disciples, grand-disciples, or trainees of one or the other of Dao brothers.

Being part of the same lineage and often coming from the local area, they are strongly connected to local lore and culture in their approach and views of Daoism. They usually share their stories while sitting around the fire in the evening, talking about some of the qualities of the old masters, the miracles or strange things that happened around the temple, the stories of their lives, and much more.

The temple being the core of the lineage, they as well as other local clerics regularly burn incense in front of the main deity and pay their respects at the tombs of previous masters. Quite commonly clerics, whose cloud wandering led them far away from their family temple, come by to check how things are going, catch up with their brethren, and pay respect to the lineage ancestors. Due its local history and its numinous efficacy (*ling* 靈), the temple is an important pilgrimage site, sometimes called Small Wudang or First Peak in southern Shaanxi. During major festivals and in the heat of summer, it is very popular: hundreds of believers come every day, thousands arrive to pray.

## Reconstruction Work

Feng Xingzhao spent several decades reconstructing temples and revitalizing the Daoist tradition in Shaanxi. In June 1996, he first went to the Taibai miao 太白廟 (Temple of Great White [Planet Venus]) in the village of Lianhua 蓮花 in Pu township 鋪鎮 of Hanzhong 漢中 municipality and raised funds for its renovation.

In the summer of the following year, Zhang Xianhou 張先厚, chairman of the Ziyang county development committee, invited Master Feng to return and assist in the redevelopment of the local Daoist religion (Ceng 2008c, 47-48). Their first project was the rebuilding of an ancient temple, originally located in the cave where Zhang Boduan, the immortal Ziyang zhenren who gave the county its name, undertook intense personal cultivation. Although high above the river, it had been submerged during the construction of the Ankang Dam of the Hanjiang River in the 1970s. Called Xianren dong 仙人洞 (Immortal's Grotto), the old temple was still remembered by villagers as a vast cave where they worshiped the Perfected (Ceng 2008c; Fang 2014).

The motivation of this ambitious project was threefold. First, the population always had strong devotion to Daoism, and there were many stories and reports of strange sightings and odd events ever since the cave temple had been submerged. For example, people would wake up at night or in the early morning to the sound of Daoist chanting, the beating of drums, and the clacking of the wooden fish. County leaders wished to put these to rest by offering a live venue for religious activities.

Second, the people no longer had a local place of worship, since most temples and shrines were either submerged or destroyed. The government thus felt the need to provide a place for the religious activities of inhabitants. Third, they also saw the tourist potential, finding in temple reconstruction a way to increase the fame and popularity of the area, especially since the county was the only one named after a Daoist immortal. The official website says,

> The creation of Ziyang county is attested in the 7th year of the Zhengde era of the Ming dynasty [1512]; to the present day, it has 500 years of history. Ziyang is the only county named after a Daoist, the founder of the Southern School, Zhang Boduan, aka Ziyang zhenren. He practiced and attained Dao here, and his title refers to the purple *qi* that comes from the east, the yang radiance that illuminates all things.[12] (Ziyang renmin 2014b)

On 10 June 1998, the local government issued a report on the project, officially giving permission to open the reconstruction as a place of worship, called Xianren dong Zhenren gong 仙人洞真人宫 (Palace of the Perfected in the Immortal's Grotto; shown below) while also emphasizing its importance for the development of local tourism (Ceng 2008c, 47).

---

[12] 紫阳置县于明正德七年（公元 1512 年），迄今已有 500 年的历史。紫阳是全国唯一用道教名号命名的县份，因道教南派创始人张伯端（号紫阳真人）在这里修行悟道而得名，意为"紫气东来，阳光普照。

70 / Chapter Three

Outside of government offices, however, the work had already started a few months earlier. In January 1998, Feng Xingzhao returned to Ziyang to look for a good place on the river close to where the original cave had been submerged. He duly found an abandoned chemical factory and decided that the fengshui was suitable for a Daoist project. Working with many different government departments, he obtained authorization to buy the old factory and the surrounding land for 120,000 RMB (US $20,000). It included 3.7 *mu* 亩 (2,500 square meters or 22,500 square feet) of building with a total of twenty-one rooms, plus 19 *mu* (1.25 hectares or half an acre) of mountain area. A group of lay disciples immediately started to clean the damaged place and set up furniture, while Master Feng carved the name "Ziyang zhenren" on a stone stele and placed an incense burner before it.

Thus, the process began to bring the deity back to the area and install him in his new home. Later in the year, on the 28th of the 12th lunar month (*layue* 臘月), a lay disciple was able to retrieve the original statue of the god from its watery grave. On New Year's Day, it was officially installed in a public ritual that drew well over a thousand people. On 17 August 1999, an official ceremony renewed the statue's consecration, supported by popular donations of over 10,000 RMB.

In February 2002, Feng Xingzhao hired a team of builders from the Hanzhong area who were particularly known for their high expertise in temple building to erect a new sanctuary for 300,000 RMB. Some of this money came from private donations; the remainder was a mortgage granted by a local bank. The process advanced quickly. Within a year, on 8 February 2003, the final consecration ceremony was held for the completion of the main hall and a set of nine new statues. They included the Perfected himself, the other four patriarchs of the Southern School as well as four popular deities such as the King of Medicines, the God of Wealth, and the Goddess of Mercy. It took over a year for the statues to be sculpted from 15,000 pounds of special local clay.

Feng's first reconstructed temple soon became financially independent. In 1998, it had a yearly donation revenue of 60,000 RMB, and from 2001 onward, this exceeded 100,000 RMB. While he chaired the committee that supervised the temple's financial management, it included several other clerics, lay disciples, and members of the local Daoist association (Ceng 2008c, 61). They not only held the keys to the donation boxes, each secured with three locks, but also made the decisions on how to use the incoming funds.

Beyond this, they were in charge of a smaller temple on the cliff of a gorge about three kilometers from the town, known as Guanyin'ai 觀音崖 (Guanyin Cliff, shown below). Built in the mid-17th century, it consists of a stone structure, set up to protect a natural rock formation that resembles the features of Guanyin, the Goddess of Mercy (Ceng 2008c, 62; Li H. and Zhang

2009). Although the place had been empty and isolated for years, many believers continued to visit it and pray there.

On 7 June 2001, the local government decided to recognize the temple officially as a place of worship and bestowed its management on the priests of the Zhenren gong. Since then, one priest has lived there to take care of the place and provide religious services to the pilgrims.

Beyond all these projects, Master Feng was also involved in the management of another village temple, the Sansheng miao 三聖廟 (Temple of the Three Sages) in Hengkou, located 57 km northwest of Ziyang.[13] Originally built in 1766 and first associated with the God of Fire (*huoshen* 火神), it is located on the main street of the village and served as a place to worship the three sages after whom it is named—Buddha, Laozi, and Confucius—before being closed down and left to decay during the Cultural Revolution.

In early 2002, the president of the Hengkou chamber of commerce, Cheng Shiyin 程世銀, contacted Master Feng with the request to restart the religious activities of the temple. He himself donated 400,000 RMB to rebuilt it both as a place of worship for the villagers and as a museum where he could store and exhibit his collection of antiques from the Qing dynasty (Hengkou 2009). The temple was duly registered as a protected historical site on the provincial level and as a center for the conservation of Hangkou and Ankang

---

[13] See Hengkou 2009; Hengkou daojiao xiehui 2012. See also Li H. 2012; Li H. and Sun 2013.

culture (Hengkou daojiao xiehui 2012). It contains numerous inscribed and painted boards, both horizontal (*bian'e* 匾額) and vertical (*duilian* 對聯) and is accordingly also called Ankang baibian tang 安康百匾堂 (Ankang Hall of the Hundred Boards; see Hengkou daojiao xiehui 2012).

Based on his strong personal beliefs in the deity worshiped at Leigutai, Master Feng reorganized the altar structure and pantheon of the Sansheng miao, making it more specifically Daoist. He had the three original sages relocated to an honorary hall in the back while dedicating the main sanctuary to the worship of Zhenwu. The deity is positioned in the center of the altar, with the Daoist version of Guanyin, here called Cihang daoren 慈航道人, on his right and the God of Wealth (Caishen 財神) on his left (see the picture below).

After the official reopening in 2002, Master Feng made a point to spend two or three months of each year at this temple, especially during its main festival for Zhenwu's birthday, held on the 3rd day of the 3rd month (Hengkou daojiao xiehui 2012). While there, he would typically recruit lay disciples and teach them to chant the morning and evening services. He also arranged for some older Dao brothers to stay there permanently and take care of the temple's affairs: they are not complicated since it is small and attracts visitors mainly on the 1st and 15th days of the lunar month.

## Later Projects

In 2010, Master Feng tackled yet another project, the reconstruction of the Xianyue si 顯月寺 (Bright Moon Monastery).[14] Located beneath a shrine called Qibao zhai 七寶寨 (Refuge of the Seven Treasures), which sits on a wooded peak, in the village of Huangjin 黄金 in Haoping 蒿平 township, it got its name from a well, in which the moon could be seen during the day while it was invisible in the sky.

The temple was originally built in 1531, during the Ming dynasty, and still has some stone steles from the Qing. Originally, a Buddhist temple, it integrated various Daoist deities over the years, becoming gradually more syncretistic. During the Cultural Revolution, it was defaced and its statues smashed to pieces. Its building became a school for local children, but after a few years a new and bigger school was built, leaving the temple to serve as an office for village leaders, with a small clinic in one of its rooms.

---

[14] On its history, see Li H. and Zhang 2009. For its modern situation, see Ziyangxian haoping 2013a; 2013b; Xu 2014. The picture shows the temple with Master Feng and his disciple Huang Shizhen.

74 / Chapter Three

In 2010, Master Feng heard of its fate and initiated the necessary administrative steps to reopen it as a place of religious activities. While Chinese law provides that ancient places of worship can be rehabilitated to serve as temples, it took him four years to receive the authorization to proceed. On his part, the process involved lots of patience, numerous meetings with government agencies, and strong powers of conviction. The local leaders, on the other hand, had to find a new place for the clinic and their administrative offices. They resolved the latter by building a whole new office block nearby.

By this time, Master Feng had a strong reputation for being a major player in the reconstruction of religion. Over the years, his activities in the area had proven his excellent managerial skills and tireless efforts. It had become clear that his projects benefited the local believers who were happy to receive the religious services provided. And he had demonstrated that the rebuilt temples were quick to become financially independent and profitable.

For all these reasons, local government leaders recognized his projects as important contributions to the social integration and cultural development of the area. They understood the advantages of having a temple in their village that would provide historical value as well as religious activities. Beyond that, the local population strongly expressed the wish to have a proper place to pray. Without an officially recognized temple where they could burn incense, they would often climb the peak that housed the unregistered Qibao zhai shrine: it had been rebuilt in a simple fashion and was taken care of by an old monk from Leigutai. They were much looking forward to performing their worship legally again, in an accredited and renovated temple that had been part of their religious beliefs for many generations. Master Feng's motivation is similarly straightforward. He says,

> The opportunity arose, so I took it. It is important to develop sacred places of worship. To achieve good results, one should practice nonaction. I first started the process and then waited with patience for things to take shape. You see, in the end, one of the officials who became interested in the project made all the difference: soon the other departments started to become interested and then the papers were signed. (Interview on 4 October 2014)

At the end of 2013, the local government finally moved their offices to the new center, and Master Feng could officially start temple construction. He first organized a dedication ceremony on the 23$^{rd}$ of the 1$^{st}$ month to signal the erection of the main sanctuary. Then, working with the same builders and the same architect as those in charge of Leigutai, he commenced the project.

In the summer of 2014, he moved his headquarters there to be close to the work. The only Daoist in the place, he took over one of the old offices, got rid of the rats, and set up a cot for himself. Then he installed an incense burner in the courtyard and placed ritual bowls on a simple altar, welcoming villagers who come to burn incense and make a wish.

By October 2014, the main sanctuary was complety and fully decorated, ready for the installation of the statues. Again, Zhenwu was positioned in the center, accompanied by Yuhuang 玉皇 (Jade Emperor), Wenchang dijun 文昌帝君 (Imperial Lord of Literature), and Leishen 雷神 (Thunder God). Liu Shitian found donations to pay for the statues and ordered them to be made in bronze in a special factory in Fujian. The old priest who took care of the shrine at Qibao zhai moved back home due to age, and a young disciple replaced him. Master Feng came to manage both places, in addition to all his other temple commitments.

With him spending more time in Huangjin village, the day-to-day management of the Siwang miao 泗王廟 (Temple of the King of [the River] Si) fell under the responsibility of his disciple Maomao, in close cooperation with a group of lay followers. Daoist believers in Ziyang were getting increasingly busy as the number of reconstructed temples increased. Often they would come at 5:30 in the morning to sweep the temple and cook breakfast. In the afternoons, they would bring fruit to be offered the next morning for the festival of the 15th day of the month.

They then would rush to the two temples across the river, the Wuzhen guan 悟真觀 (Temple of Awakening to Perfection, shown above) on Mount Wenbi 文笔 and the Zhenren gong, the resurrected cave temple to Zhang Boduan, to do the same—sweep the floor and prepare offerings. The next day, on the 15th, they again would go to the Siwang miao at 5:30 am to perform

76 / Chapter Three

the morning services and cook breakfast for the numerous believers. In the afternoon, they would go again to the other temples to burn incense and help out. In addition, they organized transportation and visited Master Feng whenever they could, deeply concerned that he had no one to take care of him.

In sum, Master Feng was the first member of the Thunder Drum lineage to leave the mountain and actively contribute to the reconstruction of Daoist temples in the local area. He singlehanded transformed its religious landscape, moving it from a scene of widespread destruction to one of vitality and expansion. Due to his untiring efforts, Daoism went from having no functioning place whatsoever to at least six active centers, supported vibrantly by a growing community.

During all this, he also contributed to the expansion of the veneration of two particular deities, Zhenwu and Ziyang zhenren. He managed to maintain the traditional way of transmission in that he took few disciples and submitted them to strict tests, followed by a long and slow apprenticeship. The way he ran his temples also followed the old ways of focusing on sincerity and ethics in both actions and words. Overall, his goal was to foster a strong belief in his students rather than a cultural or literary understanding of Daoism. His training was based on burning incense, sweeping the floor, and meditating rather than reading books or attending conferences.

Master Feng's success in reviving Daoism in the Ziyang area had much to do with his personal development. He made fruitful connections with leading clerics and institutions during his years of cloud wandering, particularly with Min Zhiting, and learned the ways of temple management from the bottom up when he held various positions in the major monastery of Baxian gong. Beyond that, he also gained respect and charisma by being one of the few selected to attend the 1989 ordination ceremony at Baiyun guan where he emerged third in rank among all attendees. Last but certainly not least, his strong dedication and charisma combined fruitfully with the will of the people and leaders of the Ziyang region to enhance the touristic and cultural value of the area, setting a model for temple and religious projects throughout the country.

# Chapter Four

# Lineage Diffusion

The Thunder Drum lineage reached a turning point in terms of diffusion when some disciples moved to the Baxian gong in Xi'an, following Feng Xingzhao who settled there in 1985 for five years. In 1990, his Daoist brother Liu Xingdi arrived, bringing two young disciples along: Liu Shitian and Huang Shizhen. Both took advantage of the opportunities offered by this big insti-tution and went on to become influential figures, their activities and careers providing telling examples of the new type of Quanzhen cleric that emerged after the Cultural Revolution. Their methods, moreover, followed the model and suggestions of the CDA, showing just how local Daoists worked in tandem with the authorities' guidance at the national level.

## The Xi'an Area

The key figure in spreading the Thunder Drum lineage to various temples in the Xi'an area was Liu Shitian. He was born in 1973 in a village in the Ba 巴 mountains in Ankang municipality and grew up in a family of Daoist believers. Inspired by his family's devotion, became a Daoist he in March 1989 when he moved to the Leigutai temple and became the disciple of Liu Xingdi and thus a grand-disciple of Yang Faxiang (Liu S. 2009b).

Liu Shitian

Liu Xingdi with the author

78 / Chapter Four

A few months after his initiation, he followed Liu Xingdi to Baxian gong and did not return to Leigutai for twenty years. In 1990, he and Huang Shizhen were selected to attend the first training course at the Daoist College in Beijing. After his graduation in 1992, Liu went back to Baxian gong, where he served on the temple's management committee. Being involved in the supervision of this and other important temples of the province and assisting in the reconstruction of several more, he quickly became well-known for his skills and charisma, then rose along the official ladder to become chairman of the Xi'an Daoist Association, vice chairman of the Shaanxi Daoist Association, and vice secretary of the CDA. His greatest efforts, moreover, were in temple reconstruction and lineage diffusion.

His first temple project began in 1992, when Min Zhiting, then abbot of the Baxian gong and also chair of the CDA, engaged him to manage the construction of the Mingsheng gong. The temple is located on Mount Li, twenty-five kilometers east of Xi'an, a peak that forms part of the Qinling range. Rising to a height of 1302 meters, it overlooks the Huaqing chi 華清池 (Pool of Florescent Clarity), a Tang-dynasty palace and hot springs complex. Not far from there is the tomb of the First Emperor of the Qin with its famous Terracotta Warriors. Legend has it that the creator goddess Nüwa 女娃 repaired the wall of heaven from here. Its central place of worship is the Laomu dian 老母殿 (Hall of the Old Mother), an ancient Daoist sanctuary dedicated to Lishan laomu 驪山老母 (Old Mother of Mount Li) (Baidu baike 2015a; Lishan 2015).

The Mingsheng gong project was initiated by a temple of the same name near Beiqing tan 北青潭 (North Green Lake) in Taipei, dedicated to a deity called Xie Yingdeng 謝映登, a Tang-dynasty official born in the town of Lishan near Mount Li. Guided and funded through the efforts of Yan Wuxiong 顏武雄, the leader of the Taipei site, the project included the construction of a school as well as a hospital and involved more than five billion RMB (Shijie daoxue 2013; Wang and Fu 1996).

Construction began in 1992 and took fourteen years to complete. The most complicated part was to obtain legal authorization to perform religious services. At the time, only places that had been acknowledged as historical sites were granted permission for reconstruction and could obtain religious authorization. Since the Mingsheng gong was a brand-new site and dedicated to a deity otherwise unknown in mainland China, the legal process occurred in two phases. First, the Daoists obtained formal recognition of the site as a historical memorial for Xie Yingdeng as a highly meritorious Tang official. Second, after a few years, they applied to establish the temple as a religious center. Once all this was done successfully, the official opening ceremony was held on 31 October 2004.

Liu Shitian became its abbot in 1997, and soon the temple evolved into one of the biggest complexes in northwest China and became a popular tourist destination, generating significant financial revenue. To keep up the good work, Liu cooperated closely with various tourist organizations which included the temple in their one-day trips from Xi'an to the Terracotta Warriors site nearby, which meant busloads and busloads of visitors every day.

Even before this project was fully complete, Liu Shitian expanded his vision and got involved in the restoration of the Xi'an City God Temple, whose management was handed over to the Xi'an Daoist Association in March 2003. On 17 June 2005, he officially became the temple's legal representative at the Xi'an Bureau of Religious Affairs and then put all his efforts into its renovation.

The total budget was 600 million RMB, including 50 million for the renovation of the temple itself. As in other big reconstruction projects at the time, major funds came from Daoists outside of mainland China, notably Taiwan and Hong Kong and in particular from the Quanzhen-affiliated temple Fungying Seenkoon. When it reopened in 2005, it gained the legal permission to host religious activities and receive donations. Pilgrims increased from 10,000 in 2003 to over 30,000 in 2005, most attending the annual temple fair on the 8th day of the 4th lunar month (Fan 2012). The full renovation project lasted quite a few years: the grand opening ceremony was only held on 21-22 October 2013 (Xi'an Chenghuang miao 2013).

## Further Afield

While managing the ongoing affairs of the Mingsheng gong and the renovation of the City God Temple, Liu Shitian also kept an eye open for further opportunities to reopen other sites. Around 2007, he got involved in the bureaucratic process of restarting Daoist activities at the Zhang Liang miao 張良廟 (Temple of Zhang Liang) in Luoba 留埧 county.[1] A famous and quite ancient public monastery in northwest Shaanxi, about 100 kilometers from Hanzhong, it sits at the foot of Mount Zibai 紫柏. In Daoism listed as the third grotto heaven (*dongtian* 洞天), it was designated a national protected historic site on 25 May 2006.

However, at the time, the temple had not yet obtained official recognition as a religious institution. Liu Shitian worked hard, and the temple received formal authorization on 16 April 2008 (Liu S. 2008b). A splendid opening ceremony followed on 20 May 2009 in the presence of Liu

---

[1] Information collected during an interview with Liu Shitian on August 17, 2007. See also Liu S. 2008b; Liu Z. 2009; Lu 2013; Zhangliang miao guanwei hui 2013. On the early history of the site, see Fan 2010a.

as main organizer and important Daoist leaders, such as the chairman of the CDA Ren Farong as well as the then-abbot and leader of the temple's management committee, Liu Zhikun 劉至堃 (Liu Z. 2009).

Born in 1980 in the same area as Liu Shitian, Liu Zhikun was quite close to him (Liu Z. 2009; Zhangliang miao guanwei hui 2013) and like him slowly moved up along the administrative ladder after graduating from the Daoist College in Beijing in 2007. In 2014, he was chairman of the Hanzhong Daoist Association and abbot of the Qinglong guan 青龍觀 (Green Dragon Monastery) (Lu 2013). At the same time, the Zhang Liang miao was run by a management committee and slowly developed more and more religious activities, such as the annual ceremony on the birthday of its main deity, the Han-dynasty immortal Zhang Liang.

Liu Shitian, then in his late thirties, continued his activities in Shaanxi province, coming to focus increasingly on his home county, that is, he returned to his roots (*huigen* 回根) and went back home (*huigui* 回歸), eager to give back to the society that raised him. Having attained success and found widespread recognition in the Daoist community, he started to look back to where it all started.

His most important project in this context was the renovation of his first temple, Leigutai. Using his now well-established charisma and power, he joined local Daoists and government leaders in a strong communal effort. Leigutai had been damaged quite a bit during the years of trouble but nobody had done anything about renovating it. This had to do with major complications not only due to its isolated mountain-top location, difficult dirt-road access, and lack of electricity and running water but also because of local regulations and difficult relationships among institutions.

In addition, in September 1997, Mount Fenghuang was classified as a protected forest park and, in February 2004, promoted to an AA-level tourist spot. This caused the local government to build an entrance gate to the mountain and set up a ticket booth that blocked the main road to the temple (Fenghuang shan 2014). As a result, only those willing to pay the entrance fee could enter, making it harder for devotees and believers to visit the sanctuary. The situation soon caused tensions in the relationship between the Daoists and the local government.

Starting in 2009, Liu Shitian made contributions to its renovation, both financially and symbolically. First, he donated a new bronze statue of the main deity, Zhenwu, as well as set of cast-iron incense burners.[2] Next, he negotiated with all the different agencies involved to start the renovation process and hire a team of local builders. They worked as much as they could, given the scant availability of water and the often-harsh mountain weather. During winter, all construction ceased, since a thick layer of snow

---

[2] Field observation on 5 April 2009.

covered the ground and blocked the road. In spring and summer, water was often short, delaying progress for weeks at a time. After each pause, the work would only start again after rain had filled the well.

Proceeding under these difficult conditions, reconstruction took four years. On 6 August 2013, the main sanctuary was complete, the Sanqing dian. Liu Shitian had ordered new bronze statues, which arrived that day and were immediately installed on the altar, honored in a short ceremony.[3] Soon after, he set up an electric system based on solar power and invited a new team of builders and architects. Upon spending more time there, he found that the first round of renovation was of rather poor quality and did not respect the fengshui of the place to a sufficient degree. The new renovation project, fully managed by Liu himself, also involved the construction of a new dormitory, a hall for Wang Lingguan, and a proper gate. A new management team was put in place, several junior clerics having relocated from Mingsheng gong and the City God Temple.

## Tourist Development

Ziyang county at the time aimed to develop tourism particularly based on the fact that it was the only county in China named after a Daoist perfected. This made Daoism a central feature in its marketing and development program. As part of this, the county sponsored the erection of a ten-meter statue of Ziyang zhenren, consecrated on 16 April 2012. Made from 4.2 tons of bronze, it was installed halfway up the slope of Mount Wenbi, at a spot that provides a wide overview of the valley and the village (He 2012). At the same time, the ceremony also celebrated the official opening of Mount Wenbi Forest Park, the result of a new tourism initiative that also included the establishment of a Ziyang Culture Park and a project celebrating local methods of nourishing life.

The Forest Park is a public venue located along the Hanjiang River and rising up along the mountain. Besides the bronze statue, it sports a lookout tower on the peak (shown below) and a temple devoted to Ziyang zhenren, the Wuzhen guan—reopened on 18 April 2014 in conjunction with the Fourth International Daoist Forum, which had a strong focus on ecology (CDA 2014i). A trail along the valley known as Yangsheng gu 養生谷 (Valley of Nourishing Life) leads along a stream to the two other local Daoist temples, Zhenren gong and Guanyin'ai. The whole project was funded by an investment of 50 million RMB (Ziyang renmin 2014c).

---

[3] Field observation in the summer of 2013.

The complex of projects was called "one valley, three Daoist temples, five hot spots" (*yigu sandao wuke* 一谷三道五核). Its goal was to develop the valley to the point where it housed three temples and five cultural hot spots. The three temples, then, were Zhenren gong near the river bank, Wuzhen guan on Mount Wenbi, and Guanyin'ai on the high cliffs. The five hot spots were dedicated to the culture of Daoism, nourishing life, mountains and rivers, and selenium tea (*fuxi* 富硒) (Lu 2013).

The project, moreover, formed part of a larger plan to develop the county's economy. Since the area housed a major reservoir, no polluting industries were allowed, and tourism became an important resource. This caused the local government to make best use of all the various cultural and historical buildings along the Hanjiang River (shown below), offering tourists an experience of so-called Han River Culture (*hanshui wenhua* 漢水文化). Besides the five hot spots, this also featured popular songs and local drama to be performed in a new concert hall as well as buildings or artifacts related to the river, such as local paintings exhibited in the community hall (Ma 2014; TUM 2014). Beyond this, there was also mountain and river scenery, to be explored by boat, bicycle, and on foot. Overall, the goal was to create a 4A-level tourist park, costing approximately 1.5 billion RMB.[4]

With this line of development, Ziyang did not stand alone. Many localities engaged in developing their tourist industry, and Daoist sites often played a major role in this effort due to their cultural, historical, and architectural value. Most mountains sacred to Daoism duly came to be

---

[4] See Ankang 2013; Ziyang fazhan 2014; Ziyang renmin 2014a; 2014c; CDA 2014i.

managed through tourist-based projects, some embracing them more readily than others (see Johnson 2014).

As regards the Thunder Drum lineage, Liu Shitian's role was essential. Not only did he give back to his hometown and the temple where he entered the Dao, but he also enhanced positive relations with the community and encouraged bright and engaging young people to get involved in the religion. This was increasingly common in Daoism at the time and formed an important aspect of Quanzhen ethics. There was a strong sense that the temple was home and that the local area must develop for the spiritual community to flourish. I met many clerics who saved money from ritual and other services to send back to the small temple they originally came from. Some also would get involved in the process of restoring the local temple of their village and support their community in various other ways. On occasion they might even travel back and forth to help in the renovation and development process while also supporting their old masters.

## Overseas Connections

All these various activities, limited to various areas in Shaanxi province, are only part of the greater picture since the Thunder Drum lineage also spread over-seas. This began in the mid-1990s, when it became involved in the creation of the British Taoist Association, the second such organization to be established in a Western country after the Chiesa Taoista d'Italia, which was founded in 1993. The karmic connection between Master Feng and Westerners started in 1995, when a group of six British enthusiasts took the strenuous climb to Leigutai, led by the young master Huang Shizhen, shown below.

Huang was born in 1968 in a mountain village near Ziyang.[5] He left the family to enter the Daoist community at Leigutai in 1989, becoming an apprentice of Liu Xingdi, a 30$^{th}$-generation Longmen master and disciple of Yang Faxiang, that is, a Dao brother of Feng Xingzhao. Soon after, Huang went with Liu to the Baxian gong in Xi'an where, in 1990, he was selected with Liu Shitian to attend the first advanced training course at the Daoist College in Beijing. He graduated in 1992, returned to Xi'an, and soon rose through the ranks of temple management. His superiors decided he would make a good ambassador of Daoism and sent him to study English at the local College of Foreign Languages.

Having learned of his proficiency, the Shaanxi Daoist Association asked him in 1994 to lead a group of eighteen visitors around famous Daoist sites of China. The group contained six British nationals, who had written

---

[5] Information on his life and work is based on field work and interviews, 2001-2014. See also Huang 2015; Smith 2001.

to the CDA, stating their intention to discover more about Daoism in its homeland.

Their leader was Alan Redman (below, on left), a long-term practitioner of Chinese healing exercises, taijiquan, and Daoist meditation, who had learned these methods from the Chinese-American Gia-Fu Feng 馮家福 (1919-1985).[6] Feng came originally from Shanghai where he first encountered Daoism; he emigrated to the US in 1947. After completing a degree in international finance and working in this field, he connected to the counterculture of the time, associating with famous beatnik figures such as Jack Kerouac, Abraham Maslow, and Alan Watts. Later, he worked on translations of Daoist classics for Alan Watts at the Association of Asian Studies and founded his own center of Daoist practice, called Stillpoint, in the mountains near Santa Cruz, California (Komjathy 2003).

Alan Redman spent quite a few years going back and forth to this center and after Gia-Fu Feng's death started his own group of Daoist practice in England. His first visit in China was in 1994, after which he decided to undertake a more extensive trip together with his young disciple, Peter Smith, during which they first met Huang Shizhen in Xi'an.

Following this, in 1995, Redman contacted the CDA to obtain permission for another visit, this time accompanied by five disciples. Huang became their leader in Shaanxi and managed to get authorization to take them to Leigutai, a place usually not accessible to foreigners. Upon arrival, Master Yang Faxiang greeted them with the words, "What took you so long?" Years before, he had seen in a dream that six Westerners would come to Leigutai to be ordained in his lineage, so he was ready for them and had

---

[6] On the relationship between the two, see Redman 1997b; Smith 2001; 2013.

86 / Chapter Four

already started preparations for an initiation ceremony. Redman immediately made the formal request to become his disciple, and two days later all six were initiated, each receiving a name containing the Chinese character *shi* 世, matching the 31st character of the Longmen lineage poem. They were accordingly named Shijing 世静 (Alan Redman), Shiran 世然 (Paul Dun-nett), Shizhi 世之 (Hooileng Dunnett), Shitao 世道 (Peter Smith), Shiqing 世清, and Shizi 世自.

Having vowed to develop Daoism in the West, the fresh initiates returned to England and soon decided to invite their master to teach a training class there. To facilitate the process, they created the British Taoist Association in 1996. In the summer of that year, the invited Feng Xingzhao to conduct a one-week retreat in Dartmoor. Master Feng came together with Huang Shizhen as translator and Zhang Minggui 張明貴, the vice chairman of the Shaanxi Daoist Association and abbot of the Baiyun guan on Mount Baiyun as official representative (Zhang 2009; 2010). They stayed for one month, during which they conducted various Daoist events, gave interviews, met government leaders, and enjoyed the sights.

Following this, the British Taoist Association became very active. Its central committee, chaired by Shijing, also included Shiran as vice chair, Shizhi as treasurer, and Shitao as secretary. It began to organize meditation retreats and training sessions in internal cultivation throughout the year, mostly taught by Shijing, as well as workshops on various topics run by visiting Daoists. It also initiated the publication of a magazine titled *The Dragon's Mouth* (Redman 1996) and continued to raise funds to support the rebuilding of various Shaanxi temples, such as the Zhenren gong, the reconstructed cave temple in Ziyang (Redman 1997a).

In 2004, two further members received formal initiation into the Thunder Drum lineage by Master Feng at the Sansheng miao: Shiqiao 世橋 (Graeme McCracken) and Shihan 世航 (Justyna Gorska). Huang Shizhen in the meantime left the Baxian gong to renovate and run his own temple, the small Qinghua gong 青華宮 (Palace of Green Efflorescence) on the outskirts of Xi'an. Around 2008, he was promoted to abbot of the major religious center Taiqing gong 太清宮 (Palace of Great Clarity) in Luyi 鹿邑, Henan, well known for honoring the site of Laozi's birth.

His encounter with the six Westerners and his facilitation of their successful connection to the Thunder Drum lineage, moreover, inspired him to continue various activities on the international level. Whenever he got the chance, he would travel abroad or receive Westerners in China. Over the years, he recruited numerous Western disciples, some of whom established Daoist associations in their own countries. Most prominent among them are Hervé Louchouarn, the founder of the Mexican Daoist Association located in Guernavaca south of Mexico City, Jose Barreno of the

Portuguese Daoist Association centered in Lisbon, and myself of the French Daoist Association with its main sanctuary in Montluçon near Vichy.

## New Temple Functions

All these various undertakings of outreach and development changed the way Thunder Drum lineage temples function in modern society, forming part of a larger transition between masters active before the Cultural Revolution and those later. In fact, it represents a shift of temple function from places of worship to platforms for the transmission of traditional Chinese culture and tourist development.

Feng Xingzhao was on the conservative end of this spectrum. He often emphasized how important it was to open sacred places in the community so that villagers and visitors could worship properly. His main goal was always to develop Daoist sites as places of communication between deities and villagers rather than between people and culture or tourists and locals. Temples to him contained an intrinsic power that connected heaven and earth. On this basis, he noted, they could best contribute to the well-being of society, providing answers to devotees' prayers. As he said,

> Daoist temples are places where people can communicate with the deities. What allows this communication? It is like using a mobile phone. When we install the statues, we perform the consecration ceremony of Opening the Light (*kaiguang* 開光). This invites the deities' power to come into the statues. Then, when people come and pray with sincerity and burn incense, it is like dialing on a mobile phone to contact this power. You cannot see it, but it is there. It is like the transmission of your mobile phone, you cannot see it either, but it still works. Therefore, it is important to set up temples and use the proper techniques and rituals to consecrate them.

Based on this fundamental perspective, he taught lay disciples three main principles with strong rigor.

> First, the temple is the place where the deities live. You must take care of just as well as you take care of your own home. You as priests are key caretakers of the temple. You must take care of them just as much as you take care of your family members.
>
> Second, always remember that the temple will be there for generations to come; the clerics are temporary office-holders in its overall lifetime. Protecting the temple is thus as much your responsibility as theirs.
>
> Third, your actions are always under scrutiny of the deities so that, according to the law of retribution, both your own well-being and that of your family and descendants depend on the sincerity and the charity of your actions.

88 / Chapter Four

Teachings such as these are visually present right in the temple's decoration. Thus, Master Feng had one stele engraved specially with the *Ganying pian* 感應篇 (Treatise of Impulse and Response), a Song-dynasty classic that outlines basic moral guidelines and explains the positive effects of following them and the disastrous consequences of ignoring or violating them. Another stone he had carved with the *San guiyi wujie* 三皈依五戒 (Five Precepts and Three Refuges) to remind all and every one of the importance of keeping the precepts and maintaining devotion to Dao, masters, and scriptures.

Beyond that, Master Feng made his teachings come to life through his very own behavior, including the way he managed his resident temples. He always worked right alongside a group of lay disciples from the local village, in particular a group of women over forty who would come in to run the day-to-day activities. He was good friends with them, and they were his personal followers, having studied with him continuously for over ten years ever since he first arrived at the Zhenren gong. Two of them went to the temple every day at 5:30 in the morning to bring fresh vegetables for offerings, sweep the floor, and clean the halls. They would bow to the deities, offer incense, and make a small donation. Feeling that they performed their duty to their faith, they would find themselves ready to face the day and go back to the village. Once there, around 7:30 am, they would send their grandchildren off to school, cook breakfast for their husbands, and go to work.

To celebrate the first and full moon, on the 1st and 15th day of each lunar month, in addition to this routine, the women would also bring more extensive offerings on the day before, then stay longer on the day itself to chant the scriptures along with Master Feng and his clerical disciple Maomao. Typically, fifty to a hundred villagers would come and join them to pray for blessings. They also had breakfast there, specially prepared by the women. By 11 o'clock, it was usually all over, the temple returning to its baseline tranquility. Only five or ten devotees might stay longer to attend the ritual noon meal and maybe the evening services.

Whenever a new community member arrived and expressed an interest, senior ones happily taught her how to perform these various activities and modes of worship. They would share how they solved problems in their family by praying to the deity as well as through the application of principles Feng taught them, such as non-contention, understanding, and forgiveness. They would tell many stories about the efficacy of the god Zhenwu in curing ailments, their own or those of a family member. Still, they also warned new arrivals that just burning incense was not enough: they must live a moral life and take good care of the temple.

Master Feng lived in his temple with only one disciple, but quite often other adepts would come to stay for a few weeks. Some were farmers who had time during the fallow season of winter and wished to enhance their spiritual prowess. Others were handicapped mentally or physically and had nowhere else to go. Master Feng always took them in until their situation improved. Sometimes a British or other foreign disciple passed by and stayed for a while. In other words, the temple was a place with its own rhythm of quiet activity that also served as a temporary refuge.

Master Feng trained his celibate clerics in the traditional way, accepting and nurturing them one at the time. Any disciple had to spend a certain number of years by his side to learn just how to take best care of the temple. At first, he or she only performed menial tasks such as cleaning the halls and preparing food or growing vegetables. Later, they were given more responsibilities, such as burning incense before the deities. After about three years, they were allowed to study the scriptures. In other words, the sacred knowledge was transmitted not so much in words but by living example. Master Feng did not talk much, which challenged disciples to develop a keen sense of observation and intuition. Only in this manner could they connect to the deep wisdom he exhibited in his daily activities.

Master Feng insisted that the first three years were most important, a period of growth in sincerity and proper dedication to the Daoist path. This, plus a strong belief in the power of the immortals and a deep commitment to service, to him formed the foundation of all progress toward the ultimate goal of Daoist initiation and ordination, which assembled all masters and disciple in a great joint celebration (as shown below).

He felt deep regret deeply that this traditional way was increasingly falling by the wayside. To him, the new generation of clerics did not have sufficient sincerity and lacked perseverance. Still, he was willing to adapt to the changing times and even started teaching the scriptures before a disciple had been with him for three years. Also, after quite a bit of resistance and many tentative trials, he eventually agreed to let lay believers participate in the daily temple rituals.

Liu Shitian in contrast was more concerned with the large-scale diffusion of Daoist values, not only through temple renovation and reactivation but also through cultural events. His vision of what the role of a temple should be differed significantly, so that temples under his guidance grew into sites of community fairs, historical lectures, seminars on longevity techniques, and tourist activities. Daoist values, spiritual cultivation, and deity worship were still present, but the overreaching hope was that by making a temple attractive within a modern cultural context, more people would be guided to embrace Dao and join the devotional community.

# Chapter Five

# From Religion to Culture

Under the guidance of the CDA and influenced by the teachings of the Daoist College, many younger abbots and Daoist leaders, both of larger teaching monasteries and smaller temples, adopted a different approach to the revival and ongoing adaptation of Daoism. Seeing the religion as an important aspect of Chinese culture and as a useful tool to social development, they hoped to contribute to its transformation and evolution on a larger scale. The key representative of this approach within the Thunder Drum lineage was Liu Shitian, whose activities closely reflected what happened on the national level in terms of Daoist transformation, showing just how the new role of Daoism in society was construed in the early decades of the 21$^{st}$ century.

Typically, this involved five key aspects of redefinition: Daoism came to be presented as a charitable entity, as the protector of Chinese culture that supports traditional philosophy and creative arts, as an ethical system that could remedy key failings of modern society, as a tool to solve ecological problems, and as a way of enhancing and promoting healthy living. Overall, new-generation masters presented it as an active and mo-dern partner, intensely participating in discussions of secular society and striving for its improvement. Many large-scale events sponsored by Daoist temples accordingly involved charitable activities, health workshops, academic conferences, ecological forums, as well as musical concerts, art exhibitions, and theater productions.

## Clerical Training

The education of young progressive abbots came to differ greatly from that of priests before the Cultural Revolution. Thus, Liu Shitian had barely entered the order when he was selected to attend the first two-year course at the Daoist College, which began in March 1990, becoming one of 500 clerics who attended this advanced course over the next fifteen years. As prescribed in its constitution, the College training consisted of classes on religious Daoism to 70 percent of its curriculum, the remainder focusing on political doctrine and cultural subjects (see Wang 2009).

After graduation, Liu had further opportunities to advance his education by attending various short training seminars. One example was the Advanced Training in Daoist Culture and Management, held first in the

92 / Chapter Five

summer of 2006 (Liu 2007). A three-week annual program, this served to promote modern management techniques among temple leaders, organized by Centre for Studies of Daoist Culture of the Chinese University of Hong Kong in close cooperation with the Fungying Seenkoon temple. Besides teaching different approaches to management to young religious leaders, it also enhanced the cooperation between the Daoist communities of Hong Kong and mainland China (Wang K. 2011).

Another venue of continuing education and enhanced training was the opportunity, offered by the government, for clerics to enroll in specific university programs for religious leaders. In this context, Liu Shitian was selected to study for a Master's degree at the Philosophy Department of People's University (Renmin daxue 人民大學) in Beijing. This particular program—as much as most other training courses and educational opportunities for clerics—formed part of an incentive to improve the educational level of Daoist leaders, sponsored by the government in conjunction with the CDA.

Young leaders tended to be very busy with these classes and often spent relatively little time at their home institution. While it still involved travel, the transmission of knowledge was different from the traditional slow mode of learning through a master-disciple relationship as preferred by senior Daoists like Feng Xingzhao. On the other hand, the new modes of training were more centralized and allowed for a standardization of methods and knowledge. As a result, the activities and presentations of younger clerics and Quanzhen abbots closely matched the guidelines established by national institutions, creating a much more uniform image of Daoism in society and making the religion relevant in various aspects.

Liu Shitian clearly summarized this approach in his final paper for the 2006 Advanced Training in Daoist Culture and Management (Liu 2007; 2008c). He began by stating that "the root of Chinese culture lies with Daoism." Due to historical events including the Cultural Revolution, Daoism declined drastically. "This situation seriously demands that we [the new generation of Daoist clerics] look closely at the value and place of Daoism in order to keep its essence and discard all waste, to weed out the chaff and make renovations."

From here he presented three points that he considered the essence of Daoism. First, the immortals as much as Dao itself treasure life and strive to bring people to salvation. On the individual level this means the cultivation of personal health and longevity; on the social level it manifests as ethics and virtues, the pursuit of a compassionate and caring attitude. Second, one can enhance and perfect spirit by honoring Dao and valuing ethics and virtues through charitable deeds. This promotes the idea of Daoism as a source of charitable activities. Third, heaven and humanity join in oneness and society is in harmony. This emphasizes the importance of the connection between people and the environment as well as of the creation of a peaceful society.

Liu as much as other young clerics took these principles very seriously and organized various events and activities to feature them prominently and promote them within Chinese society.

## Major Conferences

His first step into this direction was his involvement with the First International Daoist Forum on the *Daode jing*, held in Xi'an and Hong Kong on 22-27 April 2007 (Liu 2009a). Supported by the government, it was the first of its kind to be fully organized on a national scale and considered a major sign that the government was embracing the development of Daoism as an active player in Chinese society (Wang K. 2011).

Liu Shitian participated in its organization as a member of the Shaanxi Daoist Association, while his teachers Feng Xingzhao and Zhang Xingde came as invited participants. Observing the statue of Laozi on the main stage of the forum, the two old Thunder Drum masters commented, "This is a young Laozi." For them, as for other clerics ordained before the Cultural Revolution, such events were new and symbolized a form of Daoism that actively pursued different ways of expressing itself and playing its role in civil society.

The theme of the Forum was "Constructing a Harmonious World through Dao." It focused on the *Daode jing*, particularly in relation to a culture of harmony, environmental protection, modern ways of management, and the enhancement of health. Being the first international gathering on Daoism in China, many academic institutions were also involved. They included the Institute of World Religions, the Chinese Academy of Social Sciences, the Centre for the Study of Daoism at the Chinese University of Hong Kong, the Shaanxi Academy of Social Sciences, the Institute for the Study of Chinese Daoism and Religious Culture of Sichuan University, the Center for the Study of Daoism and Traditional Culture at Xiamen University, the Religious Culture Press, and the China Religion Journal (see Xinhua 2007; Zhongguo wang 2007a; 2007b).

The Forum was organized on a grand scale and encompassed a large crowd, consisting of a thorough mixture of academics and clerics. It had a huge influence over the following years and triggered the creation of numerous cultural events within the Daoist community, such as the national "Discussion of Scriptures of the Mystery Gate" that soon became an annual occasion (Yin 2008).

In its wake, Liu Shitian was inspired to organize something similar at his home temples, Mingsheng gong and the City God Temple. He not only established charitable associations at these two institutions but also began to sponsor various cultural events to show just how Daoism could promote traditional Chinese culture. A vivid example was the series of conferences called "Questions about Dao on Mount Li" (Lishan wendao 驪山問道). The first meeting was held on 29-30 June 2009 and focused on "Harmonious Development through Dao in the World" (shown below).

A hundred clerics joined fifty academics, mostly members of the Chinese Academy of Social Sciences, the Shaanxi Academy of Social sciences, the Shanghai Academy of Social Sciences and the Sichuan University Religious Studies Department, all presenting papers on various aspects of Daoist culture (Liu 2009a).

The program proceeded in four sections: a ceremony called "Ritual for the Celebration of the 60th Anniversary of the New China and Prayer for World Peace;" the conference proper, on the role of Daoism in the development of the new, fully harmonious society; a special session on "Dao and Nourishing Life" (Liu and Li 2009); and a discussion forum on the role and power of Daoist scriptures, combined with a dialogue with Buddhists and Confucians on how to best create social harmony.

## Scriptural Discussions

Soon scriptural discussions soon became all the rage. The first one Liu was involved in occurred during the 2009 conference and focused on the *Yinfu jing* and the *Daode jing*, both connected to Shaanxi province since they presumably were compiled at Louguantai and on Mount Li. However, it was not the first of its kind. This mode of bringing Daoist discourse into the modern age, a new trend within the Daoist community, began with the 2007 Forum and officially started on 10 October 2008, when the CDA organized a formal session on Mount Lao in Shandong (Wang K. 2011; Yin 2008). Its goal was to stimulate clerics to interpret the theories embedded in Daoist texts in a more intellectual manner and open a discussion of their contents with lay thinkers and academics.

In a religion where teachings are mostly based on examples, metaphysical experiences, and master-disciple transmission, this kind of intellectual articulation of theories and concepts is an entirely new skill, a particular way of communication and expression required in 21st-century society. The 2008 meeting, therefore, started a trend that continued to spread at the provincial and local level within the Daoist community. Many more events of the same type were in due course held yearly at various Daoist centers.

On the national level, scriptural discussions evolved through a series of further meetings: a second one on Mount Lao in 2009, a third at the Zhongyue miao 中岳廟 (Temple of the Central Peak) in Henan in 2011, a fourth on Mount Wudang in 2012 as part of the Grand Offering to the Heaven of Grand Network (*Luotian dajiao* 羅天大醮) (Huang 2012), a fifth on Mount Hua in 2013 with a focus on the moral treatise *Ganyin pian* (CDA 2013a), and a sixth on Mount Tai in 2014 with particular attention to the *Wenchang dijun Yinzhi wen* 文昌帝君陰騭文 (Divine Lord Wenchang's Text of Potent Stallions) (CDA 2014b).

On the provincial level, scriptural discussions were also held on an annual basis. For example, the Shaanxi Daoist Associations started their series of events on 25 November 2010 on Mount Hua (see the picture below), working closely with the Shaanxi Academy of Social Sciences (Shaanxi sheng and Wei 2010).

Eleven young clerics, including also the Thunder Drum master Chen Jingzhan 陳景展, a disciple of Huang Shizhen, presented Daoist teachings from a religious perspective while academics like Fan Guangchun 樊光春 examined the scriptures from historical, linguistic, and philosophical viewpoints, actively participating in the jury panel. This again shows the general trend to combine religious and academic presentations and integrate the two dimensions in a fruitful and harmonious manner.

Beyond these meetings, many provincial Daoist associations also selected a small team of three young clerics to travel around their province each year to expound scriptural teachings. Known as *xunjiang tuan* 巡講團, they journeyed from one local Daoist association to the next, visiting four or five different cities to explain various scriptures in four-hour sessions, each expressing their views on a particular subject. In this manner, Daoist ideas and concepts came to spread to places where the local association might not yet have implemented formal discussion events or lacked the means to do so.

For example, the Shaanxi Daoist Association started a yearly tour for expounding the scriptures by focusing on a different part of the province each time (Shaanxi and Wang Yu 2013). In 2013, three young Quanzhen clerics—Feng Lihe 馮理翮 from Mount Baiyun in Jiaxian 佳 county, Lu Liqi 陸理麒 from the Qinglong guan in Hanzhong, and the Thunder Drum master Chen Jingzhan from the Zhenwu miao in Lantian 藍田—toured three cities in southern Shaanxi: Hanzhong, Ankang, and Shangluo 商洛. They spent half a day explaining a particular scripture and its key concepts— chosen originally at the national level. Their presentations would later be repeated as part of a national competition. The main scripture in 2013 was the *Ganying pian*; they key concept was "correcting oneself and practicing goodness" (Shaanxi and Wang 2013).

When the traveling group arrived in Ankang, the Leigutai abbot Zhang Xingde as well as the senior master Feng Xingzhao were invited as representatives of the local Daoist association. They both came down from the mountain to attend, bringing over twenty lay disciples along. At the end of the presentation, the locals were not very impressed, noting that true teachings were acquired by worshiping the gods with sincerity and taking care of the temple where their master resided rather than by discussions and discourses. They also believed that their own masters had a great deal more experience than those young clerics whose approach to Daoism they found academic rather than experiential. In other words, they felt that listening to the discussions was not all that useful with regard to their Daoist practice.

Liu Shitian often participated in scriptural discussions, either as a guest of honor or as a member of the jury panel. He also often sent the most articulate of his clerics to participate in various competitions and debates. In one case, during the sixth national session on Mount Tai, he was on the jury while his disciple Dong Zhiguang 董至光, from the City God Temple in Xi'an, participated in the competition (Zhao 2014). In some cases, his clerics performed exceptionally well. For example, Tao Guanjing 陶觀静, also from the City God Temple, won first prize during the second Shaanxi session in Xianyang (Shaanxi and Jin 2012).

## Classical Learning

To be successful in scriptural discussion requires expertise in two areas. One is the debate part, the active engagement with others in competition during the various organized events; the other is classical learning, an in-depth understanding of the scriptures. While the first is taught on site and also in mock debates held at individual temples, the second is the subject of a special curriculum established by the Daoist College. It was inaugurated on 4 September 2011 as a one-year training in scriptural studies, enrolling fifteen students (CDA 2011b; Chen and Zi 2011). Since then, many

98 / Chapter Five

clerics who commonly participate in scriptural competitions have been graduates of this training. Among Thunder Drum clerics, especially Chen Jingzhan stands out. After he attended the training, he participated in many discus-sion sessions all over China and succeeded in a variety of competitive debates.

Another venue to obtain expertise in classical learning was sponsored by Liu Shitian. When he organized the second session on Questions about Dao on Mount Li in 2013, he also officially opened the Mount Li Academy (Lishan shuyuan 驪山書院). Housed at the Mingsheng gong, it was to present classes on Confucianism and Daoism and increase awareness of their concepts and ideas. Liu was not a pioneer in this: many newly reconstructed temples and major teaching monasteries founded similar institutions. They were intended to offer seminars, workshops, lectures, and classes on a regular basis to both clerics and lay followers free of charge.

An early example is the Lao-Zhuang Academy (Lao-Zhuang shuyuan 老莊書院) on Mount Qingcheng in Sichuan, which opened on 22 April 2010. For years, it sponsored regular talks and classes on the *Daode jing*, the *Zhuangzi*, *Yijing* divination, Fengshui, Chinese medicine, methods of nourishing life, and other aspects of Daoist culture (Qingyang gong 2014; Bloch 2019). All its presentations and courses were recorded and uploaded on the internet to be made accessible to the public for free viewing. The Academy developed its own web channel on the popular hosting website Youku 优酷 (weibo.com/lao-zhuangshuyuan; www.wingyang gong.org). In addition, it also started to publish its own magazine, called *Lao-Zhuang*.

Scripture-based seminars and other modes of education in classical learning with the same purpose were also held in organizations outside of such academies. For example, on 23 July 2014 the Changchun guan in Wuhan opened the first Daoist Study Lecture Room (Wuhan 2014a). Held in the Daozang ge 道藏閣 (Pavilion of the Daoist Canon), lectures were free of charge, video recorded, and posted on the internet to maximize the number of attendees (Wuhan and Zhang 2014).

They featured Daoists from all different schools and venues as well as academics and university professors. Thus, the third lecture, on 12 September 2014, was given by the vice chairman of the CDA, Zhang Jiyu 張繼禹, a member of the Zhengyi tradition. His topic was "Cultivating the Heart-Mind to Embody Dao" (*xiuxin yi tidao* 修心以體道) (Wuhan 2014a). The fourth lecture, on 1 November 2014 was delivered by Professor Gu Chenghua 劉固盛 of the History and Culture Department of Huazhong Normal University 華中師範大學. He spoke at length about the *Daode jing* line, "highest virtue is like water" (Wuhan and Gu 2014).

## The Role of Academics

As part of this cultural transformation, academics came to be increasingly involved in many activities Daoist clerics organized on all different levels, local and national, as well as in a great variety of areas—management (such as the Directors' Committee), training (Daoist College), research (Academies), diffusion (websites, magazines), and more (Wang K. 2011). Their active participation in the process of revival and reconstruction was an important modality since the reestablishment of the CDA.

A major player in this context was Li Yangzheng 李養正. The only academic among thirty-nine clerics, he was elected as a national representative during the third meeting of the CDA in 1980 (CDA 1980). This recovered his earlier (1958) position of secretary and led later to a highly influential role in the organization. The author of many books and articles, he was in charge of the CDA's research center from 1985 to 1992 and also served as editor of its main organ, the magazine *Zhongguo daojiao*. In 1990, he became the associate dean of the Daoist College (Zhang W. 2014). Following his model, many academics were included as national representatives and board members of the CDA. All research centers, editorial organizations, publishing venues, and academic thus came to include professors and lecturers from various universities.

Local Daoist associations followed this lead and similarly included local academics in their research centers, publications, and training activities. Liu Shitian, for example, often worked closely with Fan Guangchun, a scholar at the Shaanxi Academy of Social Sciences, organizing events or publications sponsored by the provincial or local (Shaanxi or Ziyang) Daoist Association. This held true even more for large-scale conferences or international forums.

Another major area where academics played a key role was as teachers both at the different branches of the Daoist College (Beijing, Sichuan, Changsha) and in short-term training sessions. For example, academics were typically invited to explain the deeper meaning of certain texts during scriptural discussions, both on the national and local level, and often serve as members of the jury. They were also frequently asked to give talks at one or the other academy established by leading monasteries as noted earlier.

In this context the question arises why clerics would feel the need to include academics at most levels of their activities, especially since—as I found in a number of interviews—some did not hesitate to present themselves as communist atheists and had no faith in Daoism at all. The main reason, it turns out, was the great pressure placed on the religious community to identify itself as an important part of Chinese culture in order to gain governmental support. The official discourse was quite clear on what position it wished Daoists and their teachings to take in Chinese society. In official talks and publications, political leaders never tired of presenting

Daoism as a mainstream aspect of Chinese culture. SARA officials, who until 2018 held all power over religious organizations, insisted with considerable force that Daoism be identified first and foremost as a part of Chinese traditional culture and only secondarily as a religion (Wang Z. 2011).

Even in 2014, the pressure to present Daoism primarily as a cultural movement was sometimes overwhelming, so that its mystical and spiritual components began to be neglected. The religion was valued mainly in terms of how much it contributed to a moral society by influencing the behavior of people, the Daoist belief system being used to create a more "ethical and harmonious society." A case in point is Liu Shitian's article on the role of the belief in the City God, where he presented all faith in divine entities as a tool to create a harmonious and ethical society, matching academic views and government discourse (Liu 2013a). In contrast, Feng Xingzhao always maintained a more traditional and thus religious position, presenting faith in gods as a means of release from suffering and a way of dealing with the underworld and issues of reincarnation.

Considering that most publications on Daoism were written by academics and that they formed an important component of the teaching materials at Daoist colleges, it is not surprising that clerics of the new generation came to understand the religion more as a social factor than a way toward personal realization or spiritual attainment. This trend being so widespread and deeply embedded in the Daoist community, the next question is: Where did that leave the religious discourse?

During scriptural discussions, sacred texts were analyzed in term of their philosophical values and cultural aspects. Both the theme of the events and the talks presented by young clerics during competitions were secular and academic in nature, serving the diffusion of government mottoes, doctrines, and positions. The contents of the sacred texts were presented as secular and cultural tools to maintain and enhance a harmonious society. For example, the Fifth National Competition of Scriptural Discussion, held on 11-13 September 2013 on Mount Hua, focused on the slogan "correct the self to transform humankind, let the masses practice goodness!" The scripture under debate was the moral treatise *Ganying pian*. Most papers presented by young clerics included titles that closely matched government slogans and explained the text from a sociological perspective.[1] The exact same trend was obvious during the Sixth National Competition, held on 3 September 2014 on Mount Tai (CDA 2014).

However, already at this meeting, the tendency to shift the understanding of Daoism from the religious to the secular started to be criticized, not only privately and in the corridors but also quite publicly and in official addresses, the key catchphrase being the over-secularization of Daoist

---

[1] CDA 2013a. On presentations with a sociological view of Daoist texts, see Liu C. 2013; Song 2013.

discourse. The most relevant indicator of this new trend was the closing speech, delivered by the Quanzhen master Liu Huaiyuan 劉懷元, then chairman of the Shandong Daoist Association and vice chairman of the CDA (2013).

In his address, which was published on the official CDA website, he made seven strong points, beginning by encouraging all attendees to distance themselves from a purely academic approach to interpreting the scriptures. Next, he insisted that all juries should be composed of Daoist clerics and expressed his relief that over the years they had gradually included more clerics and fewer academics, so that the 2014 panel was made of eight priests and one scholar. Third, he demanded that the competing teams should include only religious Daoists.

In the later part of his speech, Liu further reminded his audience that this as much as other events of its kind was not a goal in itself but rather served as a tool to accelerate the reintegration of the tradition, which required that scriptural teachings be expounded and discussed within the temples themselves. He noted that the inherent purpose of scriptural discussions was to educate, guide, and transform the people who come to listen to them, which meant that the act itself had an intrinsic power of salvation. This to him made it that much more important to follow the traditional approach of understanding the scriptures through personal practice and intuition. Liu concluded by emphasizing that the study and explanation of the scriptures must not rely on academic analysis but come from personal practice and go hand in hand with observing the precepts and applying the teachings in an environment of actual living (Liu H. 2014).

Liu Huaiyuan was not the only cleric to raise his eyebrows and question the role of purely academic readings of Daoist teachings within the religious community. In his wake, many others posted similar articles on the internet and gave related speeches during conferences. A new motto arose within the Daoist community that can be summarized as: "Daoism should be presented by Daoists and in a Daoist way!"[2]

Some who agreed with this and were similarly critical of an overly academic approach were themselves scholars. A case in point is Wang Chi 王馳, the vice dean of the Shanghai Daoist College with a Ph. D. in philosophy from Nanjing University (Wang C. 2014). In many speeches he expressed his position as a fervent proponent of Daoist religious discourse.

For example, he presented an hour-long talk during a six-day training course on Daoist experience, held at the Mount Mao Academy from 27 August to 1 September 2014 and organized by the Qianyuan guan 乾元觀 (Monastery of Heavenly Prime; see Maoshan 2014b) for a delegation from the Singapore Daoist College. He strongly criticized the academic inter-

---

[2] I often heard this during my field work, especially during the sixth National Competition, but also while attending various other meetings.

102 / Chapter Five

pretation of Daoist teachings and warned Daoist believers to exert caution about what they read or heard coming from the academic field. He insisted that there was a significant difference in scriptural discourse as presented by academics and the more spiritual information gleamed from them by religious masters and serious devotees (Maoshan 2014a).

A most striking example he presented to illustrate the dichotomy between religious and academic discourse was the date of the beginning of Daoism. From the academic point of view, Daoism was just about 2000 years old, since it began with the establishment of the first major organized Daoist organization, the Celestial Masters, by Zhang Daoling 張道陵 in 142 CE. However, from a religious perspective as expressed in the scriptures, it went back much further and was over 5000 years old, beginning with the revelatory encounter of Guangchengzi, one of the many transformations of Lord Lao, with the Yellow Emperor.[3]

Based on this and similar cases, Wang Chi encouraged believers to examine closely just what their position was within this and other complicated matters and to read academic publications with a careful and critical mind. His overall opinion was that a member of the Daoist community, one who studied the scriptures and believed in Dao and the gods, should base his or her understanding on the information provided by the sacred materials as revealed by the gods and contained in the Daoist Canon. He vehemently advocated that the religion should understand and express itself based on its own tradition and not on historical, philosophical, or academic readings by people who were professed atheists, card-carrying communists, or came from an altogether different religious background. In addition, he stressed the role and power of the deities and the miraculous encounters that often happen along the Daoist path. As I noted while listening to his talk, to him belief in the gods was not merely a tool to promote harmony in contemporary society but a way to free oneself from suffering and attain Dao.

---

[3] The same example also appears in an article by the Zhejiang cleric Wan Jingyuan 萬景元, widely disseminated on the internet (Wan 2014).

# Chapter Six

# Social Relevance

In the early decades of the 21st century, Daoists worked hard to adapt to the changing political climate and undertake various activities seen as making a positive contribution to modern society. They revived orchestras of Daoist music at various temples, making this expression of Chinese culture accessible to wider audiences to great acclaim. They engaged in charitable activities and donations, supporting the poorer segments of Chinese society. In addition, they supported and spread methods of nourishing life—an important aspect of traditional practice—helping people recover from illness and maintain their health. Beyond that, Daoists also engaged powerfully in ecological efforts, raising environmental awareness in accordance with their inherent honoring of natural processes. Plus, they established a more active online presence, fitting temples with Wi-Fi, constructing websites, and participating in social media.

## Traditional Music

The emphasis of the government and the CDA at the time was to promote Daoism as a protector of traditional Chinese culture. This created a movement to revive some cultural aspects such as Daoist music (see Cao 1996). For example, when Liu Shitian became abbot of the City God Temple, he revived its Daoist orchestra by assembling older clerics, notably those who had lived there before the Cultural Revolution. The group grew to about forty members and was invited to participate in concerts both in China and abroad, performing at large-scale public events such the Europe-Asia Economic Forum, the Macao Daoist Festival (Aomen 2014; personal observation), and the 2014 Daoist Music Festival at the Baiyun guan in Lanzhou, Gansu (Daojiao zhiyin 2012). Through the promotion of its music, Daoism earned international recognition. For example, in 2008 the City God Temple orchestra was recognized by the UNESCO as an Intangible Cultural Heritage (Fan 2012, 117-19).

The Quanzhen monastic order in general played an important role in the revival and promotion of Daoist music. Thus, after the reopening of religious activities, the Baiyun guan in Beijing was the first to officially establish an orchestra, which performed on 22 August 1988 at the Beijing Concert Hall. This stimulated other temples, such as the Zhengyi sanctuary

Xuanmiao guan 玄妙觀 (Temple of Mystery and Wonder) in Suzhou 蘇州 to set up their own ensembles and perform in public.

Within the Quanzhen order, the most important orchestras were those of the Qingyang gong 青羊宮 (Black Sheep Palace) in Chengdu, Zixiao gong 紫霄宮 (Palace of the Purple Empyrean), on Mount Wudang, the Qianyuan guan on Mount Mao, and the Baiyun guan on Mount Baiyun. In the 1990s, the trend moved overseas, and affiliated temples outside of China began to set up their own orchestras. Thus, in 1996, the Fungying Seenkoon created the Hong Kong Daoist Orchestra and, in 2001, under the inspiration and guidance of Liu Hong 劉紅, professor at the Music Department of the Chinese University of Hong Kong, began to sponsor an annual Daoist music festival. Held in different cities—including Taipei, Beijing, Singapore, Guangzhou, Chengdu, Hong Kong, Nanchang, Wuhan, Jingtan, Guangzhou, Hong Kong, Shanghai, and more—it emerged as an important Daoist music event.

Regular and large-scale gatherings such as this allowed the diffusion of Daoist music into general society, far beyond the temples. While originally performed only as part of temple rituals, it soon became a major cultural asset. The Quanzhen order contributed greatly to its revival, aiding in its renaissance and promoting it widely both nationally and internationally. Leaders such as Liu Shitian contributed vastly to enable Daoist music to be recognized internationally, even at UNESCO level.

# Charitable Activities

Various other factors further highlight the image of Daoism as a key player in modern society, most importantly the engagement in charitable activities and social giving. In the 2000s, many temples established formal charity organizations, literally "societies of compassionate love and meritorious virtue " (*ci'ai gongde hui* 慈爱功德會). For example, Liu Shitian as abbot of the Mingsheng gong arranged for the temple to support people in need and in many interviews emphasized the importance of donating and giving, often citing the statement that "charity is the basis of religion." In 2009, he received a prize for his activities at a ceremony honoring Ten Charitable Personalities of Shaanxi. It is estimated that he donated a total of 3 million RMB between 2004 and 2010, 70 percent of which went into education, such as scholarships for university students (Liu and Hua 2010).

On 9 October 2012, he formally established the Charitable Society of the Mingsheng gong in Xi'an's Lintong 臨潼 district. Its activities included financially supporting students in poor areas and helping old people (He and Lishan 2014). For the most part, it provided financial support through monetary donations or material succor in the form of direct help, notably in case of disasters. For example, after the 2008 Sichuan earthquake, he led eight priests and ten trucks with first aid kits and tents to the disaster area (Lou 2008a; Shaanxi and Meng 2008).[1] Such activities were considered part of the religion's role in society and strongly encouraged by the government through the CDA (Wang K. 2011).

According to official statistics, Daoist institutions donated around 400 million RMB since the reopening of their activities in 1979, with 300 million being raised between 2007 and 2012 (Chen 2103b). In 2012, the establishment of a specific government regulation for the involvement of religious institutions in charities stimulated an increase in the registration of Daoist charitable organiztions.[2]

In June of the same year, six departments of the central government, including the SARA, issued a joint notice that actively encouraged and supported religious groups to engage in charitable activities, suggesting that policies be implemented to guide such works along the principles of "active support, equal treatment, and lawful administration." According to the notice, the government would provide preferential policies for such endeavors (Huang and Zhang 2014.) Soon there were over twenty charitable societies established by various Daoist temples as well as those run by national and local Daoist associations (Chen 2013b).

---

[1] For a general discussion of the CDA on charity events, see Chen 2013a; 2013b.

[2] Its text can be found online: Guojia shuiwu zongju 国家税务总局, "Guanyu guli he guifan zongjiaojie congshi gongyi cishan huodong de yijian" 关于鼓励和规范宗教界从事公益慈善活动的意见.

# Nourishing Life

Nourishing life was another area where Daoists expanded into civil society. Liu Shitian, like many other new abbots, made use of the concept on three levels: tourism, intellectual presentation, and cultivation practice. He did so by developing of tourist projects with a focus on health, organizing conferences, and setting up training sessions.

As regards the first, in the early 2010s, Liu was involved with the creation of the Ziyang Daoist Nourishing Life and Culture Park (Ziyang daojiao yangsheng wenhua wang 紫陽道教養生文化園) on Mount Wenbi. On 26 August 2012, he was invited by the local government to attend a meeting on planning and development, which was also attended by Fan Guangchun of the Shaanxi Social Sciences Academy and by Master Feng Xingzhao. The project consisted of creating a cultural environment to develop a strong tourist industry in the county (Chen G. 2012). It was quite similar to efforts in other places, as for example on Mounts Mao and Longhu, that often centered around a scenic area, duly called Yangsheng gu (Valley of Nourishing Life). The nourishing life aspect of Daoism had great tourist value and came to be quite popular in Chinese society (see Daojiao zhiyin 2015; Yichun renmin zhengfu 2014; Zhong 2011; Wang R. 2014).

In terms of conferences, Liu participated in the 2009 event known as Questions about Dao on Mount Li, which included a session entitled "Dao and Nourishing Life." Citing the classical phrase, "the highest medicine has three aspects, spirit, $qi$, and essence," Liu explained that the regular practice of meditation would benefit health and demonstrated the practice of "sounding the heavenly drum" (*wu tiangu* 嗚天鼓) (Liu and Li 2009; Liu 2012).

A more practical effort occurred when Liu introduced nourishing life practices to university students during the National Youth Summer Camp on Daoist Culture (Quanguo dao wenhua qingnian xia lingying 全國道文化青年夏令营), initiated in 2014 with by the help of He Jianming 何建明 of the Department of Philosophy at People's University, and thereafter held annually (Lishan Mingsheng gong 2015a; Yang 2014). Hoping to spread Daoism more widely in society, he brought young people into the temples, inviting them to spend some time in a monastic setting and get a taste of Daoist culture and long-life practices (He and Lishan 2014; Wuhan 2014c; He 2014).

For example, on 13 July 2014, a group of thirty-six university students unpacked their bags and settled into the dormitories of the Mingsheng gong for five days. This was not their first Daoist endeavor: as part of the project, they had already spent six days on Mount Wudang and visited the Changchun guan in Wuhan. After Mingsheng gong, they would further head to Mount Wufeng 五峰 near Jinan in Shandong. At each place, they were to experience the daily life of a Daoist temple, practice various arts such as calligraphy, taijiquan, meditation, and healing exercises, and also attend classes on Daoist worldview.

The whole idea for this project was inspired by Buddhist organizations such as the Wooden Fish Program, which had been going on since 1993. It also echoed traditional activities, since in ancient times, young people would naturally be exposed to Daoist temples from an early age as they accompanied their parents to pray and practice cultivation or spend the summer in their cooler mountain setting. Nowadays, the parents were brought up outside of any religious environment and no longer attended temples. As a result, many young Chinese never set foot in a temple, a situation remedied by this Summer Camp on Daoist Culture.

## Online Presence

As the revival process of monastic Daoism led to enhancing its cultural aspects and adapting it to the modern age, the internet became a major promotional tool. Many new-generation clerics mastered computers to create websites, blogs, and chat rooms. Even masters of the older generation had to adapt: Feng Xingzhao installed Wi-Fi in his small temple to please his young disciples. Typically, Daoists would use the internet to facilitate communication between clerics during cloud wandering through email, promote temple activities on specific websites, spread traditional scriptures that may be hard to find in electronic format, inform the public about courses and textual explanations through videos and articles, spread knowledge of rituals and ceremonies as well as taijiquan and nourishing life practices in visual media, and make information on Daoism widely accessible.

108 / Chapter Six

Within the Thunder Drum lineage, Liu Shitian set up websites for both his temples and established a variety of other internet tools such as blogs, micro blogs, mobile apps, and chats on sites like WeChat (Weixin 微信) (Lishan Mingsheng gong 2015b; Xi'an Chenghuang miao 2014). He also established his own private blog and began to utilize various other venues, mostly under the name Baoyi daoren 抱一道人 (see Liu 2015a; 2009a). His website specifically dedicated to the transmission of Daoist culture is called *Zhidao* 知道 (Utmost Dao) (Liu 2015b), officially launched on 21 October 2013, during the official opening ceremony and consecration of the City God Temple.

The use of internet to propagate Daoist teachings and news flourished vibrantly in the 2010s. Many temples, big and small, as well as provincial and local Daoist associations all came to have their own websites. This trend owed a great deal to the new generation of clerics who grew up in an era pervaded by modern technology. Some even created their own video channels on the popular website Youku to post rituals, musical performances, talks, and lectures. Thus, the Baiyun guan in Beijing developed a whole web network that included microblogs, chat rooms, websites, and more. Its unique video channel with postings of talks and rituals logged several million views (Baiyun guan 2015).

A smaller temple like the Dadao guan in Wuhan, managed by Ren Zongquan, one of the most famous Quanzhen ritualists of his generation, also set up a popular video channel on Youku and regularly posted lectures and rituals, gaining half a million views (Ren 2015). This channel, too, formed part of a larger internet-based system of communication that included micro-blogs and websites.

Beyond websites of clerics and institutions, secular web-platforms arose that focused on publishing news, videos, writings, and other information on Daoism, most importantly *Daojiao zhiyin,* whose presenters would tour temple festivals and religious conferences. Another secular website was the Daoist section of the Chinese Traditional Culture Channel, established around 2013 by Tencent. Called *Tengxun daoxue* 騰訊道學, its team of reporters established close collaboration with Daoist temples to better pro-mote their culture. For example, it published an interview with a reporter and senior editor, Ms Li 李 and Guo Yunjie 郭雲洁, on 13 November 2014. Held at the Fungying Seenkoon temple in Hong Kong, it covered their tour of temples in Hong Kong and Guangdong to establish collaboration for the diffusion of their activities.

The internet, therefore, grew into a major tool to popularize monastic Daoism and spread many texts and rituals that used to be kept hidden within monastery walls. It documented the intention to develop an image of the religion that differed from its traditional position of being secluded and mysterious. Monastic Daoists tried hard to demonstrate that their activities were less strange than secular people might think and that they were willing to open the gates to all.

## Ecological Engagement

On 18-19 April 2014, the Fourth International Daoist Forum with a focus on ecology was held in Ziyang county on Mount Wenbi, part of the reopening ceremonies of the Wuzhen guan and the occasion of Ziyang's joining the Green Pilgrimage Network. It also included the redaction of the Ziyang Declaration (Ziyang daojiao xiehui 2014). The website states,

> Three Daoist pilgrimage cities joined the Green Pilgrimage Network last month, at a Daoist ecological meeting in the remote city of Ziyang in the Qinling mountains. The cities include Ziyang, the sacred site where Zhang Ziyang wrote the famous *Wuzhen pian* in 1075.
>
> Today, it is also important for housing one of the reservoirs that supplies northern China with water. It does not allow any polluting industries, and its GDP is not calculated in the official economic assessment. The town has a lively tourist industry, with a focus on ecological and cultural tourism. . . It is similar to other forest parks, where polluting industries are banned. (ARC 2014)

The forum was organized by the CDA in cooperation with the SARA and the ARC or Alliance of Religions and Conservation (Shijie zongjiao yu huaibao qijin hui, 世界宗教與环保基金會). Founded in 1995 by Prince Philip of England, this secular body helps major world religions in the development of environmental programs, based on their various core teachings, beliefs, and practices. It helps them link up with key environmental organizations, creating alliances between faith communities and conservation groups (see ARC 2005).

Ziyang was selected as part of the Green Pilgrimage Network that also includes Houzhenzi 厚畛子, a district in Shaanxi where Mount Taibai 太白 is located. A sacred Daoist mountain with a number of prominent grottos and temples, it hosts a national park forest and panda nursery and provides water for the whole of Xi'an. Thus, it strongly preserves local biodiversity, ecology, and environmental integrity, not allowing any polluting industries but giving preference to organic agriculture and tourism (ARC 2014).

Another prominent site in the Network is Mount Mao in Jiangsu, one of the most famous Daoist mountains. At one point in history, it held over 900 temples and still receives over a million visitors annually. To protect its natural habitat, measures have been taken to minimize human influence on the environment. For instance, all electric wires are buried, all advertising boards are made from recyclable materials, and all street lamps use solar energy. When new temples are built, protection of trees and large rocks is essential, so that structures are erected around them. No private cars are allowed, and all visitors are advised to take public transportation or cycle (ARC 2014).

Ziyang was very proud to be a member of this elect group, redefining itself as an important place that promoted the values of ecological and cultural tourism. This was not only because it housed one of the largest reservoirs for northern China and prevented polluting industries in the area but also due to its strong Daoist presence, properly reflecting the values promoted by ARC.

The Ziyang forum was the biggest since the first one at Mount Taibai in 2007. There were four groups of speakers: government leaders, academics, senior Daoists, and ARC representatives. Top representatives included government leaders such as Zhao Jianzheng 趙建政 from the SARA, academics such as Ren Zongzhe 任宗哲 of the Shaanxi Academy of Social Sciences, Fan Guangchun of the Academy's Daoist Studies Center, Xie Yangju 謝陽舉 from Northwest University as well as Daoist leaders such as the chairman of the CDA Ren Farong, the vice chairman Yuan Zhihong 袁志鴻, the leader of the Jiangsu Daoist Association Yang Shihua 楊世華, and the chief of the Huashan Daoist Association and vice chairman of the Shaanxi Daoist Association Zou Tongxuan 鄒通玄. ARC was represented by its secre-tary general, Martin Palmer.

Each presented their views on the role of Daoism in ecology. Zhao Jianzheng talked about the destruction of the natural habitat being the most important factor threatening endangered wildlife. Master Yuan Zhihong called on people to make an effort to clean up the environment, taking both small and big steps, including building eco-temples and engaging in civilized, that is, moderate incense burning.

Allerd Sticker of the Valley Foundation outlined the history of the first Daoist eco-temple on Mount Taibai, which he helped sponsor, and announced the launch of *Sacred Mountains*, a book dedicated to the history of environmental work by Daoists in China. Martin Palmer talked about Daoism and the protection of endangered wildlife species and announced three new members of the GPN network, suggesting that the Daoist eight-year plan should in fact be at least an eighty-year plan. He Xinping, chairman of the Xi'an Daoist Association, spoke about herbal Chinese medicine as a Daoist tradition and noted that it is an obligation of the Daoist community to find herbal alternatives to animal ingredients in medicines.

Other major topics included wildlife protection, carbon reduction, nourishing life practices, and Chinese medicine. There were also talks on what has become known as "civilized worship" (*wenming jingxiang* 文明敬香), encouraging temple visitors to be ecologically thoughtful, especially by reducing the amount of incense they burn (Guojia 2014d; CDA 2014a).

This forum was one of a major series created by the ARC. The series began on 26 July 2006, with an inaugural workshop on Daoism and the environment, attended by fourteen local clerics and a small number of

## 112 / Chapter Six

academics on Mount Taibai (ARC 2006). It led to a second workshop in 2007, joined by eighteen Daoist leaders, which started the tradition of signing a Declaration of Ecological Intent. On 31 May 2007, attendees signed the Qinling Decla-ration: it contained seven points related to the involvement of the Daoist community in the promotion of ecological awareness, including one on the impact of temple construction on the ecological system (ARC 2007).

In 2008, the ARC workshop was held on Mount Mao in collaboration with the United Nations and expanded to included sixty-nine Daoists leaders at the national level. It resulted not only in a declaration (ARC 2008a), but also in an eight-year Daoist ecological protection plan, officially signed by the CDA on 9 September 2009. The document was then presented during an ARC event held in the UK in November 2009, entitled titled "Many Heavens, One Earth: The Windsor Celebration."

The plan describes the different areas where Daoists can contribute to the development of ecological awareness. It includes actions such as pro-viding ecological education, raising environmental awareness, maximizing ecological benefits from Daoist resources, promoting Daoist ecological traditions and wisdom, living daily life with strong environment awareness, cooperating with environment-related departments to incorporate environ-mental protection into Daoist networks, and celebrating the international environment day as part of the religious calendar (Ding 2011).

While the Daoist ecological forum began only in 2006 through collaboration with the ARC, there were various precursors encouraging participation of the community in environmental discourse. Thus, as early as 1993, the CDA included certain ecological concepts in its management. They first surfaced at a meeting in Gansu called "First Report on the Advance of Daoism," held during the fourth major board meeting and urged Daoists to participate in reforestation projects.

Following this, in 1995, the CDA participated in the World Religions and Ecology Meeting held during a grand celebration at Windsor Castle which also saw the inauguration of the ARC. It marked the first inter-national presence of Daoism in the field of ecology, signified by the presen-tation of the "Declaration of Intention of Chinese Daoism for Ecology and Environmental Protection." Then again, in 2003, the organization set up a reforestation project in Shimin 市民 county, Wuwei 武威 prefecture, Gansu which helped to protect the area from increasing desertification (Ding 2011).

Beyond these activities, Daoist leaders were also increasingly involved in the discourse on ecology at the national level. For one, the Beijing Daoist Association under the guidance of Huang Xinyang sponsored both the Fourth and Fifth International Symposium on Traditional Culture and Eco-Civilization, organized by the China Society of Environmental Sciences (Zhongguo huanjing kexue cuehui 中國環境科學學會) (Zhongguo huanjing 2013; 2014).

In addition, many large-scale events and discussion platforms organized by the Daoist community included ecological themes. For example, it was one of the four main topics during the Third International Daoist Forum, described as "The Axis of All Things: Ecological Wisdom in the Daoist Religion" (*Wanwu yiti: Daojiao de shengtai zhihui* 萬物一體：道教的生态態智慧 (Fenghuang 2014; Liu 2104a). Zhang Jiyu of the CDA, Liu Zhongyu 劉仲宇 of Huadong Normal University, Lin Anwu 林安梧 of Taiwan Ciji University, and Martin Palmer of the ARC all spoke on the subject and took part into a TV program titled "The Dao of Heaven and Humanity" (*Tianren zhidao* 天人之道; see CDA 2014d; Guojia 2014b).

Even before this, the theme of ecology played an important role in Daoist events. Thus, during the First International Daoist Forum in 2007, a major area of discussion was "The *Daode jing* and the Protection of Our Living Environment" (Zhongguo wang 2007a). The Second Forum, held at Nanyue in 2011, similarly featured a TV broadcast on "Daoism and the Dao of Harmony with Nature" (CDA 2011a; Guojia 2011; Li Yao 2011).

Local Daoist associations, too, participated actively in the discourse on ecology. For example, the Guangdong Daoist Association organized a conference on "Daoist Culture and Civilized Ecology" during its annual Daoist festival held on Mount Luofu 羅浮 on 15-16 November 2013 (Zhongguo huanjing 2013; Guangdong daojiao xiehui 2013).

## Public Relations

One of the earliest books on ecology was published by CDA vice-chairman Zhang Jiyu (1998). After that, the theme became very popular in Daoist writings, so that the term *shengtai* 生態 appears close to 4000 times on the website *Daojiao zhiyin*.

Presentations usually link the environment with philosophical teachings of ancient texts such as the *Daode jing* and the *Zhuangzi*. In the 2010s, articles also started to cite the views of Chinese government leaders on the importance of Daoism in solving the problems of modern society (see Liu 2014b). This matches patterns in the official political discourse.

For instance, at the 17th Congress of the CCP in October 2007, it was officially proposed to build an "ecological civilization." The goal was to form "an energy- and resource-efficient as well as environmentally friendly structure of industries, patterns of growth, and modes of consumption." This idea reflects an important change in the government's understanding of development. Rather than emphasizing economic construction as the core, as they did in the past, CCP leaders stressed that sustainable development must be based on a relationship between humanity and nature (Hu and Xinhua 2007).

At the 18th National Congress, 8-14 November 2012, "the construction of an ecological civilization" was written into the Party's constitution for the

114 / Chapter Six

first time. President Hu Jintao said, "We must give high priority to making an ecological civilization, work hard to build a beautiful country, and achieve lasting and sustainable development of the Chinese nation" (2012). He gave ecological civilization a prominent position by incorporating it into the country's five-year plan 2011-2015 together with economic, political, cultural, and social progress. In his report, Hu called for efforts to keep more farmland for farmers and leave a beautiful homeland with green fields, clean water, and blue skies to future generations. Xi Jinping, too, supported this vision at the time, noting that building an ecological civilization would "benefit both contemporary and future generations" (2014).

Daoist activities further paralleled the discourse of influential academics who supported the idea that traditional wisdom was of value in providing strong moral support for ecological civilization and environmental regulation (Wang, He, and Fan 2013). More and more people realized the important roles traditions and religions can play in creating an ecological civilization. In the words of Pan Yue:

> From the Daoist view of Dao respecting nature to the Confucian idea of the oneness of humanity and nature and the Buddhist belief that all living beings are equal, Chinese religions have helped our culture to survive for thousands of years. Their doctrines and practices can be powerful weapons in preventing environmental crises and building a peaceful harmonious society. (2001)

In sum, Daoist activities in ecology and environmental protection were organized in close relation with government guidelines and matched concepts presented by academics.

## Conclusion

Liu Shitian and other leading Daoists in their activities provide a window into the creative process of building Daoism so it would the new Chinese society and work in accordance with government guidelines. The themes he presented in his 2006 graduation paper show the vision he later implemented through various activities: orchestras of Daoist music, charities of the Mingsheng gong, conferences on Mount Li, the culture park of nourishing life in Ziyang, the Daoist ecological forum, and more. All these contributed to the promotion of Daoism defined by visions of charity, ethics, culture, ecology, and nourishing life.

# Chapter Seven

# The Third International Daoist Forum

In the same way that the activities of one man reflect the trends in the entire community, so do presentations at the Third International Daoist Forum offer a window into the definition of Daoism by national institutions such as the SARA and the CDA and the official understanding of how monastic Daoism served as a tool toward the attainment of Xi Jinping's China Dream.

Held on Mount Longhu on 25-26 November 2014, it was attended by numerous dignitaries as well as Thunder Drum leaders, notably Liu Shitian (Zhongguo wang 2014; Guojia 2014b; CDA 2014g; SARA 2014).

## Background

The series of international forums, organized by the SARA in cooperation with the CDA, began on 22-27 April 2007 with the First Forum on the *Daode jing* in Xi'an and Hong Kong (Zhongguo wang 2007a). Topics centered on the *Daode jing* in relation to a culture of harmony, the protection of the living environment, modern management, and health. The first large-scale international event in fifty years, it assembled over 500 Daoist leaders and scholars. As a prelude, 13,839 citizens recited the *Daode jing* jointly at the Hong Kong Stadium on 21 April, setting a new Guinness record for "the most

116 / Chapter Seven

people reading aloud simultaneously in one location." The forum also held the largest *Daode jing* exhibition in the world, showing over 300 different editions and versions of the philosophical classic, including the *Bamboo Laozi*, its earliest edition known so far, dated to about 350 BCE (Xinhua 2007).

Focusing on "Constructing a Harmonious World through the Dao," the Forum's rationale was to promote an image of Daoism as the root teaching of Chinese culture through its most important text, the *Daode jing*. It also aimed to enhance the relationship between Hong Kong and the mainland, coinciding both with the tenth anniversary of the British hand-over and the renovation of the Louguantai temple near Xi'an, the presumed location where Laozi transmitted the *Daode jing* (Zhongguo wang 2007b). Since this was the first time in many years that the Chinese government organized a conference on a major document of its own history, high-ranking CCP officials publicly stated that the wisdom expressed in the text was invaluable for modern China and that its ancient worldview should return to the heart of modern society.

In its wake, the Second International Daoist Forum was held on 24 October 2011 at Nanyue (CDA 2011a). With a key theme of "Respect the Dao and Honor Virtue," it aimed at attracting a large audience and was presented by CCTV as focusing on ecology and the development of Daoism abroad (Li Y. 2011).

Three years later, the Third Forum took place on Mount Longhu with an emphasis on nourishing life and the contributions Daoism could make toward the realization of the China Dream. On 24 November 2014, over 500 participants from twenty-seven countries arrived (CDA 2014f). The Thunder Drum lineage was represented by Liu Shitian who had also attended the two previous occasions and was invited to join this one as a representative of the CDA and the Shaanxi Daoist Association and to offer a paper in the section on ecology (Liu 2014a; 2014b).

The place of the forum had been carefully chosen for its historical, cultural, and tourist value. Mount Longhu in a southwestern suburb of Yingtan 鷹潭, Jiangxi is a state scenic region and major tourism area as well as a national forest and geological park. It is also the head-quarters of the Zhengyi school, as which it emerged in the 9th century based on the strong presence of a temple to the original 2nd-century founder Zhang Daoling and the claim that his descendants had settled there (Goossaert 2021). Today the mountain houses ten major Daoist palaces, eighty-one temples, and thirty-six small monasteries (Zhang 2014b).

The main theme of the Forum was "Promote the Dao and Establish Virtue, Aid the World and Benefit Others" (*xingdao lide jishi liren* 行道立德 济世利人). It began with an outdoor opening ceremony that included speeches by political and CDA leaders. This was followed by a ceremony of blessing for world peace, during which the chairmen of the Daoist associations of China, Macao, Hong Kong, and Mount Longhu recited a petition for peace and prosperity to be sent to the deities in the name of the CDA and the China Religious Culture Communication Association (Xu 2014; Zhang 2014a). After this, there were several Daoist-themed artistic performances.

The afternoon featured the opening presentation on the main theme of the Forum, where Daoist, political, and academic leaders gave speeches. This was followed by sessions on four secondary topics, translated by the official organizers as follows:

Health of Mind and Body: The Way of Daoist Health and Well-Being
The Axis of All Things: Ecological Wisdom in the Daoist Religion
Preserving Truth and Dispelling Falsity: Themes of Sincerity and Trust in Daoist Religious Thought
To Benefit without Causing Harm: The Spirit of Charity and Compassion in the Daoist Religion

There were also three TV forums, where selected high-ranking guests discussed specific themes in front of a live audience. Their topics were:

The Dao of Culture
The Dao of Heaven and Humanity
The Dao of Health and Well-Being

Other activities included practices of nourishing life undertaken in the main square of Yingtan, a book release on nourishing life, a calligraphy and painting exhibition, and an outdoor evening show. The Forum closed with a ceremony where a total of five academics, Daoists, and government leader gave summarizing speeches. It culminated in the reading of the forum's key declaration, also called the Longhu shan Declaration (CDA 2014h).

118 / Chapter Seven

## Media and Representation

Given vast exposure in various media, the Forum had a huge press release featuring the new Daoist image promulgated to the public. All sessions were covered by national press and television, and over a hundred journalists from thirty media companies were present. In addition to the three TV forums, there were reports on the biggest TV channels such as CCTV—both its English and Chinese branches—Phoenix TV, and the local Jiangxi TV (Guojia 2014c).

A major national and religious event, it gathered numerous important leaders. 180 major Daoist representatives and 200 special guests from twenty-seven countries attended, including the United States, United Kingdom, Germany, France, South Korea, and Japan. In addition, there were 2,500 Daoist practitioners, experts, academics, and reporters from around the world.

Among politicians the most elevated were CCP Central Committee members Yu Zhengsheng 俞正聲 and Liu Yandong 劉延東 as well as Prince Philip, the Duke of Edinburgh. UNESCO sent congratulatory letters (Zhang 2014a). In order to demonstrate government support for the development of Daoism, it sent special guests as well as academics of prestigious universities. The highest government leaders included Ma Bin 馬飚, vice chairman of the People's Political Consultative Conference; Xu Jialu 許嘉璐, the former vice chairman of the Standing Committee of the People's Congress; Wang Zuoan 王作安, minister at the SARA; as well as Jiang Jianyong, vice-minister at the SARA who also served as secretary-general and vice chairman of the China Religious Culture Communication Association.

Government leaders were involved at all levels and most sessions. High-ranking politicians gave speeches during the opening ceremony, the first breakout session, and again at the closing event. They also offered presentations and comments on TV broadcasts. For example, the TV program "The Dao of Culture" hosted three guests: Xu Jialu 許嘉璐, the former vice chairman of the Standing Committee of the People's Congress; Stephen Bokenkamp, professor at Arizona State University; and Chen Guying 陳鼓鷹, senior scholar at Beijing and National Taiwan Universities. They debated before millions of viewers on the question of how Daoist culture could contribute to a better society. Interestingly, no Daoist clerics were invited to take part in this debate, and the audience could not ask any questions related to any religious aspects.

Scholars from major Daoist research centers at various Chinese universities were also invited. Stephen Bokenkamp demonstrated the importance of Daoist studies abroad while Martin Palmer of the ARC represented foreign institutions. They were invited to speak mainly on ecology. To highlight the internationalization of the Daoist faith, moreover, leaders of associations from other countries were invited, notably coming from Singapore,

Japan, Malaysia, Thailand, France, Belgium, Switzerland, Spain, Mexico, and the United States.

The aim of the Forum was twofold, covering both national and international dimensions. On the national level, its goal was to transform the image of Daoism from that of an archaic religion based on superstitions to one of a modern contributor to the development of contemporary society, whose discourse supported the political agenda of the China Dream. On the international level, the aim was to use Daoism as part of China's soft power, that is, its drive to shape world opinion and outlook toward its particular socialist vision with non-coercive means such as cultural and philosophical values.[1]

According to Liu Jinguang, deputy principal of the Politics and Law Section of the SARA, the 18th National Congress of the CCP proposed a development strategy that included the full implementation of economic political, cultural, social, and ecological construction as comprehensive overarching goals. Religion in this system was part of overall cultural construction, with the government setting up just how religious cohesion of wisdom and cultural power could contribute to further development (Liu J. 2014). The Third Forum was organized within this specific context, serving to demonstrate how "religious cohesion of wisdom and cultural power can make contribution to China's further development."

The main government representative in charge of the forum's organization was Jiang Jianyong. His comments provided important insights into its political aims, showing the importance of working along with and contributing to the China Dream while also being available as an aspect of soft power at the international level. The overall tenor had been decided beforehand, during the first coordinating meeting on 27 February 2014. A report published on the SARA website accordingly shows the importance of Daoist dedication to the implementation of Xi Jinping's plan to increase the prestige of traditional Chinese culture. Jiang further added that organizing the forum was a way of carrying the China Dream forward and contributing to the enhancement of China's soft power (Jiang 2014).

During the press conference at the beginning of the Forum, Jiang Jianyong similarly said that it aimed at presenting the positive aspect of Daoism and its social function. He expressed his hope that the essence and wisdom of the religion could help solve modern society's problems and make a great contribution to lasting prosperity and world peace. He also emphasized his expectation that the speeches at the forum would support the innovative transformation and development of Daoist culture, the

---

[1] On the need to contribute to the China Dream, see SARA 2014; Zhao 2104; Jiang 2014. On its role in this context as seen by the CDA, see Ren 2013b. On religions in general in the China Dream according to the SARA, see Ren 2013a. On the influence of the China Dream on local Daoist associations, see Wang 2104.

exploration of Daoist ethics and moral ideals, the promotion of traditional virtues, and the promotion of Daoist patriotism. In addition, he supported the cultural uniqueness of Daoism and an overall increase in its presence internationally (Guojia 2014c; Zhang 2014a).

Speaking after Jiang, Daoist leaders followed in his footsteps and highlighted the role of Daoism in the development of Chinese society and the contributions it could make to the world by transmitting wisdom in the fields of health, ecology, harmony, ethics, and more (Huang 2014; Zhang 2014).

The theme of following the China Dream also played a part in the blessing ceremony held during the opening ceremony and its prayer petition for peace. Overall, the meeting had a rather nationalistic tone, as exemplified in expressions such as "magnificent Chinese culture," "magnificent China," "ancient country of great civilization," "highest established teaching for over 5000 years," and the like. According to this, the Dao is the body of mystery and there is nothing it does not encompass. Its function is virtue and its main action is to benefit all beings. On its wings, China would rise up with force and spirit. All people should pursue the China Dream and make it come true, so that the country would be prosperous and have a bright future (Xu 2014).

The official discourse was clearly present on all levels of the Forum: political, religious, and ritual. Enhancing Daoism was presented as a way of strengthening China's soft power internationally and contributing to the fulfillment of the China Dream nationally. An important aspect of Chinese culture, it was recast as an essential dimension of the China Dream. To be valuable in this context, though, it must be redefined appropriately. "Positive elements" must be highlighted and "superstitious elements," discarded. Daoist teachings were to be redefined, limiting its numerous concepts and philosophical theses while streamlining their outlook and purpose. The Forum did exactly that as do academics and political leaders related to the Daoist community on all different levels. After Daoists succeeded in the huge effort of rebuilding their temples, their next step would be to focus on reorganizing or even creating a Daoism that fit the political agenda.

## Tourist Values

Among the organizers of the Forum, the Mount Longhu Tourism Group (Longhu shan lüyou jituan 龍虎山旅游集團) was very much involved, utilizing it as a valuable form of advertising. Like all other agencies managing Daoist mountains in China, the Group is in charge of all tourist activities as well as of the entrance fees that believers must pay to get access to places of worship.

The Forum also featured a majestic big-budget and high-tech outdoor Daoist folk musical, entitled "Follow the Dream on Mount Longhu" (*Jinmeng Longhu shan* 儘夢龍虎山) or "Dream of the Dao" (Zhang 2014b). The show used mountain scenery as the stage, enhanced by extra-vagant lighting effects. Design and set were entirely natural, featuring rocks, trees, rivers, and hills. The seventy-minute visual feast, which centered on Daoist philosophy, involved constant movement from one place to another for both performers and spectators. There were no seats, and the audience had to walk along with the show until they settled in boats and drifted through a valley between the mountains.

Over 300 actors dressed in blinking-bulb costumes of constantly changing colors echoed the performance designed by Zhang Yimou 張藝謀 at the opening ceremony for the 2008 Beijing Olympics. Facing the world's biggest "screen," a cliff of 18,000 square meters that is 90 meters high and 196 meters wide, the show featured rising smoke, bright flashes, 3D-image projections, popular music, sound effects, ancient costumes, and a Cirque du Soleil-style performance of acrobatics—to present Daoist narratives, semi-ritual dances, and martial arts performances. The famous pop-diva Faye Wong lent her voice with a new song called "Like a Dream."

The show was produced by media proprietor and talk show host Yang Lan and his Sun Media Group in cooperation with the Mount Longhu Tourism Group. It cost 300 million RMB (US $48.9 million) and was directed by Chen Weiya 陳維亞, also in charge of the opening ceremony at the Beijing Olympics and the Summer Youth Olympics in Nanjing in 2014. Music and songs were composed by the French-Chinese composer Chen Qigang 陳其鋼, who also wrote the Olympics' theme song, "You and Me." It was first staged on 12 November 2014, scheduled to open to the public in the following spring (Zhang 2014b). It played an important part in the tourist development of the mountain, the Tourism Group investing heavily in the cultural and historical aspects of Daoism and thus transforming the sacred mountain.[2]

# Nourishing Life

Compared to its predecessors, the Third Forum focused more heavily on nourishing life, since its main theme emphasized harmonious coexistence (CDA 2014e). This is further reflected in the wide media coverage and the topics of various subsessions. More specifically, four events related directly to it, including a panel discussion, a televised forum, the release of a book published by the CDA, and a free clinic of Chinese medicine, the main public activity during the event (CDA 2014e).

On the main public square of the town of Yingtan, twelve renowned Daoists masters who specialized in nourishing life and Daoist medicine provided consultations on health matters. Another major event was the release of a book on essential Daoist techniques for health and well-being by Zhang Xingfa 張興發 and Wang Zhiyi 王哲一, entitled *Daojiao yangsheng fangfa jingcui* 道教養生方法精粹 (The Essence of Daoist Methods of Nourishing Life; 2014). This occurred during a panel session that also featured presentations by the CDA representatives Huang Xinyang 黃信陽, Ding Changyun 丁常雲, Huang Zhijie 黃至杰, Lin Zhou 林舟, and Wang Zhyi 王哲一 (Huang and Wang 2014). Huang Xinyang (shown below) presided over the official release ceremony, during which he also donated sample copies to representatives of various foreign Daoist associations. In his dedicatory speech, he said,

> Daoist nourishing life is the treasure of nourishing life culture. From the past to the present, it has always been valued highly by the people. For example, taijiquan and many other nourishing life practices have been recognized widely in China and abroad. This book, compiled by a team of the CDA, contains the best collection of theories, methods, and fundamental principles with regard to nourishing life and Daoist medicine. It holds the essence of Daoist ways of nourishing life and has been written very meticulously. (Huang and Wang 2014)

---

[2] This is also happening on other Daoist mountains, such as Mounts Hua and Mao. See Palmer 2013; Johnson 2012.

In terms of contents, the book contains many references to and citations from texts of the Daoist Canon that pertain to the medical field. Examples are the medical classic *Huangdi neijing* 黃帝内經 (The Yellow Emperor's Inner Classic), the cosmological work *Yinfu jing* as well as materials that cover various traditions of internal alchemy. Methods described include taijiquan, meditation, dietetics, hygiene, and alchemy, both external and internal. Chapter 14, entitled "Daojiao neidan yangsheng fa" 道教内丹養生法 (Nourishing Life Methods of Daoist Internal Alchemy) makes particular note of many distinct lineages of internal alchemy such as those of the Zhong-Lü, Southern, Northern, Eastern, Western, Central, Sanfeng, Wu-Liu, Qianfeng, and Nüdan traditions (Zhang and Wang 2014). It is interesting to note that most of the texts of the internal alchemy traditions presented in the book, as noted earlier, originally warn against nourishing life practices, regarding them as of limited use when it comes to profound energetic transformation.

The tendency at the Third Forum to focus so strongly on nourishing life goes back to the preferential treatment of this modality established a few years earlier by CDA leaders such as Huang Xinyang, who published his book on the subject in 1993. Daoists in general came to highlight nourishing life culture as a response to an increased interest in living longer and healthier both in China and overseas, where qigong and taijiquan have become vastly popular (see Palmer 2007).

## Daoist Characteristics

The Third Forum ended with the reading of the Mount Longhu Declaration by CDA vice-chairman, Zhang Jiyu (in Chinese) and the chairman of the American Daoist Association, Bernard Shannon (in English). It emphasized the key themes that make up the image of Daoism as presented at the forum, such as ethics, charitable activities, nourishing life, and ecology.

It also offered a set of vows as, for example, the intention "to benefit others by practicing truth and charitable love," "to reach for physical and spiritual health," and "to respect all living things." More specifically, it said,

> We aim to restore sincerity, dispel falsity, and preserve the genuine.
> We expound upon charitable love to benefit others without doing harm.
> We seek spiritual and physical health through the practice of well-being.
> We praise the axis of all living things, the natural state shared by us all.
> May we practice the Dao and establish virtue,
> Acting in concord with the heavens and feel empathy for others.
> May we work toward goodness and self-improvement,
> Always aiding the world and benefitting others! (CDA 2014d)

The Third Forum was a major media event that established an image of Daoism and its role in China and the world, following the regulations and directions for its development determined by the national CDA committee. The two work closely together, the CDA providing the software while the forum offers the hardware. Both, moreover, closely relate to the political directions as instituted by the CCP—the engineer in background who determines both software and hardware.

Along similar lines, the Fourth International Daoist Forum, held on 10-12 May 2017 on Mount Wudang, focused on five major topics: the relationship between nature and ecological ethics, physical and mental health, social welfare, and eco-friendly environment. Following this, the Fifth Forum convened on Mount Mao in Jurong near Nanjing on 23-25 September 2023. Its theme was "In Recognition of Dao and Virtue, Moving Forward with the Times," combined with a TV forum, entitled "Dao is Simplicity: Daoism and a Healthy Life." Again, the emphasis was on health and ecology with greater attention paid to innovation and adaptation, enhancing the role of Daoist in socialist society.

They all served to strengthen China's soft power internationally and contribute to the political agenda of the China Dream nationally. Daoism as the indigenous higher religion of China and an important feature of traditional culture was recognized as a useful tool and supporting factor in this endeavor. However, it also had to be redefined. Positive elements as understood by the policy makers had to be highlighted as superstitious elements, discarded. Certain concepts and practices became acceptable while others were placed aside or ostracized, its teachings clearly delimited and the entire religion transformed into a mode that fit the political agenda.

# Chapter Eight

# From Revival to Survival

Soon after the events recorded here, the Chinese government moved away from the China Dream and replaced it with a new policy called sinicization (*zhonguo hua* 中國化). Xi Jinping adopted the slogan for the first time in 2015. At the National Conference on Religious Work in 2016, he asserted that all religions must move toward sinicization and ultimately sealed it as the main characteristic of his religious policy at the 19th Congress of the CCP in 2017 (Yang 2024).

Characteristic of Xi Jinping's reign, sinicization is distinct from his predecessors' "mutual adaptation" and "harmonious society" philosophies, aiming at complete political domestication and submission to the Communist party-state. It is, in other words, a strategy "to comprehensively reshape religions to be consistent with the dominant ideology and promote loyalty to the CCP" (Yang 2024). The idea of "Chineseness" in this context is redefined "to explicitly link loyalty to the Party with being Chinese and a sharp move toward assimilationist policies directed strongly at non-Han ethnic and religious minorities" (Theaker 2024). While used to justify the intensified suppression of Tibetans and Uyghurs (USCIRF 2024; HRW 2024; Tibet 20102), it also applies to Han Chinese religious practitioners of Islam and Christianity but is not limited to them: even Chinese Buddhists and Daoists have to adjust their teachings and practices.

126 / Chapter Eight

Sinicization is administered by the United Front Work Department (Zhongyang tongyi zhanxian gongzuo bu 中央统一戰線工作部), an official entity directly under the CCP Central Committee (as shown in the chart above). Originally created in the 1920s, it was active in the early years of communist rule to train and reform intellectuals (Groot 2004, 2-8). Shut down during the Cultural Revolution, it was revived in 1979 but remained low-key until 2012, when Xi Jinping expanded and intensified it. Its so-called united front work consists of gathering intelligence on, managing relations with, and gaining influence over entities outside the CCP that hold political, commercial, or academic influence, ensuring that they are supportive of, and useful to, CCP interests (Brady 2018).

In 2018, the United Front Work Department was put in charge of the various religions of China, absorbing the SARA and the Overseas Chinese Affairs Office, whose names, structures, and employees it retained yet consolidated. It also assumed control of the National Ethnic Affairs Commission and thus became the main agency to oversee all ethnic, religious, and overseas Chinese affairs (Zhao and Leibold 2019).

As outlined in Wikipedia, the agency has over 40,000 personnel and directs eight minor political parties as well as the All-China Federation of Industry and Commerce. Below its General Office, it consists of twelve major bureaus, among which the eleventh and twelfth focus particularly on religion, while the second deals with minorities and the sixth and seventh work on Tibetans and Uyghurs. Its methods consist mainly of outreach through large-scale events, training sessions, media tours, and similar activities, but it also has powers of incarceration, confiscation, and demolition.

## Practical Application

Sinicization requires all religious organizations to modify their doctrines and activities so that they match Han Chinese culture. In concrete terms, it manifests in various dimensions. The most visible involves architecture, which now has to be entirely Chinese in style: authorities have removed crosses from churches and demolished the domes and minarets of mosques (Theaker 2024).

In 2018, the State Council, the government's administrative authority, passed regulations on religious affairs that restricted religious schooling and the times and locations of religious celebrations (CFR 2024). Unlike before, any major event or festival now not only has to be registered for approval but attendance is limited to a few hundred, and all participants have to provide identification to government officials (CFR 2024). For example, in December 2023, "authorities tried hard to contain and curb Christmas celebrations inside and outside churches, prohibited students and others from participating in Christmas activities and detained some house church leaders to prevent them from organizing congregational gatherings" (Yang 2024).

Along other lines, clergy are required to attend indoctrination courses on a regular basis that severely limit the time they can spend on the upkeep of their institutions and/or personal cultivation practice. Also, in September 2023, the Chinese government released a draft regulation that, if passed, would penalize those who wear clothes in public that "hurt the Chinese people's feelings," including vestments or religious robes regulations (Hassan 2024). Along the same lines, contact with foreigners is actively discouraged and can lead to repercussions.

In early 2020, the government intensified the campaign and installed new regulations that require religious groups to accept and spread CCP ideology and values. All clergy have to modify their teachings to that they reflect socialist values and include "Xi Jinping Thought," an abbreviation of the more formal "Xi Jinping Thought on Socialism with Chinese Characteristics for a New Era" (*Xi Jinping xin shidai zhongguo tese shehui zhuyi sixiang* 習近平新时代特色社會主義思想). Expressed in detail at the 19th CCP Congress in 2017, this involves fourteen commitments that all center around ensuring that the Party retains and even intensifies its leadership over all forms of work and thought in China. In this context, administrators plan to issue newly annotated versions of key religious scriptures, such as the Quran, that will help teachings align with what they call "Chinese culture in the new era" (Pew 2024).

Other regulations limit the organizational competence of religions. Permits for renovation, expansion, or new construction of worship halls and community centers are almost impossible to get and even if a building is completed in perfect alignment with all the regulations, authorities can (and do) order it to be torn down at a moment's notice. Donations have been severely curtailed, and religions are not allowed to receive funding from sources other than those approved by the state.

Then again, all communications are closely monitored. As Tirana Hassan notes, "Through laws and regulations, criminal punishment, harassment, intimidation, and the use of technology, the Chinese government operates one of the world's most stringent censorship regimes" (2024). China's online search platforms use 60,000 rules to censor online content; the most far-reaching political censorship among web search engines is by Microsoft's Bing, its rules less numerous but broader and affecting more search results than those applied by Chinese companies such as Baidu (Hassan 2024). Under these conditions, religious organizations are severely limited in what they can publish and in some cases are no longer able to post information on social media, such as WeChat. At the same time, academics in religious studies not only have to submit all teaching content for government approval but are highly restricted in terms of publication,

128 / Chapter Eight

as most venues have closed down. Books with religious content are destroyed *en masse*. Also, many universities are closing their religion departments, moving their faculty into philosophy or sociology.

In September 2023, even stricter laws were installed that required religious sites and activities to support sinicization policies, which included prohibiting religious activity if it could "endanger national security, disrupt social order, or damage national interests." Meanwhile, in Hong Kong, where religious groups are not required to register with the government, religious figures are facing tighter scrutiny and have increased self-censorship under the 2020 national security law (CFR 2024; USCIRF 2024).

To comply with the regulations, religious organizations tend to hold workshops and training courses to set the agenda for their adaptation. For example, on September 5, 2023, the China Buddhist Association, which is very eager to comply, arranged for a special training course on Mount Wutai, a major sacred mountain with numerous temples. It convened over a hundred Buddhist leaders from all over the country together with the always-present leaders of the United Front Work Department. Based on Xi Jinping's 2021 speech at the National Conference on Work Related to Religious Affairs, four sets of instructions were formulated to be implemented in all communities.

First, "improve ideological understanding and consolidate the responsibility for a strict management of education," which means that Marxism and Xi Jinping Thought should be taught to all monks and devotees. Second, "carry out in-depth socialist legal education," that is, teaching and enforcing all the new laws and directives on religion. Third, "strengthen system management" and build a bureaucracy from the top down to supervise even the most remote temples and their teachings and activities in accordance with the new administrative measures that are essentially aimed at converting all churches, mosques, and temples into centers of CCP propaganda. Fourth, "Sinicize academic courses on Buddhism" by making sure that they apply Xi's principles and use Marxism as an interpretive tool for religious history and doctrine (Zhao 2023).

Even more new regulations enacted in 2024 stipulate that religious adepts must "practice the core values of socialism" and "adhere to the direction of the sinicization of religions" (art. 5). Whether places of worship are being "built, renovated, expanded, or rebuilt," they should "reflect Chinese characteristics and style in terms of architecture, sculptures, paintings, decorations, and so on" (art. 26). The revisions also impose new requirements before religious institutions can apply to create places of worship (art. 20) as well as more stringent restrictions and cumbersome approval processes for building, expanding, altering and moving them (articles 22, 25). In addition, all places of worship must "deeply excavate the content of [religious] teachings and canons that are conducive to social harmony . . . and interpret them in line with the requirements of contemporary China's development and progress and in accordance with the excellent traditional Chinese culture" (art. 11).

Beyond that, the regulations prohibit religious education other than by government-approved groups (art. 13). Religious institutions need to "operate any schools with Chinese characteristics" (art. 14), which includes "cultivating patriotic religious tenets" and interpreting sacred texts "in the correct manner" (art. 15). The chapter also imposes new requirements that religious establishments must report and seek permission from the authorities to conduct religious training (art. 8) and to organize "large scale religious activities" (art. 42). The 2024 revisions empower grassroots CCP cadres to monitor society. Cadres in "village committees" and "neighborhood committees" must report to the authorities if they discover "illegal religious organizations, illegal preachers, illegal religious activities, or the use of religion to interfere in grassroots public affairs" (art. 7). These surveillance powers at low levels make repression widespread, matching Xi's "mass mobilization" style of governance and social control, a style that Chinese state media say is directly inspired by Mao Zedong, whose picture is increasingly installed in religious venues (HRW 2024).

## Monastic Daoism

Daoists, as much as devotees of all other religions in China, are severely affected by these policies. As the Regulations of Religious Affairs, revised at the 4th meeting of the Standing Council of the CDA on 28 November 2023 state, all Daoist clergy must

> love the motherland, support the leadership of the CCP, support the socialist system, abide by the constitution, laws, regulations, and rules, practice core socialist values, adhere to the directions of sinicization, and preserve national unity, ethnic unity, religious harmony, and social stability. (https://www.daoisms.com.cn/2021/06/17/28144/)

More specifically, the rules require that Daoists wear appropriate dress and exhibit correct behavior, "study and implement Xi Jinping Thought and the CCP's policy on religious work." All activities, publications, and teachings must be in strict adherence to government policies and are tightly censored, essentially making Daoism—as much as all other religions—into an organ of state doctrine.[1]

---

[1] For extensive documentation on specific organizational measures and regulations, see the CDA website http://www.taoist.org.cn/getDjzsById.do?id=1654: "Daoist Temple Management Measures," also based on the meeting of 28 November 2023.

130 / Chapter Eight

As for the concrete impact of sinicization on Daoism, in 2023, I had the opportunity to travel through many parts of China, spending almost five months in the country. During that time, I visited more than one hundred Daoist temples, traveling over 4000 km across a dozen provinces from the most southern (Guangdong) to the far northern (Heilongjiang), including also the western provinces of Gansu and Qinghai. I began my journey in Guangzhou, visited my old haunts in and around Xi'an, including the temples of the Thunder Drum lineage, and spent quite a bit of time in several places in the northeast. I also attended a CDA conference to honor the birthday of Zhenwu on Mount Wudang and traveled to Gansu to visit temples there. My field data, therefore, came to include Daoists from many different places and institutions. Sometimes I visited three or more temples in a single day, speaking directly—without any translator or government representative—to the monks and nuns.

Everywhere I went, I found temples in a state of decline and disarray. There were no devotees, much fewer clergy, and minimal activities. Buildings were in disrepair, and there was very little renovation or construction. The overall atmosphere was one of desolation and despair. Some temples, both Buddhist and Daoist, including the Wuzhen guan near Leigutai, were closed completely, their grounds starting to overgrow. Others closed officially on grounds of reconstruction, yet the clergy remain-ed inside, shielding themselves from the outside world. Yet other temples remained open, but their buildings and grounds showed serious decay—a poignant example being the Siwang miao in Ziyang.

The government has made the permit process for any kind of religious building activity so difficult that in fact neither new temples are developed nor existing ones expanded. Even repairs are often not possible, and in some cases, as for example the ancestral temple of Quanzhen, the Chongyang gong, already permitted and erected structures are subject to demolition.

To give one example, Huang Shizhen spent many years trying to get the authorization to renovate Qinghua gong, which was falling apart and constituted a safety hazard. After years of filing forms with a whole slew of different departments, he eventually managed to get the permits but was not allowed to alter the original structure or design in any way, precluding any form of expansion.

When I was there in the spring of 2023, he was ready to hold an opening ceremony, but again had to file a whole series of complicated forms with different departments that also involved providing the names of every one attending. In the end, the event happened (as shown below) with rather short-term notice and probably not quite fully official. Also, it was radically censored and neither pictures nor descriptions appeared online. This matches the official policy that only allows four Daoist temples in Shaanxi province to have an online presence. Even for them, every single post must obtain approval through a formal authorization process. As a result, temple websites—so strongly developed just a decade ago—now only speak about Xi Jinping Thought and ways of complying with government guidelines, like the Buddhist set of instructions outlined earlier.

Not only temples but also tombs are subject to suppression. After Feng Xingzhao passed away at Xianyuesi on February 19, 2023 he was buried nearby. Although there was no official announcement, thousands of people came to attend his funeral (as shown below), lining the roads three deep and causing the main highway to be closed to regular traffic.

All flowers in the greater Xi'an area were sold out completely, and the outpouring of grief was tremendous.

Since he had died sitting up in a state of deep meditation, moreover, he was buried upright in a special earthenware jar, going back to a traditional practice that had not been activated in the modern era. His tomb was accordingly rather small, as shown below. However, when I visited it to pay my respects in April 2024, I learned that the authorities not only prevented his Daoist heirs from adding a small ornamental tower, matching the one at Baiyun guan, but claimed that this tomb was too big and should be reduced in size, making it more inconspicuous.

The earthenware jar as coffin.    The tomb.

In yet another and more practical dimension, Daoist living has been seriously impacted by the new regulations. For example, since all clergy were forced to rejoin secular society during the Cultural Revolution, many got married and had children yet later returned to their monasteries. The marriages often continued, if at long distance, allowing priests to fulfill their spiritual calling while yet having families. Now this is no longer possible, and monks either have to leave the monastery or document that they have obtained a divorce and are properly celibate.

In a similar manner, Daoists used to have some leeway regarding their hair. While long hair tied up in a topknot has been the official standard since the Tang dynasty, if someone was not comfortable growing his hair out or the parents found it hard to see their child in religious accoutrements, they could keep their hair short and wear a Daoist hat. The community fully accepted this as an act of filial piety. Now all Daoists have to have long hair and tie it up in a topknot, marking them clearly as Daoist clergy.

By the same token, while Daoists must wear their garb in the temple, many are now reluctant to enter the world visibly dressed as religious practitioners, the official and popular climate increasingly turning against them. Rather than just being able to stay in seclusion, however, Daoists are forced to leave their temples to attend local meetings and resident training courses in Xi Jinping Thought. Every week there is at least one meeting and every month there is at least one course. During the latter, attendants stay for three to fourteen days in government-run hotels rented by the CDA that may even be in other cities or far-away provinces. Notice given is always very short: just ordering a certain monk or nun to show up at a certain place at a certain time within a day or two. Topics are not revealed until the event starts, which also involves exams and reports on the subject covered.

Matching this tendency, the CDA's official organ, *Zhong-guo daojiao*, in its June 2024 issue spent forty-eight of a total of eighty pages to explicate and admonish members about the ongoing process of siniciza-tion, echoing and repeating much of the official regulations found on their website.

The intensity of the meeting schedule combined with political indoc-trination and the prevention of in-depth cultivation causes many monks and nuns to leave the order, especially if they are well educated and thus able to train or work in a secular profession. Temples that had thirty to forty residents are now down to four or five, if that, causing more closures. An-other bureaucratic restriction is the addition of the epithet "religious personnel" (*zongjiao yuan* 宗教員) to the passport, which makes it impos-sible for Daoists to travel abroad, even on vacation, without obtaining various permits. All this makes life so difficult that some Daoists, including ones I met personally last year, fall into deep states of depression and, in some cases, seriously contemplate suicide.

Daoists in the West, too, are experiencing major changes. For one, many of their inspiring masters are no longer available, being restricted in communication and interaction. For another, Daoists are not allowed to interact with foreigners unless they file a large number of permit forms. During my entire stay in China, while I had many meetings with Daoists, they were always semi-secret and there were absolutely no pictures taken— in sharp contrast to the photo mania of previous years. Some even warned me to never tell the CDA that they had seen me, emphasizing the political and restrictive nature of this organization, which essentially is the executive arm of the United Front Department.

In the meantime, the CDA, at the Fifth Forum on Mount Mao in Sep-tember 2023, officially inaugurated the World Daoist Federation (Shijie daojiao lianhe hui 世界道教联合會). This serves to integrate various Daoist associations in other parts of the world that are typically founded and run by Western followers who have received initiation but, with very few exceptions, do not speak Chinese and have spent very little time in China. Taken to showcase temples such as the Baiyun guan in Beijing, they are presented with an official image and remain largely unaware of the intensity and depth of the current decline.

As regards the activities of Federation affiliates in their home countries, the CDA neither requires them to pay dues nor provides any funds or guidelines, leaving them largely part to their own devices and decisions. At the same time, it asks them to sign a formal charter, which places them under the direct control of the Chinese authorities and demands a similar commitment to the communist state and the proliferation of Xi Jinping Thought as the in-country regulations. Several Chinese Daoists told me that, in light of the repression they were suffering from the CDA and its enforced rules, they did not believe that the newly created Federation's true aim was to help spread or support Daoism. Rather, they saw it as a cover-up that would create an international smokescreen and hide what was really happening in China. How, they asked, can a government agency repress a religious organization in its own country, on the one hand, and endeavor to spread it abroad, on the other? For this reason, even in the light of this international effort, they felt quite hopeless concerning the survival of the religion.

Just as Daoists in China are split into those eager to support the new doctrine and those retreating in an effort to hold on to the old ways, so Western Daoists are now divided into those transforming their teachings to adhere to the Party line and those supporting more traditional ways. Adepts who move away from politics and continue to follow established ideas and practices, including myself, may no longer be welcome in the motherland but are the greatest hope for the survival and eventual resurgence of Daoism once this new "cultural revolution" has passed.

# Conclusion

# A Tradition Transformed

The Leigutai abbot and lineage master Feng Xingzhao, a monastic who was trained before the Cultural Revolution and thus experienced and learned the traditional ways, was an icon promoting a "Daoism of proximity." His relationship with the local community was of a personal nature and he interacted and taught on an individual level. To him, temples were a home that must be taken care of like one's own by both clerics and lay followers. Temples were also places of sacred power, where deities and immortals dwelled and believers could access and merge with transcendental powers. His teachings contained a strong religious flavor, the belief in immortals and deities being of central importance. As far as he was concerned, one must learn how to pray, develop strong beliefs, follow the teachings and values promoted by the deities, and communicate properly with them. He made very few references to the cultural or political aspects of Daoism and taught more through action and example than by providing theory and discourse.

Liu Shitian, although from the same lineage, emerged as a representative of the new generation of clerics who entered the Dao after the Cultural Revolution. Much more in line with modern values and Party policies, he approached the renewal of the religion through actions on a larger scale with a strong emphasis on promoting it as an essential element of Chinese culture as well a contributor to the needs of modern society, especially through charitable activities, nourishing life practices, and ecological awareness. Liu Shitian, one could say, stood for the promotion of a "cultural Daoism at the provincial level." To him, temples were a place of development and protection of culture, an approach closely related to the position of the central government (Wang Z. 2011). As such, they were also places where events such as conferences, musical performance, and scripture readings should be held.

Throughout his career, Liu Shitian actively supported the main guidelines and directions set up by the CDA in line with Party policies, presenting the religion as a supportive partner in solving the problems faced by modern society. His activities accordingly included participation in the discourse on the development of ecological awareness, the protection and promotion of Chinese cultural values and traditional arts (philosophy and music), charitable works, protection of historical buildings, and an active support of local economic development. These activities over the last several decades contributed to presenting Daoism as a modern and socially conscious partner of the development of the country.

136 / Conclusion

# Lineage Diffusion

Studying the diffusion of the Thunder Drum lineage, two major turning points emerge, both connected to lineage members leaving the mountain.

The first was the departure of Master Feng. Leaving the isolated peak to go cloud wandering allowed him to increase his knowledge, expand his mind, get acquainted with the ways of the world, and thus enhance his ability to run negotiations involved in the complex bureaucracy of temple reconstruction. It also allowed him to increase his charisma; he became known and recognized by local government leaders due to his managerial position at the Shaanxi Daoist Association and the management committee of the Baxian gong in Xi'an. Spending some time with Min Zhiting, who later became head of the CDA, further increased his official connections (*guanxi* 關系), an extremely important aspect of Chinese culture, always essential when developing or running projects. Furthermore, having obtained a high ordination level through the 1989 consecration ceremony at the Baiyun guan, he developed a prestigious aura and a good name within the Daoist community.

The second turning point was the departure of Liu Xingdi in 1989, when he left the mountain to live at the Baxian gong. Master Liu was a hermit-like Daoist who focused intensively on meditation practice and stayed locked up in his room. Although he did not have a direct impact on the diffusion of the lineage, he yet exerted an indirect influence. His move to the monastery, bringing along his two novices Huang Shizhen and Liu Shitian, was the stepping stone that led to a much-enhanced diffusion of the Thunder Drum lineage.

His first novice, Huang Shizhen, in due course became the link that connected the lineage to the rest of the world. This role evolved due to two personal characteristics. For one, he was one of the first (maybe the very first) Quanzhen Daoist who spoke some English; for another, from an early age he developed a great interest in teaching foreigners. He thus played a major role in the lineage diffusion abroad, when he connected Feng Xingzhao to the British Taoist Association. Furthermore, over the years he continued to pursue his connective role between foreigners and Daoists as he helped to set up other Daoist groups and took in disciples from all over the world.

Liu Xingdi's second novice, Liu Shitian, contributed to the development of the lineage mostly at the provincial level, exercising his three main characteristics. First was his ability to raise huge amounts of money. Second was his knack for developing tourist projects that were attractive to the civil authorities and involved building large temples in the greater Xi'an area, such as the Mingsheng gong on Mount Li and the City God Temple in Xi'an as well as others on Mount Wenbi in Ziyang. And third, he had the gift to follow trends of the CDA and quickly develop new ways of transmitting cultural aspects of Daoism, thus establishing conference series such as "Questions about Dao on Mount Li" and musical orchestras such as the one of the City God Temple.

While the departures of Feng Xingzhao and Liu Xingdi from the mountain were important factors in the diffusion of the lineage, it also benefited greatly from its connection to the Baxian gong. It was here that Master Feng established long-term relationships and proved himself to the community through his service on the management committee. He was able to make sure that both Huang Shizhen and Liu Shitian were sponsored by the monastery to study at the Daoist College, which in turn speeded up their recognition in the community.

The Leigutai temple thus gave its members a traditional and rigorous training that, like the strong root of a tree, would ensure that they could flourish as further nourishment was provided by various local monasteries and personal connections, official training sessions, and community positions.

## Cultivation Practice

Quite a number of monks and nuns I met over the years mentioned that they thought of themselves as the generation that had to rebuild temples in order to give their successors the opportunity to focus on internal alchemy, an important aspect of the interest and career of any Quanzhen Daoist, yet traditionally highly esoteric. Since its founding by Wang Chongyang in the 12th century, the order has insisted that knowledge of internal cultivation should be imparted only to the worthy and through oral and secret processes. It further highlighted how internal alchemy involved much higher and purer methods than nourishing life techniques, which served mainly to enhance health and prolong life. In contrast, the more powerful internal transformation procedures opened access to immortality and the ability to ascend into heaven in broad daylight.

The Cultural Revolution led to the disappearance or death of many old masters who held this sacred and rare knowledge. The abrupt discontinuity in the transmission created a huge loss for the order. Not only are techniques of internal cultivation acquired primarily through oral transmission from master to disciple, but they can only be developed properly through experience and intense ascetic practice. The Cultural Revolution stopped masters from transmitting their expertise and kept disciples from acquiring their own internal experiences. Furthermore, after the reopening in 1979, the lack of temples and suitable retreat opportunities that would allow clerics to focus on internal practices presented another major obstacle for the new generation to grow in internal cultivation.

138 / Conclusion

Within the community, even today its most important aspects are still solely transmitted in secret and only to those considered worth—partly because anyone else would not understand them anyway. Adepts must have reached the proper stage and their destiny must have arrived clearly before the essence of the practice can be imparted. However today, since there are so few highly trained masters, this restriction has become a liability, presenting a risk to the very continuity it is supposed to ascertain. In order to make sure the teachings are not lost, some masters have resorted to spread them more widely through various media, including public lectures, books, and online presentations. A case in point is Zhang Zhishun who, once he turned a hundred years old, began to focus on "transmitting the knowledge from one generation to the next to prevent its complete loss."

One aspect of Daoist-inspired training that came to the fore in Chinese society after the Cultural Revolution was the practice of qigong, which grew massively in the 1970s and 1980s. It utilizes ideas of nourishing life and incorporates a variety of health and healing practices that spread through all ranges of society, making "nourishing life" a household term. Internal alchemy in the meantime continued to be kept secret among Daoists and was not popularly known. Later, in order to enhance communication about their tradition, monastic Daoists endeavored to present the heart of their doctrines in terms familiar to the general public. Thus, in publications of the Quanzhen headquarters at the Baiyun guan, the term "internal alchemy" came to be replaced by "nourishing life," and in many treatises, more esoteric practices were rebranded as a form of health support. At the same time, patriarchs who historically had nothing but disdain for the life-enhancing arts were called masters of nourishing life.

Not only was this shift visible in the writings of Baiyun guan abbots, but in the 2010s, it was also strongly emphasized as part of the official image of Daoism. Each international forum featured nourishing life as an important theme, most prominently so at the Third Forum in 2014, where several TV programs and public events were held and the release of a relevant book by the CDA was highly celebrated. Furthermore, at the central committee meeting of the CDA in 2015, Li Guangfu, leader of the Wudang Daoist Association, was elected chairman, catapulting a Daoist mountain into the national limelight that had a high level of popularity in terms of martial arts, taijiquan, and nourishing. Add to this the fact that a 100-year-old hermit spread secret teachings on the popular Youku website and the widely broadcast international forum focused strongly on nourishing life, the image of Daoism in the 21$^{st}$ century came to be strongly defined in terms of health and longevity.

# Moving Abroad

As monastic Daoists came back to their temples that had been destroyed during the Cultural Revolution and undertook the massive reconstruction and reorganization effort necessary to revive their order, they had to (and still have to) first and foremost remain in strict adherence to all government guidelines. This holds true for all organized religions in China, but is even more important for Daoists. As one old monk told me,

> The other religions could not really be destroyed by the Cultural Revolution because they had already spread all over the world. . . but for us the loss was horrific because everything that was precious and at the core of our tradition was on Chinese soil. What was lost then is lost now forever: there were no masters abroad to keep the teachings alive and was no external copies of our ancient texts and rituals. So, for me it is important to help disseminate Daoism abroad just in case such terrible events happen again in China, so that the Daoist tradition can never disappear completely.

This master, as quite a few others, was accordingly very enthusiastic to take on foreign disciples and transmit secret teachings of internal cultivation to them, hoping to save as many teachings and practices of Daoism as possible. This endeavor has become even more important today due to the impact of sinicization, when Daoists are once again limited in their aspirations and subject to suppression. Hopefully overseas Chinese and Westerners continue to practice and support the religion during this current and any future versions of the Cultural Revolution.

# Appendix 1

# The Lineage

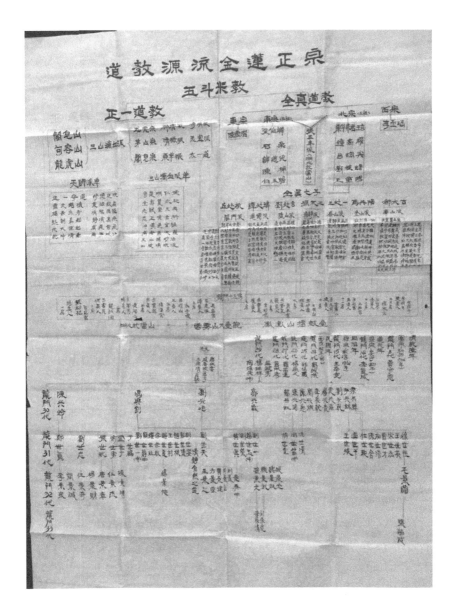

Left: Names of Thunder Drum masters on a stele engraved by Feng Xingzhao.
Right: The lineage in handwritten genealogy.

# Appendix 2

# Timeline

Ming dynasty: Tan Zhenren from the Taizi po on Mount Wudang, a 9th-generation Longmen master, develops Daoism at Leigutai. The Perfected Sun from the Tiantai guan on Mount Yunwu in Shiquan, Shaanxi develops it further.

1912: Liu Chenghong, 24th-generation Longmen master, arrives from Mount Yunwu.

1929: Xie Xincheng moves from Mount Yunwu to take up the management. He is succeeded by abbots Yang Chongyi and Luo Gaolian.

1945: Luo Gaolian leaves to return to Mount Yunwu. Management passes to Huang Sishou and Wu Siliang.

1948: Yang Faxiang (aka Wenpang), a 30th-generation Longmen master, succeeds as abbot.

1949: Only Yang Faxiang and Chen Xinzhong (aka Changdeng) remain.

1953: Yang Faxiang is requisitioned to work as a physician in a hygiene and health workers' commune. Chen Xinzhong replaces him as abbot.

1957: Yang frees himself from the workers association and returns to Leigutai.

1961: Feng Xingzhao follows Yang Faxiang as a disciple. Later, other disciples include Yin Xingshu, Chen Xinghui, Chen Xinglin, Feng Xingzhao, Zheng Xingde, and Liu Xingdi.

1963: Chen Changdeng dies of illness; Yang Faxiang resumes the abbacy.

1966: The Cultural Revolution begins. Feng Xingzhao leaves to works as kitchen staff in a commune farm, but soon manages to leave and hide out at Leigutai.

1981: Feng returns officially.

1983: Feng goes cloud wandering for two years, spending time on Mount Hua.

1985: Feng spends five years at Baxian gong in Xi'an (-1990).

1989: Feng attends the consecration ceremony at the Baiyun guan in Beijing and takes the precepts under the tutelage of transmission master Min Zhiting. He invites Min to come to Leigutai for one month to teach local clerics. Also, both Liu Shitian and Huang Shizhen become disciples of Liu Xingdi.

1990: Feng Xingzhao returns to Leigutai. He will remain abbot for six years (-1996). Liu Xingdi moves to Baxian gong in Xi'an with his two disciples, Liu Shitian and Huang Shizhen. They soon leave to attend the two-year training course at the Daoist College in Beijing.

1992: Huang and Liu return to Baxian gong. Liu begins his project of rebuilding Mingsheng gong on Mount Li, which will take him fourteen years (-2004).

1994: In the fall, Huang Shizhen accompanies Alan Redman and Peter Smith of the British Daoist Association on their first China trip.

1995: Huang Shizhen takes Alan Redman and five other British Daoists to Leigutai, where they are ordained as Quanzhen clerics. In October, Yin Xingshu goes to Mount Qingcheng to attend the consecration ceremony and take the three sets of Quanzhen precepts.

1996: The British Daoist Association is inaugurated. In the summer, Feng Xingzhao, Huang Shizhen, and Zheng Minggui spend one month in England to teach Daoism. Later, Yang Faxiang dies; Yin Xingshu becomes abbot of Leigutai (- 2003); and Feng Xingzhao goes to the Taibai miao in Hanzhong to renovate and revitalize local temples.

1997: Liu Shitian becomes abbot of the Mingsheng gong on Mount Li. In September, the area around Leigutai, Phoenix Mountain, is officially classified as a protected forest park at the provincial level by the forestry department of Shaanxi province (Ceng 2008b, 72; Fenghuang shan 2014).

1998: Feng Xingzhao returns to Ziyang to build the Ziyang zhenren gong.

2002: Feng follows the invitation of the president of the Hengkou chamber of commerce and supervises the management and renovation of the Sansheng miao, resulting in a formal opening ceremony.

2003: Liu Shitian becomes abbot of City God Temple of Xi'an. On February 8, work on the Ziyang Zhenren gong is complete, and Feng Xingzhao presides over a formal opening ceremony. Also, Yin Xingshu dies and Zhang Xingde becomes abbot of Leigutai.

2004: In February, Phoenix Mountain is classified as an AA-level tourist location, which later leads to the erection of a ticket booth, limiting

144 / Appendix 2

access to Leigutai. In March, Feng Xingzhao moves to the Siwang miao in Ziyang to begin its renovation. In October: the Siwang miao obtains the official permit to host religious activities. Also, Feng ordains two further members of the British Daoist Association at the Sansheng miao in Hengkou.

2007: In April, Liu Shitian attends the first international forum on the *Daode jing* in Xi'an.

2009: On April 20, Liu Shitian is installed as abbot of the Zhangliang miaoin Luoba; organizes a formal opening ceremony under the management of Liu Zhikun. He also presents a new bronze statue of Zhenwu and new incense burners to Leigutai.

2010: Feng Xingzhao starts the process of obtaining authorization to rebuild the Xianyue si in Haoping. It ends up taking three years.

2011: In October, Liu Shitian attends the second international forum on Nanyue.

2012: On April 16, Mount Wenbi is officially opened as a protected park; a giant bronze statue of Ziyang zhenren is consecrated

2013: On the 23$^{rd}$ day of the 1$^{st}$ lunar, the rebuilding of the Xianyue si is inaugurated. On August 6, Leigutai hosts a ceremony to install bronze statues of the Three Pure Ones in its new main hall, secured by Liu Shitian.

2014: On April 18, the Wuzhen guan on Mount Wenbi is opened officially and the fourth Daoist forum on ecology begins. In November, Liu Shitian attends the third international forum on Mount Longhu.

# Appendix 3

# Maps of Temple Locations

1. Leigutai (red dot) west of Xi'an (city in the upper right)

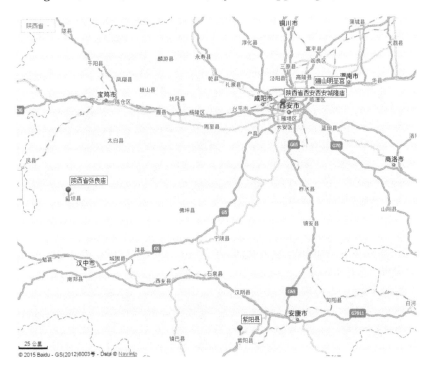

2. From top right to bottom left: Sansheng miao, Leigutai, Xianming si, Yaowang miao, and Zhenren gong (Mount Wenbi)

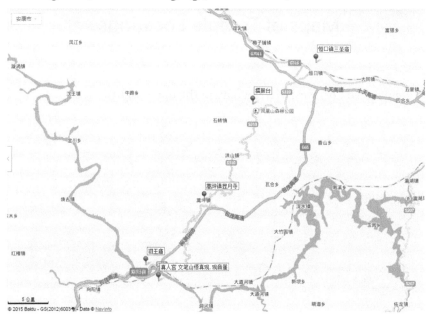

3. Detail of Mount Wenbi: Yaowang miao (top), Wuzhen guan, and Zhenren gong (near the river)

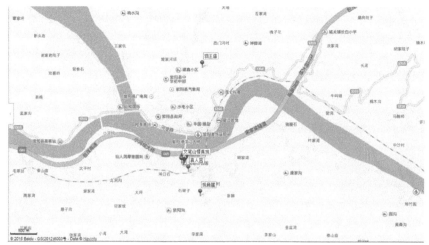

# Bibliography

Ankang 安康. 2013. "Ziyang xian laodi qiye ji zaijian ziangmu" 紫阳县落地企 业及在建项目. *Ankangshi zhaoshang wang* 安康市招商网, November 26, 2013. http://zs.ankang.gov.cn/ html/qyml/luodiqiyejizaijianxiangmu/2013/1126/10135.html

Aomen 澳门. 2014. "2014 Aomen daojiao wenhua jie 澳門道教文化節. Aomen daojiao xiehui 澳门道教协会, October 25, 2014. http://www.macaotaoist. Org.

ARC [Alliance of Religions and Conservation]. 2005. "About ARC." http://www. arcworld.org/about_ARC.asp.

_____. 2006. "ARC Projects - July 2006 Daoism and Conservation Workshop." July 26. http://www.arcworld.org/projects.asp?projectID=273.

_____. 2007. "Daoist Ecology Workshop Hugely Oversubscribed." May 31. http://www.arcworld.org/news.asp?pageID=171.

_____. 2008a. "ARC Projects: Mao Shan Declaration." October 27. http://www. arcworld.org/projects.asp?projectID=371.

_____. 2008b. "Third Daoist Ecology Forum Opens in Jurong, Jiangsu—And This One Is Country-Wide." October 27. http://www.arcworld.org/news.asp?pageID=273.

_____. 2014. "Three Daoist Pilgrim Cities Join the Green Pilgrimage Network." April 18. http://www.arcworld.org/news.asp?pageID=706.

Baidu baike. 百度百科. 2014. "Leigutai" 擂鼓台. http://baike.baidu.com/ subview/78171/9571359.htm.

_____. 2015a. "Lishan" 骊山. http://baike.baidu.com/view/50705.htm.

_____. 2015b. "Yunwu shan" 云雾山. http://baike.baidu.com/subview/52516/10990397.htm.

Beida 北大. 2014. "Beida falü yingwen wang" 北大法律英文网. http://www. lawinfochina.com/index.aspx.

Baiyun guan 白云观. 2015. "Beijing Baiyun guan guanwang de pindao" 北京白云观官网的频道. *Youku* 优酷, June 23. http://i.youku.com/u/ UNDAoMzQzNTQw.

Berkowitz, Alan. 1989. "Patterns of Reclusion in Early and Medieval China." Ph.D. Diss., University of Washington, Seattle.

Bloch, Helene. 2019. "From Daoist Asceticism to Longevity Market? 'Nourish-ing Life' on Mount Qingcheng." *Journal of Daoist Studies* 12:163-80.

Bokenkamp, Stephen R. 1997. *Early Daoist Scriptures*. Berkeley: University of California Press.

## 148 / Bibliography

Brady, Annie-Marie. 2018. "Magic Weapons: China's political influence activities under Xi Jinping." https://www.wilsoncenter.org/article/magic-weapons-chinas-political-influence-activities-under-xi-jinping?gad_source=1.

Cao Benye 曹本冶. 1996. *Zhongguo daojiao yinyue shilüe* 中国道教音乐史略. Taipei: Xinwenfeng.

CDA [Zhongguo daojiao xiehui 中国道教协会]. 1980. "Zhongguo daojiao xiehui disanjie lishi hui" 中国道教协会第三届理事会. *Zhongguo daojiao xiehui* 中国道教协会. http://www.taoist.org.cn/getDjzsById.do?id=10.

_____. 2008. "Daojiao jiaozhi renyuan rending banfa" 道教教职人员认定办法. *Zhongguo daojiao xiehui* 中国道教协会. http://www.taoist.org.cn/getDjzsById.do?id=69.

_____. 2011a. "2011 nian Nanyue guoji faojiao luntan zhuanti baodao" 2011 年南岳 国际道教论坛专题报道. *Daojiao zhiyin* 道教之音, October 23. http://www.daoisms.org/article/sort028/info-4042.html.

_____. 2011b. "Zhongguo daojiao xueyuan shoujie jingdian Jiangxi ban zhaosheng" 中国道教学院首届经典讲习班招生. *Daojiao zhiyin* 道教之音, September 4. http://www.daoisms.org/infos/3129.html.

_____. 2012. "Zhongguo daojiao xueyuan 12 ri juxing shoujie jingdian Jiangxi ban biye dianli" 中国道教学院 12 日举行首届经典讲习班毕业典礼. *Daojiao zhiyin* 道教之音, June 12. http://www.daoisms.org/article/sort028/info-6902.html.

_____. 2013a. "Diwujie xuanmen jiangjing ji Huashan lundao zai Huashan kaimu" 第五届玄门讲经暨华山论道在华山开幕. *Daojiao zhiyin* 道教之音, September 11. http://www.daoisms.org/article/sort028/info-9514.html.

_____. 2013b. "Zhongguo daojio diwu jie xuanmen jiangjing ji Huashan lundao zhuanti baodao" 中国道教第五届玄门讲经暨华山论道专题报道. *Daojiao zhiyin* 道教之音, September 11. http://www.daoisms.org/article/sort028/info-9542.html.

_____. 2014a. "Changdao wenming jingxiang jianshe shengtai siguan xinwen fabiao hui zaijing juxing" 倡导文明敬香建设生态寺观新闻发布会在京举行. *Zhongguo daojiao xiehui* 中国道教协会, January 22. http://www.taoist.org.cn/showInfoContent.do?id=575&p=%27p%27.

_____. 2014b. *Diliujie xuanmen jiangjing ji Dongyue lundao wenji* 第六届玄门讲经暨东岳论道文集. Taishan: Zhongguo daojiao xiehui.

_____. 2014c. "Diliujie xuanmen jiangjing ji Dongyue luntan dao juanti baodao" 第六届玄门讲经暨东岳论道专题报道. *Daojiao zhiyin* 道教之音, September 1. http://www.daoisms.org/article/sort028/info-13203.html.

_____. 2014d. "Disanjie guoji daojao luntan xuanyan" 第三届国际道教论坛宣言. *Zhongguo daojiao xiehui* 中国道教协会, November 26. http://www.taoist.org.cn/showInfoContent.do?id=1027&p=%27p%27.

_____. 2014e. "Disanjie guoji daojiao luntan juxing yangsheng daoyizhen huodong" 第三届国际道教论坛举行养生道医义诊活动. *Zhongguo daojiao xiehui* 中国道教协会, November 26. http://www.taoist.org.cn/showInfoContent.do?id=1023&p=%27p%27.

_____. 2014f. "Disanjie guoji daojiao luntan juxing zhu luntan fayan" 第三届国际 道教论坛举行主论坛发言. *Zhongguo daojiao xiehui* 中国道教协会, November 25. http://www.taoist.org.cn/showInfoContent.do?id=1024&p=%27p%27.

_____. 2014g. "Disanjie guoji daojiao luntan zhuanti baodao" 第三届国际道教论坛专题报道. *Daojiao zhiyin* 道教之音, November 25. http://www.daoisms.org/article/sort028/info-13985.html.

_____. 2014h. "Fenghuang wang: Disanju huoji daojiao luntan bimu fabiao Longhu shan xuanyan" 凤凰网：第三届国际道教论坛闭幕发表龙虎山宣言. *Guojia zongjiao shiwuju* 国家宗教事务局, November 26. http://www.sara.gov.cn/mtjj/192554.htm.

_____. 2014i. "Ziyang Zhenren gong Wuzhen guan qifu huodong ji disi ci Zhongguo daojiao shengtai jiaoyu zuotan hui zai Shaanxi Ziyang juxing" 紫阳真人宫悟真观祈福活动暨第四次中国道教生态教育座谈会在陕西紫阳举行. *Zhongguo daojiao xiehui* 中国道教协会, April 18. http://www.taoist.org.cn/showInfoContent.do?id=698&p=%27p%27.

Ceng Deqiang 曾德强. 2008a. *Ziyang daojiao wenhua* 紫阳道教文化. Xi'an: Sanqing chubanshe.

_____. 2008b. "Leigutai daoguan" 雷鼓台道观. *Ziyang daojiao wenhua* 紫阳道教文化 2008:70-115.

_____. 2008c. "Ziyang zhenren gong" 紫阳真人宫. *Ziyang daojiao wenhua* 紫阳道教文化 2008:44-69.

CFR (Council on Foreign Relations). 2024. "Religion in China." https://www.cfr.org/backgrounder/religion-china.

Changchunshi 长春市. 2012. "Changchunshi Changchun guan jiangzhong xing shenxian kaiguang ji Quanzhen guanjin fahui" 长春市长春观隆重举行 神像开光暨全真冠巾法会. *Daojiao zhiyin* 道教之音, May 18. http://www.daoisms.org/article/sort028/info-6623.html.

Chen Gang 陈刚. 2012. "Ziyang xian zhaokai daojiao yangsheng wenhua yuan guihua cehua zuotanhui" 紫阳县召开道教养生文化园规划策划座谈会. *Ziyang renmin zhengfu* 紫陽人民政府, August 26. http://www.ziyang-xian.gov.cn/news/jinri/2012/0827/9199.html.

Chen Jie 陈杰. 2013a. "Jicheng chuantong xia de jinqu yu chuangxin jinnian lai daojiao jie congshi gongyi cishan huodong de qingluang fenxi" 继承传统下 的进取与创新 近年来道教界从事公益慈善活动的情况分析. *Zhongguo daojiao* 中国道教 2.

150 / Bibliography

———. 2013b. "Jinnian Lai Daojiao Jie Congshi Gongyi Ceishan Huodong de Qingkuang Fenxi" 近年来道教界从事公益慈善活动的情况分析. *Zhongguo daojiao xiehui* 中国道教协会. http://www.taoist.org.cn/ showInfoContent.do?id=392&p=.

Chen Jingzhan 陈景展 and Zi Shanxi 善溪子. 2011. "Zhongguo daojiao xueyuan shoujie jingdian jiangxiban kaixue dianli jintian shangwu zhaokai" 中国道教学院首届经典讲习班开学典礼今天上午召开. *Daojiao zhiyin* 道教之音, September 4. http://www.daoisms.org/article/sort028/info-3782.html.

Chen Xiongqun 陈雄群. 1988. "Daojiao zhishi zhuanxiu ban kundao ban juxing longzhong kaixue dianli" 道教知识专修班坤道班举行隆重开学典礼. *Zhongguo daojiao* 中国道教 4:5-6.

Conze, Edward. 2001. *Buddhist Wisdom: The Diamond Sutra and the Heart Sutra*. New York: Random House.

Daobei 道碑. 2000. "Baiyun guan Chen Yukun fangzhang chuanjie beiji" 雲觀陳毓坤方丈傳戒碑記. http://www.daobei.info.

Daojiao zhiyin 道教之音. 2012. "Lanzhou Baiyun guan juxing Quanzhen guanjin fahui" 兰州白云观举行全真冠巾法会. August 1. http:/ www.daoisms.org/ article/sort028/info-7217.html.

———. 2013. "Shaanxi sheng Xi'anshi Lintong qu Mingsheng gong 陕西西安市临潼区明圣宫. *Daojiao zhiyin* 道教之音, December 1, 2013. http://www.daoisms. org/article/sort022/info-10021.html.

———. 2014. "Lanzhou Jiang Juxing di shisi jie daojiao yinyue huiyan" 兰州将举行第十四届道教音乐汇演. http://www.daoisms.org/article/sort 028/info-13722. html.

———. 2015. "Yangsheng dongtai 养生动态. June 24. http://www.daoisms.org/ article/sort012/list139_1.html.

Darga, Martina. 1999. *Das alchemistische Buch von innerem Wesen und Lebensenergie: Xingming guizhi*. Munich: Diederichs.

DeBruyn, Pierre-Henry. 2000. "Daoism in the Ming (1368-1644)." In *Daoism Handbook*, edited by Livia Kohn, 594-622. Leiden: Brill.

Despeux, Catherine. 1979. *Zhao Bichen: Traité d'alchimie et de physiologie taoïste*. Paris: Guy Trédaniel.

———. 1989. *Traité d'alchimie et de physiologie taoïste*. Paris: Les Deux Océans.

———. 2008. "Yangsheng: Nourishing Life." In *Encyclopedia of Taoism*, edited by Fabrizio Pregadio. London: Routledge.

Ding Changyun 丁常云. 2011. "Zhonghe zhidao: Daojiao de shengtai hexie lilun" 中和之道：道教的生态和谐理论. *Zhongguo gongchengdang xinwen* 中国共产党新闻. http://theory.people.com.cn/GB/14032229.html.

Engelhardt, Ute. 1987. *Die klassische Tradition der Qi-Übungen. Eine Darstellung anhand des Tang-zeitlichen Textes Fuqi jingyi lun von Sima Chengzhen*. Wiesbaden: Franz Steiner.

_____. 2000. "Longevity Techniques and Chinese Medicine." In *Daoism Handbook*, edited by Livia Kohn, 75-108. Leiden: Brill.

Eskildsen, Stephen. 2004. *The Teachings and Practices of the Early Quanzhen Taoist Masters*. Albany: State University of New York Press.

Esposito, Monica. 2009. "The *Daozang Jiyao* Project: Mutations of a Canon." *Daoism: Religion, History and Society* 1:95-156.

_____. 2014. *Facets of Qing Daoism*. Zurich: University Media.

_____. 2016. *Creative Daoism*. Zurich: University Media.

Fan Guangchun 樊光春. 1989. *Ziyang xianzhi* 紫阳县志. Ziyang: Sanqin chubanshe.

_____. 1991. *Shannan xiao wudang: Fenghuang shan Leigutai* 陕南小武当：凤凰山擂鼓台. Xi'an: Sanqin chubanshe.

_____. 2010a. "Ren Yongzhen yu Zhangliang miao" 任永真与张良庙. *Xibei daojioa shi* 西北道教史, edited by Fan Guangchun, 561-67. Beijing: Shengwu yinshuguan.

_____. 2010b. "Zhang Boduan yu neidan xue de xingcheng 第三节张伯端 与内丹学的形成. *Xibei daojiao shi* 西北道教史, edited by Fan Guangchun, 331-33.

_____. 2012. "Urban Daoism, Commodity Markets, and Tourism: The Restoration of the Xi'an City God Temple." In *Daoism in the Twentieth Century: Between Eternity and Modernity*, edited by David Palmer and Xun Liu, 108-22. Berkeley: University of California Press.

Fang Wanhua 方万华. 2014. "Ziyang daojiiao wenhua de meili" 紫阳道教文化 的魅力. *Zhongguo daojiao nanzong wenhua wang* 中国道教南宗文化网, March 4. http://www.djnzw.cn/a//2014/0304/101.html.

Fenghuang 凤凰.2014. "Fen luntan daojiao de shengtai zhihui" 分论坛道教 的生态智慧. *Fenghuang xinmeiti 凤凰新媒体*, November 26. http://fo.ifeng.com/a/20141126/40881666_0.shtml.

Fenghuang shan 凤凰山. 2014. "Shaanxi sheng Fenghuang shan Guojia senlin gongyuan" 陕西省凤凰山国家森林公园. *Fenghuangshan senlin gongyuan wangzhan* 凤凰山森林公园网站. http://fhsh.hanbin.gov.cn/Aboutus.asp? Title

Fungying Seenkoon 蓬瀛仙館. 2014a. "Chen Yingning" 陳攖寧. *Fengying xianguan daojiao wenhua zhongxin ziliaoku* 蓬瀛仙館教文化中心資料庫. http://www.daoinfo.org/wiki/陳攖寧.

_____. 2014b. "Yue Chongdai" 岳崇岱. *Fengying xianguan daojiao wenhua zhongxin ziliaoku* 蓬瀛仙館教文化中心資料庫. http://www.daoinfo.org/ wiki.

## 152 / Bibliography

_____. 2015. "Daoist Temples:." *Fengying xianguan daojiao wenhua zhongxin ziliaoku* 蓬瀛仙館教文化中心資料庫. http://en.daoinfo.org/wiki/Daoist_ Temples.

Goossaert, Vincent. 1997. "La creation du taoïsme moderne: L'ordre Quanzhen." Ph.D. Diss. Paris: École Pratique des Hautes Études.

_____. 2001. "The Invention of an Order: Collective Identity in Thirteenth-Century Quanzhen Taoism." *Journal of Chinese Religions* 29:111-38.

_____. 2004. "The Quanzhen Clergy, 1700-1950." In *Religion and Chinese Society*, edited by John Lagerwey, 1:699-771. Hong Kong: Chinese University Press.

_____. 2007. *The Taoists of Peking, 1800-1949. A Social History of Urban Clerics*. Cambridge, Mass.: Harvard University Press.

_____. 2021. *Heavenly Masters: Two Thousand Years of the Daoist State*. Honolulu: University of Hawaii Press.

_____, and David Palmer, eds. 2011. *The Religious Question in Modern China*. Chicago: University of Chicago Press.

_____, and Xun Liu, eds. 2013. *Quanzhen Daoists in Chinese Society and Culture, 1500-2010*. Berkeley: University of California Press.

Graham, A. C. 1981. *Chuang-tzu: The Seven Inner Chapters and Other Writings from the Book of Chuang-tzu*. London: Allan & Unwin.

Groot, Gerry. 2004. *Managing Transitions: The Chinese Communist Party, United Front Work, Corporatism and Hegemony*. New York: Routledge.

_____. 2016. "The Expansion of the United Front under Xi Jinping." *The China Story Yearbook 2015: Pollution*. Canberra: Australian National University Press. doi:10.22459/csy.09.2016.04a.

Guangdong daojiao xiehui 广东道教协会. 2013. "Guangdong daojiao juxing 2013 nian daojao wenhua jie" 广东道教举行 2013 年道教文化节. *Daojiao zhiyin* 道教之音. http://www.daoisms.org/article/sort028/info-9956.html.

Guojia shuiwu zongju 国家税务总局. 2012. "Guanyu guli he guifan zongjiaojie congshi gongyi cishan huodong de yijian" 关于鼓励和规范宗教界从事公益慈善活动的意见. *Guojia shuiwu zongju* 国家税务总局, February 16. http://www.chinatax.gov.cn/n810341/n810765/n812151/n812431/c1083869/content.ht.

Guojia 国家 2008. "Shaanxi sheng zongjiao shiwu tiaolie (2008 xiuding)" 陕西省宗教事务条例(2008 修订). *Beida falü yingwen wang* 北大法律英文 网, July 30. http://www.lawinfochina.com/display.aspx?lib=law&id=13444 &CGid=.

_____. 2011. "2011 guoji daojiao luntan" 2011 国际道教论坛. *Guojia zongjiao shiwuju* 国家宗教事务局, October 23. http://www.sara.gov.cn/ztzz/gjdjlt2011/index. htm.

_____. 2014a. "2014 Guoji daojiao luntan" 2014 国际道教论坛. *Guojia zongjiao shiwuju* 国家宗教事务局, November 25. http://www.sara.gov.cn/ztzz/gjdjlt/index.htm.

_____. 2014b. "Disanjie guoji daojiao luntan juxing santang dianshi luntan" 第三届国际道教论坛举行三场电视论坛. *Guojia zongjiao shiwuju* 国家宗教事务局, November 26. http://www.sara.gov.cn/ztzz/gjdjlt/xwjj_ djlt/192544.htm.

_____. 2014c. "Disanjie guoji daojiao luntan xinwen fabuhui jingtan juxing" 第三届国际道教论坛新闻发布会在鹰潭举行. *Guojia zongjiao shiwuju* 国家宗教事务局, November 24. http://www.sara.gov.cn/xwzx/xwjj/ 192447.htm.

_____. 2014d. "Guoji zongjiao shiwuju guanyu jinyi bu tuidong wenming jingxiang jianshe shengtai siguan gongzuo de tongzhi 国家宗教事务局 关于进一步推动文明敬香、建设生态寺观工作的通知. *Zhongguo daojiao xiehui* 中国道教协会, January 9. http://www.taoist.org.cn/show InfoContent.do?id=579a.

_____. 2014e. "Zongjiao shiwu tiaoli youguan zongjiao huodong changsuo de guiding" 宗教事务条例有关宗教活动场所的规定. *Guojia zongjiao shiwuju* 国家宗教事务局, May 4. http://www.sara.gov.cn/xxgk /zcfg/79731.htm.

Hackmann, Heinrich. 1920. "Die Mönchsregeln des Klostertaoismus." *Ostasiatische Zeitschrift* 8:141-70.

_____. 1931. *Die dreihundert Mönchsgebote des chinesischen Taoismus.* Amsterdam: Koninklijke Akademie van Wetenshapen.

Han Bin. 2014. "International Taoist Forum Focuses on Health and Longevity." *CCTV English*, November 27. http://english.cntv.cn/2014/11/27/VIDE 1417065722325580.shtml.

Harper, Donald. 1998. *Early Chinese Medical Manuscripts: The Mawangdui Medical Manuscripts.* London: Wellcome Asian Medical Monographs.

Hassan, Tirana. 2024. "The Human Rights System Is under Threat: A Call to Action." https://www.hrw.org/world-report/2024/country-chapters/china.

He Jianming 何建明. 2014. "He Jianming: Xialingying cujin daojiao zishen jianshe" 何建明：夏令营促进道教自身建设. *Daojiao zhiyin* 道教之音, July 8. http://www.daoisms.org/interview/13396.html.

_____ and Lishan 骊山. 2014. "He Jianming jiaoshou zai Xi'an Lishan Ming-sheng gong daojiao wenhua xialingying kaimushi shang de jianghua" 何建明教授 在西安骊山明圣宫道文化夏令营开营式上的讲话. *Daojiao zhiyin* 道教之音, July 14. http://www.daoisms.org/article/sorto28/info-13010.html.

Hengkou 恒口. 2009 "Qinbashan dishang de zhongzhen Hengkou guzhen" 秦巴山地上的重镇-恒口古镇. *Hengkou320 de boke* 恒口 320 的博客, October 12. http://hengkou320.blog.163.com/blog/static/12910993320099 12115137348/.

Hengkou daojiao xiehui 恒口道教協會. 2012. "Hengkouzhen Changgong juxing sanyue san miaohui" 恒口镇成功举行三月三庙会. *Hanbin qu gongshang lian*

汉滨区工商联, March 26. http://gsl.hanbin.gov.cn/ReadNews.asp?NewsID=475.

Herrou, Adeline. 2005. *La vie entre soi: Les moines taoïstes aujurd'hui en Chine*. Nanterre: La Société d'ethnologie.

———. 2010. "A Day in the Life of a Daoist Monk." *Journal of Daoist Studies* 2:117-48.

———. 2013. *A World of Their Own: Monastics and Their Community in Contemporary China*. St. Petersburg, Fla: Three Pines Press.

He Yuanbo 何远波. 2012. "Shaanxi Ziyang xian juxing zhixian 500 nian shengda qingdian Ji Ziyang zhenren xiang luocheng yishi" 陕西紫阳县举行置县 500 年盛大庆典暨紫阳真人像落成仪式. *Daojiao zhiyin* 道教之音, April 16. http://www.daoisms.org/article/sort028/info-6165.html.

HRW [Human Rights Watch]. 2024. "China: Religious Regulations Tighten for Uyghurs—New Laws Aim to 'Sinicize' Places of Worship, Practice in Largely Muslim Xinjiang." https://www.hrw.org/news/2024/01/31/china-religious-regulations-tighten-uyghurs.

Huang Shizhen 黄世真. 2015. "Daojiao qishi Huang Shizhen" 道教奇士黄世真. *Daojiao zhiyin* 道教之音. http://www.daoisms.org/article/sort010/info-2738.html.

Huang Xinyang 黄信阳. 1993. *Xiudao yangsheng zhenjue* 修道养生真诀. Beijing: Beijing shifan daxue chubanshe.

———. 2000. *Daojiao quanzhen bidu* 道教全真必讀. Hong Kong: Xinde Yinzhi chang youxian gongsi.

———. 2006. "Daojiao Quanzhen dao 道教全真道. *Huang xinyang de boke* 黄信陽的博客. http://blog.sina.com.cn/s/blog_68dd00750100mpmp.html.

———. 2007a. *Daojiao changzhi wenda* 道教常识问答. Beijing: Beijingshi daojiao xiehui.

———. 2007b. "Quanzhen daoshi weishenme yao guanjin" 全真道士为什么要冠巾. *Daojiao changzhi wenda* 道教常识问答. Beijing: Beijingshi daojiao xiehui.

———. 2011. "Disanjie Xuanmen jianjing ji Zhongyue lundao zai Henan Song-shan juxing" 第三届玄门讲经暨中岳论道在河南嵩山举行. *Huang xinyang de boke* 黄信阳的博客, November 16. http://blog.sina.com.cn/s/blog_68dd00750102dunf.html.

———. 2012. "Wudangshan daxing liubai nian luotian dajiao ji disijie xuanmen jiangjing huodong kaimushi" 武当山大兴六百年罗天大醮暨第四届玄门讲经活动开幕式. *Huang xinyang de boke* 黄信阳的博客, October 17. http://blog.sina.com.cn/s/blog_68dd00750102e230.html.

———. 2014. "Huang Xinyang daozhang zai disanjie guoji daojiao luntan xinwen fabuhui shang de zhici" 黄信阳道长在第三届国际道教论坛新闻发布会上的致

辞. *Daojiao zhiyin* 道教之音, November 24, 2014.
http://www.daoisms.org/plus/view.php?aid=13996.

_____ and Wang Jinmei 王金梅. 2014. "Daojiao yangsheng fangfa jingcui shoufa Huang Xinyang jieshou Zhongguo wang zhuanfang "道教养生方法 精粹首发 黄信阳接受中国网专访. *Zhongguo zhengxie* 中国政协, Novem- ber 26. http://cppcc.china.com.cn/2014-11/26/content_34159277.htm.

_____ and Zhang Hui. 2014. "Taoist Master: Positive Publicity Helps Religious Charity." *Zhongguo wang* 中国网, March 13. http://www.china.org.cn/ china/NPC_CPPCC_2014/2014-03/13/content_31772685.htm.

Hudson, Clarke. 2007. "Spreading the Dao, Managing Mastership, and Perform-ing Salvation: The Life and Alchemical Teachings of Chen Zhixu." Ph. D. Diss., Indiana University, Bloomington.

Hu Jintao 胡锦涛. 2012. "Di babu fen: Dali tuijinshengtai wenming jianshe-shipin zhongguo" 第八部分：大力推进生态文明建设- 视频中国. *Zhong-guo wang* 中国网, November 8. http://v.china.com.cn/18da/2012-11/11/ content_27074139.htm.

_____, and Xinhua News Agency. 2007. "Hu Jintao's Report at 17th Party Congress. "*Zhongguo wang* 中国网, October 25. http://www.china.org.cn/ english/congress/229611.htm.

Jiang Jianyong 蒋坚永. 2014. "Jiang Jianying fuzhu zhang fu Jiangxi kaocha disanjie guoji daojiao luntan choubei gongzuo" 蒋坚永副局长赴江西考察 第三届国际 道教论坛筹备工作. *Guojia zongjiao shiwuju* 国家宗教事务局, February 27. http://www.sara.gov.cn/xwzx/xwjj/ 63253.htm.

Johnson, Ian. 2012. "Two Sides of a Mountain: The Modern Transformation of Maoshan." *Journal of Daoist Studies* 5:89-116.

Kim, David, ed. 2015. *Religious Transformation in Modern Asia: A Transnational Movement*. Leiden: Brill.

Kohn, Livia, ed. 1989. *Taoist Meditation and Longevity Techniques*. Ann Arbor: University of Michigan, Center for Chinese Studies.

_____. 1993. *The Taoist Experience: An Anthology*. Albany: State University of New York Press.

_____. 2001. *Daoism and Chinese Culture*. Cambridge, Mass.: Three Pines Press.

_____. 2002. "Quiet Sitting with Master Yinshi: Medicine and Religion in Modern China." In *Living with the Dao: Conceptual Issues in Daoist Practice*, edited by Livia Kohn, 151-65. Cambridge, Mass.: Three Pines Press.

_____. 2003. "Monastic Rules in Quanzhen Daoism: As Collected by Heinrich Hackmann." *Monumenta Serica* 51:1-32.

_____. 2004a. *Cosmos and Community: The Ethical Dimension of Daoism*. Cambridge, Mass.: Three Pines Press.

156 / Bibliography

_____. 2004b. *Supplement to Cosmos and Community.* Cambridge, Mass.: Three Pines Press.

_____. 2004c. *The Daoist Monastic Manual: A Translation of the Fengdao Kejie.* New York: Oxford University Press

_____, ed. 2006. *Daoist Body Cultivation: Traditional Models and Contemporary Practices.* Cambridge, Mass.: Three Pines Press

_____. 2008. *Chinese Healing Exercises: The Tradition of Daoyin.* Honolulu: University of Hawaii Press.

_____. 2012. *A Source Book in Chinese Longevity.* St Petersburg, Fla.: Three Pines Press.

_____. 2020. *The Zhong-Lü System of Internal Alchemy.* St. Petersburg, Fla.: Three Pines Press.

Komjathy, Louis. 2003. "Daoist Teachers in North America. *Center for Daoist Studies,* 2003. www.daoistcenter.org/advanced.html.

_____. 2007. *Cultivating Perfection: Mysticism and Self-Transformation in Early Quanzhen Daoism.* Leiden: Brill.

_____. 2008. *Handbooks for Daoist Practice.* Hong Kong: Yuen Yuen Institute.

_____. 2013. *The Way of Complete Perfection: A Quanzhen Daoist Anthology.* Albany: State University of New York Press.

Lai Chi Tim, ed. 2021. *Daozang jiyao tiyao* 道藏輯要提要.Hong Kong: The Chinese University Press.

Li Houzhi 李厚之 and Zhang Huijian 张会鉴. 2009. "Shaanxi Ankang Ziyang xian gusha jianjie" 陕西安康紫阳县古刹简介. *Foyuan wang* 佛缘网, April 12. http://www.foyuan.net/article-114513-1.html.

Li Huanlong 李焕龙. 2012. *Ankang bai bian tang cangpin shangxi yu bian wenhua yanjiiu* 安康百匾堂藏品赏析与匾文化研究. Xi'an: Sanqin chubanshe.

_____ and Sun Hong 孙鸿. 2013. "Shoucang bohu yanjiu chuancheng Ping Ankang Baibian tang cangpin shangxi yu bian wenhua yanjiiu" 收藏保护研究传承评安康百匾堂藏品赏析与匾文化研究. *Xibu xuekan* 西部学刊 2.

Li Wencheng 李文成. 1988. "Zhongguo daojiao xiehui li wencheng mishu zhang zai kundao ban kaixue dianli shang de jianghua" 中国道教协会 李文成秘书长在坤道班开学典礼会上的讲话. *Zhongguo daojiao* 中国道教 4:7-8.

Li Xinjun 李信军. 2013a. *Zhonghua daoxue baiwen* 中華道學百問. 3 vols. Beijing: Baiyun guan.

_____. 2013b. "169 shenme shi yangsheng" 169 什么是养生？In *Zhonghua daoxue baiwen* 中華道學百問, 100-03. Beijing: Baiyun guan.

Li Yangzheng 李養正. 1993a. *Dangdai zhongguo daojiao* 当代中国道教. Beijing: Zhongguo shehui kexue chubanshe.

_____. 1993b. "Dangdai daojiao shi: Zhongguo daojiao xiehui (si)" 当代道教 历史-中国道教协会（四. *Shanyou qingjun boke* 山幽清君博客. http://blog.sina.com.cn/s/blog_4c7cf72101007y9j.html.

_____, ed. 2003. *Xinbian beijing baiyunguan zhi* 新編北京白雲觀志. Beijing: Zongjiao wenhua chubanshe.

Li Yao. 2011. "Taoist Forum Looks at Environment." *China Daily*, October 23. http://europe.chinadaily.com.cn/china/2011-10/24/content_13959045.htm.

Lin Zhou 林舟, Xie Ying 谢樱, and Li Jianmin 李建敏. 2011. "Zhongguo daojiao pingwen fazhan xian you jīn 10 wan daoshi-guoji daojiao luntan xinwen fabuhui" 中国道教平稳发展 现有近 10 万道士-国际道教论坛 新闻发布会. *Guojia zongjiao shiwuju* 国家宗教事务局, October 25. http://www.sara.gov.cn/ztzz/gjdjlt2011/mtjjgjdjlt2011/10718.htm.

Lishan 骊山. 2015. "Lishan guojia senlin gongyuan wanwang zhan" 骊山国家森林公园官方网站. http://www.xalishan.com/gyzt/jdjs.php.

Lishan Mingsheng gong 骊山明圣宫. 2013. "Mingsheng gong zuzhi daozhong kanwang pinkun laoren" 明圣宫组织道众看望贫困老人. *Daojiao zhiyin* 道教之音, November 10. http://www.daoisms.org/article/sort028/info-9890.html.

_____. 2015a. "Dierjie quanguo daojiao wenhua qingnian xilingying" 第二届全国道文化青年夏令营. *Zhidao wang* 知道網, July 4. http://www.realdao.cn/msg/index.php?s=/tcsc/detail/id/297.

_____. 2015b. "Lishan Mingsheng gong de boke weibo 骊山明聖宫的微博-微博. http://www.weibo.com/msabbey.

Liu Chengjie 刘诚洁. 2013. "Liu Chengjie: Zhengji huaren zhongshan fengxing bangzheng shihui zheng nengliang (shipin)" 刘诚洁：正己化人、众善奉行—助增社会正能量（视频）. *Daojiao zhiyin* 道教之音, September 11. http://www.daoisms.org/article/sort025/info-9547.html.

Liu Huaiyuan 刘怀元. 2013. "Shandong sheng daojiao xiehui huizhang Liu Huayuan" 山东省道教协会会长刘怀元. *Daojiao zhiyin* 道教之音. http://www.daoisms.org/article/sort010/info-5492.html.

_____. 2014. "Xuanmen jiangjing xuanyai gengshen de sikao yu geng gao de zhuiqiu (zai diliujie xuanmen jiangjing ji dongyue lundao huodong bimushi shang de zongjie fayan)" 玄门讲经，需要更深的思考与更高的追求 (在第六届玄门讲经暨东岳论道活动闭幕式上的总结发言). *Zhongguo daojiao xiehui* 中国道教协会, September 3. http://www.taoist.org.cn/showInfoContent.do?id=916&p=%27p%27.

Liu Jinguang. 2014. "The Strategic Thinking on the Involvement of Religions in the Comprehensive Social Construction." Paper presented at the conference on Religion in China Today: Resurgence and Challenge November 3. http://fudan-uc.ucsd.edu/research/conference-2014.html.

Liu Shitian 刘世天. 2007. "Xiandao guisheng zundao guide yu tianren heyi: Jiandai shehui zhong de daojiao jiazhi" 仙道貴生尊道貴德與天人合一: 現代社會中的道教價值. In *Daoguan guanli yu jiandai shehui: Shoujie shoujiao wenhua ji shuqi yanxiuban daoshi xueyuan lunwen ji* 道觀管理與現代社會: 首屆首教文化及暑期研修班道士學員論文集. Xianggang: Xianggang zhongwen daxue daojiao wenhua yanjiu zhongxin.

———. 2008a. "Tianjiang danan shanhe lei daoyi rushanbei chuanxing" 天降大难 山河泪道义如山北川行. 新浪博客. *Baoyi Daoren de boke* 抱一道人的博客, May 12. http://blog.sina.com.cn/s/blog_4efca68b01009yht.html.

———. 2008b. "Hanzhong Zhangliang miao huifu wei daojiao huodong changsuo" 汉中张良庙恢复为道教活动场所. *Zhongguo daojiao* 中國道教 4.

———. 2008c. "Xiandai shehui zhong de daojiao jiazhi" 現代社會中的道教價值. 新浪博客. *Baoyi daoren de doke* 抱一道人的博客, July 21. http://blog.sina.com.cn/s/blog_4efca68b01009ydi.html.

———. 2009a. "Hexie fazhan tianxia you dao: Zhongguo xian 2009 Lishan wendao zai Lintong Mingsheng gong changgong juxing" 和谐发展·天下有道-中国西安2009 骊山问道在临潼明圣宫成功举行. 新浪博客. *Baoyi daoren de boke* 抱一道人的博客, June 29. http://blog.sina.com.cn/s/blog_4efca68b0100 evo9.html.

———. 2009b. "Leigutai daoguan" 擂鼓台道观. *Baoyi daoren de boke* 抱一道人的博客, October 11. http://blog.sina.com.cn/s/blog_4efca68b0100ewqn.html.

———. 2012. "Tianren heyi dao yangsheng kaitan ludi" 天人合一道养生开坛绿地. *Xinliang wang* 新浪网, May 20. http://sx.house.sina.com.cn/news/2012-05-17/184245465.shtml.

———. 2013a. "Chenghuang miao xinyang zai chuantong shehui zhong de zuoyong" 城隍信仰在传统社会中的作用. *Zhongguo daojiao* 中国道教 6.

———. 2013b. "Fen luntan: Daojiao de tai zhihui" 分论坛: 道教的生态智慧. *Fenghuang xin boti* 凤凰新媒体, November 26. http://fo.ifeng.com/a/20141126/40881666_0.shtml.

———. 2014a. "Jianxing rudao liangxing zhutui wenhua fuxing dui dangdai daojiao wenhua jianshe de xin sikao" 践行儒道两行助推文化复兴—对当代道教文化建设的新思考. *Proceedings of the Third International Taoist Forum Conference* 第三届国际道教论坛论文集, 332-38. Longhu shan: Zhongjiao wenhua chubanshe.

———. 2014b. "Jianxing rudao liangxing zhutui wenhua fuxing dui dangdai daojiao wenhua jianshe de xin sikao" 践行儒道两行助推文化复兴—对当代道教文化建设的新思考. *Daojiao zhiyin* 道教之音, November 26, 2014. http://www.daoisms.org/article/lundao/info-14661.html.

———. 2015a. "Lishan Baoyi daoren de boke-weibao" 骊山抱一道人的微博-微博. http://www.weibo.com/u/2896856355.

_____. 2015b. "Zhidao wang" 知道网. http://www.realdao.cn/index.php?m=about&a=index&id=20.

_____ and Hua Shangbao 华商报 2010. "Cishan shi zongjiao lishen zhi ben" 慈善是宗教立身之本. *Baoyi daoren de boke* 抱一道人的博客, February 9http://blog.sina.com.cn/s/blog_4efca68b0100ix75.html.

_____ and Li Fenrong 李粉荣. 2009. "Yangsheng jiushi ren zhi shenxin yu ziran de hexie tongyi: 2009 Lishan wendao xilie huodong zhi Sandao yu yangsheng jiangzuo zuori kaijiang" 養生就是人之身心与自然的和谐统一: 2009 骊山 问道系列活动之三'道与养生讲座'昨日开讲. *Huasheng bao*, June 24. http://hsb.hsw.cn/2009-06/24/content_7365265.htm.

Liu Xiao 刘潇. 2013. "Ziyang daojiao wenhua luyou yangsheng gu xiangmu jianshe qidong gongzuohui zhaokai" 紫阳道教文化旅游养生谷项目建设启动 工作会召开. *Ziyang renmin zhengfu* 紫陽人民政府, August 29. http://www.ziyangxian.gov.cn/news/jinri/2013/0830/15892.html.

Liu, Xun. 2009. *Daoist Modern: Innovation, Lay Practice, and the Community of Inner Alchemy in Republican Shanghai.* Cambridge, Mass.: Harvard University Asia Center.

Liu Zhikun 刘至堃. 2009. "Zhangliang miao kaiguang da dian" 张良庙开光大典. *Liuzhikun* 刘至堃, April 20. http://liuzhikun1980.blog.163.com/blog/static/87409572200943155288/.

Lu Liqi 陆理麒. 2013. "Hanzhongshi daojiao xiehui dierci daibaio hui shengli zhaokai" 汉中市道教协会第二次代表大会胜利召开. *Daojiao zhiyin* 道教知音, January 22. http://www.daoisms.org/article/sort028/info-8138.html.

Lu, Kuan-yü. 1970. *Taoist Yoga: Alchemy and Immortality.* London: Rider.

Ma Linyan. 马琳燕. 2014. "Shaanxi Ziyang bei wusheng huiguan bihua baohu xiufu xiangmu" 陕西紫阳北五省会馆壁画保护修复项目. *Zhongguo wenwu bao* 中国文物报, September 19. http://eng.oversea.cnki.net/Kcms/detail/detail.aspx?filename=CWWB201409190080&dbcode=CCND&dbname=CCNDTEMP.

Major, John S., Sarah A. Queen, Andrew S. Meyer, and Harold D. Roth. 2010. *The Huainanzi: A Guide to the Theory and Practice of Government in Early Han China.* New York: Columbia University Press.

Maoshan 茅山. 2014a. "Xinjiapo daojiao Xue yuan lilin Maoshan Qianyuan guan tidao" 新加坡道教学院学员莅临茅山乾元观体道. *Changzhou daojiao* 常州道教, August 27. http://www.czdj.org/plus/view.php?aid=305.

_____. 2014b. *Maoshan Qianyuan guan* 茅山乾元观. http://www.msqyg.com/.

Mi Jingzi 米晶子. 2012. *Qiben yuanliu* 炁体源流. 2 vols. Shenzhen: Shenzhen baoye jituan chubanshe.

_____. 2013. *Babu jingang gong* 八部金刚功. Shenzhen: Shenzhen baoye jituan chubanshe.

Min Zhiting 閔智亭. 1990. *Daojiao yifan* 道教儀範. Beijing: Zhongguo daojiao xueyuan.

_____. 2000. *Xuanmen risong zaowan gongke jing zhu* 玄門日诵早晚功课经注. Beijing: Zongjiao wenhua chubanshe.

Mozias, Ilia. 2020. *The Literati Path to Immortality: The Alchemical Teachings of Lu Xixing*. St. Petersburg, Fla.: Three Pines Press.

Mu Mu 木木. 2012. "Shundao erwei zizai xiuxing: Fang Ziyang xian Ziyun gong Lao daozhang feng xingzhao" 顺道而为自在修行：访紫阳县紫云宫老道长冯兴钊. *Xuanmen daowu zhazhi* 玄门道语杂志, 2012. http://blog.sina.com.cn/s/blog_659461ef01018dr3.html.

Neswald, Sara Elaine. 2009. "Internal Landscapes." In *Internal Alchemy: Self, Society, and the Quest for Immortality*, edited by Livia Kohn and Robin R. Wang, 27-53. Magdalena, NM: Three Pines Press.

Palmer, David A. 2006. "Review of Adeline Herrou, *La Vie entre soi. Les moines taoïstes aujourd'hui en Chine*." *China Perspectives* 63.

_____. 2007. *Qigong Fever: Body, Science and Utopia in China*. New York: Columbia University Press.

_____. 2013. "Globalizing Daoism at Huashan: Quanzhen Monks, Danwei Politics, and International Dream Trippers." In *Quanzhen Daoists in Chinese Society and Culture, 1500-2010*, edited by Vincent Goossaert and Xun Liu. Berkeley: University of California Press, 2013.

_____, and Xun Liu, eds. 2012. *Daoism in the Twentieth Century: Between Eternity and Modernity*. Berkeley: University of California Press.

Pan, Yue. 2001. "Marxist Notion of Religion Must Catch up with Time." *Huaxia Times*, December 15.

Paynter, Joshua M., Ross Rosen, and Jack D. Schaefer. 2020. *Daoist Morning and Evening Altar Recitations*. New York: Parting Clouds Daoist Press.

Pew. 2024. "10 things to know about China's policies on religion." https://www.pewresearch.org/short-reads/2023/10/23/10-things-to-know-about-chinas-policies-on-religion.

Phillips, Scott. Park. 2019. "The Zhang Sanfeng Conundrum: Taijiquan as Enlightenment Theater." *Journal of Daoist Studies* 12:96-122.

Porter, Bill. 1993. *The Road to Heaven: Encounters with Chinese Hermits*. San Francisco: Mercury House.

Qingyang gong 成都青羊宫. 2014. "Qingyang gong Laozhuang shuyuan de pindao" 青羊宫老庄书院的频道. *Youku* 优酷 2014. http://i.youku.com/u/UMzI5NzI2OTcy.

_____. 2010. "Qingyang gong laozhuang shuyuan yi yu 2010 nian 4 yue 22 ri duiwai kaifang" 青羊宫老庄书院已于 2010 年 4 月 22 日对外开放. *Qingyang gong ba* 青羊宫吧, April 22. http://tieba.baidu.com/p/863754240.

Redman, Alan. 1996. "About the British Taoist Association." http://www.taoists.co.uk/main_files/aboutus.htm.

_____. 1997a. "The Dragon's Mouth." http://www.taoists.co.uk/main_files/dragonsmouth.htm.

_____. 1997b. "Interview with Gia Fu Feng. *The Dragons's Mouth.*

Ren Farong 任法融. 2013a. "Fahui zongjiao zheng nengliang xieshou gongyuan Zhongguo meng" 发挥宗教正能量携手共圆中国梦. *Guojia zongjiao shiwuju* 国家宗教事务局. http://www.sara.gov.cn/xwzx/xwjj/20223.htm.

_____. 2013b. "Huakai youshi yuanmeng youqi" 花开有时圆梦有期. *Zhongguo zongjia* 中国宗教 4.

Ren Zongquan 任宗權. 2006. "Guanjin keyi 冠+巾科仪. In *Daojiao keyi gailan* 道教科仪概览, 234-40. Beijing: Zongjiao wenhua chubanshe.

_____. 2011. "Xinmao tan Huashan Quanzhen gaogong bozhi midian ji guanjin da fahui zai Huashan Yuquan guan jiangzhong juxing" '辛卯坛华山全真高功拨 职秘典暨冠巾大法会'在华山玉泉院隆重举行. *Daojiao zhiyin* 道教之音, June 10. http://www.daoisms.org/article/sort028/info-3318.html.

_____. 2015. "Shanyou qingjun de pindao" 山幽清君的频道. *Youku* 优酷, June 23. http://i.youku.com/u/UMjMyOTkyMjUy.

Robinet, Isabelle. 1989. "Original Contributions of *Neidan* to Taoism and Chinese Thought." In *Taoist Meditation and Longevity Techniques*, edited by Livia Kohn, 297-330. Ann Arbor: University of Michigan, Center for Chinese Studies,

SARA [State Administration of Religious Affairs]. 2014. "Guoji daojiao luntan" 国际道教论坛. November 25. http://www.sara.gov.cn/ztzz/gjdjlt/index.htm.

Schipper, Kristofer M., and Franciscus Verellen, eds. 2004. *The Taoist Canon: A Historical Companion to the Daozang.* Chicago: University of Chicago Press.

Seidel, Anna. 1970. "A Taoist Immortal of the Ming Dynasty: Chang San-feng." *Self and Society in Ming Thought*, edited by Wm. Th. DeBary, 483-531. New York: Columbia University Press.

Shaanxi dianshi tai 陕西电视台, and Meng Ye 梦野. 2008. "Sichuan, wo bu wangji ni" 四川，我不能忘记你. *Mengye de boke* 梦野的博客, June 6. http://blog.sina.com.cn/s/blog_4dd043f201009m8n.html.

Shaanxi sheng daojiao xiehui 陕西省道教协会. 2015. *Xuanmen daojao zhazhi* 玄门道语杂志. http://blog.sina.com.cn/xuanmendaoyu.

162 / Bibliography

_____ and Jin Mao 金苗. 2012. "Shaanxi daojiao 2012 nian xuanmen jingjing zai Xianyang Zhongwu tai daoguan juxing" 陕西道教 2012 年玄门讲经在咸阳中 五台道观举行. *Daojiao zhiyin* 道教之音, July 4. http://www.daoisms.org/ article/ sort028/info-7040.html.

_____ and Wang Yu 王宇. 2013. "Shaanxisheng daojiao disanjie xuanmen jiangjing shannan xunjiang huodong yuanmen jieshu" 陕西省道教第三届玄门讲经 陕南巡讲活动圆满结束. *Daojiao zhiyin* 道教之音, August 17. http://www. daoisms.org/article/sort028/info-9459.html.

_____ and Wei Wei 魏 伟. 2010. "Shaanxisheng juban daojiao xuanmen jiangjing Huashan jiantan" 陕西省举办道教玄门讲经华山讲坛. *Daojiao zhiyin* 道教知音, November 25. http://www.daoisms.org/article/sort028/info-2067.html.

Shaanxi sheng zongjiao shiwu ju 陕西省宗教事务局. 2009. "Shaanxisheng daojiao jiben qingkuang" 陕西省道教基本情况. *Shaanxi sheng minzu shiwu weiyuan hui* 陕西省民族事务委员会, December 14. http://www.sxmzzj.gov.cn/ newstyle /pub_newsshow.asp?id=29003563&chid=100228.

Shidao 世道. 2005. "An Interview with Shi Jing," *The Dragon's Mouth.*

Shijie daoxue 世界道学. 2013. "2013 Lishan wendao huodong zai Xi'an Lingtong mingsheng gong juxing" 2013'骊山问道活动在西安临潼明圣宫举行. *Shijie daoxue wang* 世界道学网, August 18. http://www.worlddao.com/?p=1348.

Smith, Peter. 2001. "An Interview with Huang Shizhen. *The Dragons's Mouth.*

_____. 2013. "Recognising the Path an Interview with Shi Dao. *The Dragons's Mouth.*

Songshan Zhongyue miao 嵩山中岳庙供稿. 2013. "Zhi shengwang zhi daohang yiguan wenming Songshan Zhongyue miao juban di shijie guanjin fahui" 知圣王之道行衣冠文明—嵩山中岳庙举办第十届冠巾法会. *Daojiao zhiyin* 道教之音, December 22. http://www.daoisms.org/article/sort028/info-10294.html.

Song Xiaolong 宋小龙. 2013. "Song Xiaolong zuo shanshiren xing shanshi chuan shanfa yixiao weixian" 宋小龙： 做善事人行善事传善法以孝为先. *Daojiao zhiyin* 道教之音, September 11. http://www.daoisms.org/article/sort025/info-9544.html.

State Council. 1997. "Freedom of Religious Belief in China." *Law of China,* http://www.lawinfochina.com/display.aspx?lib=dbref&id=15&EncodingName= big5.

Stein, Stephan. 1999. *Zwischen Heil und Heilung: Zur frühen Tradition des Yangsheng in China.* Uelzen: Medizinisch-Literarische Verlagsgesellschaft.

Theaker, Hannah. 2024. "China's Sinicisation Campaign Puts Islamic Expression on the Line." https://eastasiaforum.org/2024/05/13/chinas-sinicisation-campaign-puts-islamic-expression-on-the-line.

Tibet. 2024. "2024 Two Sessions Show China will Continue Plans to Sinicize Tibet." https://tibet.net/2024-two-sessions-show-china-will-continue-plans-to-sinicize-tibet.

TUM [Technische Universität München]. 2014. "Lehrstuhl für Restaurierung, Kunst-technologie und Konservierungswissenschaft" 紫阳北五省会馆. http://www. rkk.ar.tum.de/index.php?id=250.

USCIRF [US Commission on International Religious Freedom]. 2024. "Annual Report 2024: China." https://www.uscirf.gov/sites/default/files/2024-05/China. pdf.

Valussi, Elena. 2008. "*Daozang jinghua*." In *Encyclopedia of Taoism*, edited by Fabrizio Pregadio. London: Routledge.

Vervoorn, Aat Emile. 1990. *Men of the Cliffs and Caves: The Development of the Chinese Eremitic Tradition to the End of the Han Dynasty*. Hong Kong: Chinese University Press.

Wang Chi 王驰. 2014. "Shanghai shi daojiao xiehui dier qi Changxuan jiang daoban qigao" 上海市道教协会第二期畅玄讲道班启告. *Shanghai daojiao* 上海道教. http://www.shtaoism.com/news.asp?id=890.

Wan Jingyuan 万景元. 2014. "Daijiao qiyuan yu shenme shihou" 道教起源于什么 时候？. 新浪博客. *Qingqiu daoren de boke* 青丘道人的博客, December 9. http://blog.sina.com.cn/s/blog_485ee7470102vv6q.html.

Wang Jianting 王建廷 and Fu Gengshi 傅庚时. 1996. "Taibao wuxong juanzi 100 wan yuan xiujian yingdeng yiliao dalou" 台胞颜武雄捐资 100 万元修建映登医疗 大楼. *Shuxue tushu guan* 数字图书馆. http://lib.cnki.net/cyfd/N200604075 3002425.html.

Wang Ka 王卡. 2011. "Daojiao fazhan de xin qixiang yu xin jiyu" 道教发展的新气 象与新机遇. *Daojiao zhiyin* 道教之音, September 5. http://www.daoisms.org/article/zatan/info-3788.html.

Wang Renhe 王仁和. 2014. "Longhu shan jiang zhutui daojjiao yangsheng you" 龙虎山将主推道教养生游. *Daojiao zhiyin* 道教之音, March 19. http://www.daoisms.org/article/sorto28/info-11346.html.

Wang, Robin R. 2009. "To Become a Female Daoist Master: Kundao in Training." In *Internal Alchemy: Self, Society, and the Quest for Immortality*, edited by Livia Kohn and Robin R. Wang, 165-80. Magdalena, NM: Three Pines Press.

Wang Xiping 王西平. 1989. *Daojiao yangsheng gongfa jiyao* 道家养生功法集要. Xi'an: Shaanxi kexue jishu chubanshe.

Wang Zhi'an 黄至安. 2014. "Ningxin juli Zhongguo meng Hunan daojiao pu Huazhang: Hunan sheng daojiao xiehui diwu jie lishi hui gongzuo baogao" 凝心聚力中国梦湖南道谱华章:湖南省道教协会第五届理事会工作报告. *Hunan daojiao xiehui* 湖南省道教协会, September 22. http://www.hunandj.com/zzjg/40/2014922173153.htm.

## 164 / Bibliography

Wang Zhihe, He Huili, and Fan Meijjun. 2014. "The Ecological Civilization Debate in China: The Role of Ecological Marxism and Constructive Postmodernism— Beyond the Predicament of Legislation." *Monthly Review* 66.6. https://monthlyreview.org/2014/11/01/the-ecological-civilization-debate-in-china/.

Wang Zuoan 王作安. 2011. "Zhichi daojiao jie kaizhan xuanmen jiangjing huodong: Zai disan jie xuanmen jiangjing ji Zhongyue lundao shang de zhici" 支持道教界开展玄门讲经活动—在第三届玄门讲经暨中岳论道上的致辞. *Guojia zongjiao shiwu ju* 国家宗教事务局, November 17. http://www.sara.gov.cn/ldxx/wza/ldjh/11379.htm.

Ware, James R. 1966. *Alchemy, Medicine and Religion in the China of AD 320*. Cambridge, Mass.: MIT Press.

Watson, Burton. 1968. *The Complete Works of Chuang-tzu*. New York: Columbia University Press.

Wong, Eva. 1992. *Cultivating Stillness: A Taoist Manual for Transforming Body and Mind*. Boston: Shambhala.

Wong, Shiu Hon. 1982. *Investigations into the Authenticity of the Chang San-feng ch'uan-chi*. Canberra: Australian National University Press.

Wu, Baolin, and Michael McBride. 2020. *The Soul of Taiji: Zhang Sanfeng-Wu Baolin Taijiquan*. St. Petersburg, Fla.: Three Pines Press.

Wuhan 武汉. 2014a. "Changchun guan daoxue jiangtang disan jiang jinri kaijiang shi you Zhongguo daojiao xiehui fuhui zhang Zhang Jiyu zhujiang xiuxin yi tidao" 长春观道学讲堂第三讲今日开讲！是由中国道教协会副会长张继禹主讲《修心以体道》. *Wuhan Changchun guan* 武汉长春观, September 12. http://www.whccg.com/news/bencandy.php?&fid=11&id=1881.

———. 2014b. "Changchun guan daoxue jiangtang jianshi" 长春观道学讲堂简介. *Wuhan Changchun guan* 武汉长春观. http://www.whccg.com/news/bencandy.php?&fid=48&id=1918.

———. 2014c. "Shoujie daxue sheng xialing ying zai Changchung guguan lakai weimu" 首届大学生夏令营在长春古观拉开帷幕. *Wuhan Changchun guan* 武汉长春观, 2014. http://www.whccg.com/news/bencandy.php?fid=1 1&id=1860.

———. 2014d. "Wuhan Changchun guan daoxue jiantang jiangzhong kaijiang" 武汉长春观道学讲堂隆重开讲！. *Wuhan Changchun guan* 武汉长春观, July 23. http://www.whccg.com/news/bencandy.php?&fid=11&id=1864.

——— and Gu Chenghua 刘固盛. 2014. "Daoxue jiangtang disi jiangkai jiangle 道学讲堂第四讲开讲了. *Wuhan Changchun guan* 武汉长春观, November 1. http://www.whccg.com/news/bencandy.php?&fid=10&id=1924.

——— and Zhang Jiyu 张继禹. 2014. "Zhang Jiyu: Xiuxin yi tidao" 张继禹：修心以体道. *Daojiao zhiyin* 道教知音, October 9. http://www.daoisms.org/article/sort025/info-13561.html.

Wu, Jiao. 2007. "Religious Believers Thrice the Estimate. *China Daily*, February 7. http://www.chinadaily.com.cn/china/2007-02/07/content_802994.htm.

Xi'an Chenghuang miao 西安城隍庙. 2013. "Xi'an shidu Chenghuang miao juxing xiufu kaifang bing juxing shenxiang kaiguang dadian" 西安都城隍庙举行 修复开放并举行神像开光大典. *Daojiao zhiyin* 道教之音, October 20. http://www.daoisms.org/article/sort028/info-9789.html.

———. 2014. "Xi'an shidu Chenghuang miao de weibo" 西安市都城隍庙的微博. http://www.weibo.com/xapct?from=page_100505_profile&wvr=6&mod=like.

Xiao Tianshi 蕭天石. 1974. *Daohai xuanwei* 道海玄微. Taipei: Ziyou chubanshe.

———. 2007 [1963]. *Daojia yangsheng xue gaiyao* 道家养生学概要. Beijing: Huaxia chubanshe.

Xi Jinping 习近平. 2014. "Xi Jinping tan shengtai wenming" 习近平谈生态文明. *Renmin wang* 人民网, August 29. http://cpc.people.com.cn/n/2014/0829/c164113-25567379-2.html.

Xinhua. 2007. "International Forum on *Daode jing* Winds Down. *Zhongguo wang* 中国网, April 27. http://www.china.org.cn/english/news/209384.htm.

Xu Caijin 徐才金. 2014. "Disanjie guoji daojiao luntan Qifu fahui qishou wen" 第三届国际道教论坛祈福法会祈祷文. 道教之音, November 25. http://www.daoisms.org/article/zatan/info-14033.html.

Xu Haichang 许海昌. 2014. "Ziyang daojiao gaoren feng xingzhao" 紫阳道教高人 冯兴钊. *Zhongguo daojiao nanzong wenhua wang* 中国道教南宗文化网, March 25. http://www.djnzw.cn/a//2014/0319/122.html.

Xu Shangshu 许尚枢. 2013. "Fu quanguo weiyi daohao mingming de Ziyang xian kaocha jilue" 赴全国唯一以道号命名的紫阳县考察纪略. *Daojiao zhiyin* 道教知音, April 16. http://www.daoism.org/article/sort028/info-8604.html.

Yang, Fenggang. 2024. "Xi Jinping Is Not Trying to Make Christianity More Chinese."https://www.christianitytoday.com/ct/2024/january-web-only/china-christianity-xi-religion-policy-sinicization.html/.

———, and Anning Hu. 2012. "Mapping Chinese Folk Religion in Mainland China and Taiwan." *Journal for the Scientific Study of Religion* 51.3:505-21.

Yang Xinran 杨信然. 2014. "Shoujie quanguo dao wenhua qingnian xialing ying jiang zai sida daochang tongqi juxing" 首届全国道文化青年夏令营将在 四大道场同期举行. *Daojiao zhiyin* 道教知音, May 13. http://www.daoisms.org/article/sort028/info-12012.html.

Yichun Renmin Zhengfu 宜春人民政府. 2014. "Zongtouzi 10 yi yuan de dongbai yuan daojiao yangsheng gu xiangmu luohu suijing" 总投资 10 亿元的东白源 道教养生谷项目落户靖安. *Daojiao zhiyin* 道教之音, May 16. http://www.daoisms.org/article/sort012/info-12045.html.

## 166 / Bibliography

Yin Zhihua 尹志華. 2008. "2008 Zhongguo Laoshan lundao ji shoujie xuanmen jiangjing huodong zai Qingdao Laoshan Taiqing gong juban" 2008 中国崂山论道暨首届玄门讲经活动在青岛崂山太清宫举办. *Zhongguo daojiao* 中国道教 5.

Yuan Zhihong 袁志鸿. 2000. "Ji Zhongguo daojiao xiehui disansi jie huizhang Li Yuhang daozhang" 记中国道教协会第三,四届会长黎遇航道长. In *Dangdai daojiao renwu* 当代道教人物, 38-66. Beijing: Huawen chubanshe.

Zhang Hui. 2014a. "3rd International Taoist Forum Begins." *Zhongguo wang* 中国网, November 25. http://www.china.org.cn/china/2014-11/25/content_34147111.htm.

_____. 2014b. "Dazzling Outdoor Show Promotes Taoist Culture." *Zhongguo wang* 中国网, November 26. http://www.china.org.cn/arts/2014-11/26/content_34156845.htm.

Zhang Jiyu 张继禹. 1998. *Daofa ziran yu huanjing baohu: jian lun daojiao jishi guisheng sixiang* 道法自然与环境保护:兼论道教济世贵生思想. Beijing: Huaxia chubanshe.

_____. 2014. "Daojiao xiehui fuhui zhang Zhang Jiyu zhici" 道教协会副会长张继禹致辞. *Taishang*, November 25. http://www.taishang9.com/news/5386.html.

Zhang Minggui 张明贵. 2009. "Mingdao: Zhang Minggui 名道: 张明贵. *Baiyun shan* 白云山. http://www.bysdg.com/bys/byzs/2009/0712/225.html.

_____ 2010. *Baiyunshan daojiao yinyue* 白云山道教音乐. Xi'an: Shaanxi luyou chubanshe.

Zhang Rui. 2011. "China Promoting Taoism's Influence Abroad CCTV News. *CCTV English*. http://english.cntv.cn/20111024/101803.shtml.

Zhang Weiwen 章伟文. 2014. "Dangdai zhuming daojiao xuezhe li yangzheng xiansheng jilu"e 当代著名道教学者李养正先生记略. Zhongguo daojiao xiehui 中國道教協會. http://www.taoist.org.cn/showInfoContent.do?id=369&p=.

Zhang Xingfa 张兴发 and Wang Zhiyi 王哲一. 2014. *Daojiao yangsheng fangfa jingcui* 道教养生方法精粹. Beijing: Zhongyi gujian chubanshe.

Zhang Zhishun 张至顺. 2014. "Hainan yuchan gong fangzhang Zhang Zhishun daozhang" 海南玉蟾宫方丈张至顺道长. *Hainan Yuchan gong* 海南玉蟾宫. http://yuchangong.com/yuchangong/daozhang/315.shtml.

Zhangliang miao guanwei hui 张良庙管委会. 2013. "Zhangliang miao juban Zhang Liang zushi shengdan qigu fahui" 张良庙举办张良祖师圣诞祈福法会. *Daojiao zhiyin* 道教之音, May 4. http://www.daoisms.org/article/sort028/info-8575.html.

Zhao Peng 赵芃. 2014. "Diliujie xuanmen jiangjing ji Dongyue lundao dianping zongjie" 第六届玄门讲经暨东岳论道点评总结. *Bixiaci*, September 5. http://www.bixiaci.org/newsfile/bxc_new627.html.

Zhao, Taotao, and James Leibold. 2019. "Ethnic Governance under Xi Jinping: The Centrality of the United Front Work Department and Its Implications." *Journal of Contemporary China* 29.124: 487-502.

Zhao Xuechen 赵雪晨. 2014. "Disanjie guoji daojiao luntan jiang zai Jiangxi jingtan Longhu shan juxing" 第三届国际道教论坛将在江西鹰潭龙虎山举办. *Guojia zongjiao shiwuju* 国家宗教事务局, September 12. http://www.sara.gov.cn/mtjj/157424.htm.

Zhao, Zhangyong. 2023. "New Campaign for 'Sinicization of Buddhism' Starts in China." https://bitterwinter.org/new-campaign-for-sinicization-of-buddhism-starts-in-china/?gad_source=1.

Zhongguo huanjing 中国环境. 2013. "Di sijie chuantong wenhua yu shengtai wenming guoji yanjiuhui jianzhong zhaokai" 第四届传统文化与生态文明 国际研讨会隆重召开. *Daojiao zhiyin* 道教之音, October 19. http://www.daoisms.org/article/sort028/info-9739.html.

_____. 2014. "Diwujie chuantong wenhua yu shengtai wenming guoji yanjiuhui zai Jinan juxing 第五届传统文化与生态文明国际研讨会在济南举行. *Daojiao zhiyin* 道教之音, October 18. http://www.daoisms.org/article/sort028/info-13627.html.

Zhongguo wang 中国网. 2007a. "Guoji *Daode jing* luntan" 國際道德經論壇. http://www.china.com.cn/aboutchina/zhuanti/gjddjlt/node_7017047.htm.

_____. 2007b. "The Way to Harmony: International Forum on the *Daode jing*. *Zhongguo wang* 中国网, April 22. http://www.china.org.cn/english/daodejing forum/207901.htm.

_____. 2014. "Xingdao lide jishi liren disanjie guoji daojiao luntan" 行道立德济世 利人—第三届国际道教论坛. *Zhongguo wang* 中国网, November 25. http://cppcc.china.com.cn/node_7216874.htm.

Zhong Xueman 钟学满. 2011. "Tuxian daojiao wenhua youshi dazao zhongghua yangsheng fudi" 凸显道教文化优势 打造中华养生福地. *Daojiao zhiyin* 道教 之音, August 25. http://www.daoisms.org/article/sort028/info-2055.html.

Zhuo Xinping. 2014. "Religion in Contemporary China: Resurgence and Challenge." Paper presented at the Religion in Contemporary China: Resurgence and Challenge, University of California, San Diego. http://chinafocus.us/2014/11/19/religion-contemporary-china-challenge-hope-title-sure-title-event/.

Ziyang daojiao xiehui 紫阳道教协会. 2014. "Ziyang xuanyan" 紫阳宣言. *Zhongguo daojiao xiehui* 中国道教协会, April 18. http://www.taoist.org.cn/showInfo Content.do?id=811&p=%27p%27.

Ziyang fazhan 紫阳发展. 2014. "Ziyangxian yanjiang chanye jingji dai zhongdian jianshe xiangmu guihua biao (2014)" 紫阳县沿江产业经济带重点建设项目 规划表（2014 年). *Ziyangxian fazhan he gaigeju* 紫阳县发展和改革局, May 17http://www.zyfgj.gov.cn/zcfg/2014/07/28/267.html.

Ziyang haoping 紫阳蒿坪. 2013a. "Fuzianzhang gu xueyong dao wo zhen jiancha zhidao xianyuesi huifu chongjian gongzuo" 副县长贾学勇到我镇检查指导 显月寺恢复重建工作. *Ziyangxian haoping renmin zhengfu* 紫阳县蒿坪人民 政府, April 25. http://www.zyhp.gov.cn/Article/ShowArticle.asp?Article ID=733.

———. 2013b. "Ziyang xian xianyuesi huifu chongjian gongcheng kaigong" 紫阳县显月寺恢复重建工程开工. *Ziyang xian haoping renmin zhengfu* 紫阳县蒿坪人民政府, August 29. http://www.zyhp.gov.cn/Article/ShowArticle.asp?ArticleID=807.

Ziyang renmin 紫阳人民. 2014a. "Ziyang daojiao wenhua luyou yangsheng gu xiangmu kaigong jianshe" 紫阳道教文化旅游养生谷项目开工建设. *Ziyangxian renmin zhengfu* 紫阳县人民政府, April 18. http://www.ziyangxian.gov.cn/news/jinri/2014/0420/19663.html.

———. 2014b. "Ziyang gaikuang /lishi yange" 紫阳概况 / 历史沿革. *Ziyangxian renmin zhengfu* 紫阳县人民政府. http://www.ziyangxian.gov.cn/plus/list.php?tid=242.

———. 2014c "Ziyang Wenbis han jingqu chengwei guojiao 3A ji luyou jingqu" 紫阳文笔山景区成为国家 3A 级旅游景区. January 28. http://www.ziyangxian.gov.cn/news/jinri/2014/0128/18489.html.

# Index

academia, 4-5, 11-12, 16, 54, 91, 94-97, 99-102, 117, 126, 128

academics, 53, 54, 94, 95, 96, 98, 99, 101, 102, 110, 112, 114, 117, 118, 121, 127

adaptation, of Daoism, 2, 10, 16, 90, 103, 107

administration, of religion, 4, 16, 17, 18, 60, 74, 80, 126, 128

All-China Federation of Industry and Commerce, 126

ancestors, 23, 30, 31, 36, 64, 67

Ankang, 58, 66, 68, 71, 77, 82, 97

ARC, 109-13, 118

architecture, regulations of, 126, 128

Association of Asian Studies, 85

Baiyun guan, 17, 18-19, 22, 35-36, 43, 54-55, 62-63, 66, 76, 86, 103-04, 108, 132-38, 143

*Bamboo Laozi*, 116

*Baopuzi neipian*, 45

Baoyi daoren, 108

Barreno, Jose, 86

Baxian gong, 20, 38, 39, 62-63, 66, 76-78, 84, 86, 136, 137, 142-43

Beijing, 17, 18, 19, 63, 66, 78, 80, 84, 92, 99, 103-04, 108, 112, 118, 121, 134, 143,

Beiqing tan, 78

Biyun'an, 38

Bokenkamp, Stephen, 118

breathing, 43, 44, 45, 46, 48, 49, 51, 53

Buddhism, 6, 11-12, 16, 24-25, 45-46, 71-73, 95, 114, 128, 130

Bureau of Daoist Registration, 17

*Cantong qi*, 51

CDA, see Daoist Association, Chinese

Celestial Master, 18

Celestial Worthy, 6

censorship, 16, 127, 128

Center on Contemporary China, 12

Central Committee, 118, 126

Centre for Studies of Daoist Culture, 19, 92

Centre for the Study of Daoism, 94

Changchun guan, 22, 98, 107

Changsha, 19, 45, 99

Chen Guying, 118

Chen Jingzhan, 96, 97, 98

Chen Qigang, 121

Chen Weiya, 121

Chen Xinghui, 66, 142

Chen Xinglin, 66, 142

Chen Xinzhong, 65, 142

Chen Yingning, 19, 52

Chen Yukun, 17

Cheng Shiyin, 71

Chengdu, 104

Chenghuang miao, *see* City God Temple

Chiesa Taoista d'Italia, 84

China Buddhist Association, 128

China Dream, 11, 13, 115, 116, 119, 120, 124, 125

*China Religion Journal*, 94

China Religious Culture Communication Association, 117, 118

China Society of Environmental Sciences, 112

Chinese Academy of Social Sciences, 12, 94

Chinese Communist Party, 11, 14, 113-19, 124-29, 134-35

Chinese Traditional Culture Channel, 108

Chongyang gong, 63, 130

*Chongyang lijiao shiwu lun*, 8, 55

*Chongyang zhenren jinguan yusuo jue*, 8

Christianity, 12-13, 16-17, 125

*Chuzhen jie*, 8, 52

Cihang daoren, 72

City God Temple, 67, 79, 81, 94, 97, 103, 108, 136, 143

clerics, 2-5, 9, 10-11, 22-23, 32-33, 39, 55, 58, 64, 66-67, 70, 76, 81, 83, 87-103, 107-08, 111, 118, 135, 137, 143

cloud wandering, 3, 9, 39, 66, 67, 76, 107, 136, 142

170 / Index

communism, 5, 11, 13, 18, 19, 99, 102, 126, 134, 126
competitions, 97, 98, 100
completion, levels of, 30-32
Comprehensive Daoist Assembly, 18
conferences, 2, 4, 12, 76, 91-95, 101, 106, 108, 114-16, 119, 130, 135, 137
Confucianism, 45, 46, 71, 114
control, of religion, 9, 16, 17, 45, 46, 126, 129, 134
cost, of projects , 70, 71, 78, 79, 81, 82, 105, 121
Cultural Revolution, 1, 5, 9, 10, 12, 19, 42, 55, 65, 71, 73, 77, 87, 91-93, 103, 126, 133, 135-39, 142
culture, and Daoism, 5, 10-13, 16, 36, 40, 45, 54, 67, 72, 82, 87, 91-95, 98-99, 103, 107-08, 114-20, 122-27, 129, 135-36; Western, 4-5, 9-10, 13, 84-86, 123, 134
*Dadan zhizhi*, 29, 30, 31, 32, 51
Dadao guan, 3, 108
*Danyang zhenren yulu*, 48, 50, 53
*Daode jing*, 6, 9, 38-39, 93-95, 98, 113-16, 144
Daoist Association: American, 123; Beijing, 112;British, 10, 84, 86, 89, 116, 136, 143-144; Chinese, 2-5, 10-11, 17-21, 52, 58, 63, 66, 77-85, 91-92, 95-101, 103, 105, 109-17, 119, 122-24, 129-36, 138; foreign, 122; local: 2-4, 22, 37, 40, 62, 66, 70, 86, 96-98, 105, 108, 113, 116, 119; French, 87; Guangdong, 113; Huashan, 110; Jiangsu, 110; Longhu, 116; Mexican, 86; Portuguese, 87; Shaanxi, 4, 62, 78, 84, 86, 93, 96-97, 110, 116, 136; Shandong, 101; Wudang, 138; Xi'an, 78-79, 111
Daoist Canon, 6, 7, 46, 52, 98, 102, 123
Daoist College, 19, 37, 66, 78, 80, 84, 91, 97, 99, 101, 137, 143
Daoist Culture and Management, 91, 92
Daoist Forum, 18, 2, 10, 39, 81, 93, 109, 113, 115, 116, 124

Daoist Music Festival, 103
Daoist name, 21, 22, 54, 65
Daoist Studies Center, 110
*Daojia yangsheng mizhi daolun*, 53
*Daojia yangsheng xue gaiyao*, 52
*Daojiao neidan yangsheng fa*, 123
*Daojiao yangsheng fangfa jingcui*, 122
*Daojiao yangsheng gongfa jiyao*, 53
*Daojiao zhiyin*, 4, 22, 103, 106, 108, 113
Daozang ge, 98
*Daozang jinghua*, 26, 53
*Daozang jiyao*, 7, 8, 9, 32, 34, 52
Dartmoor, 86
debates, 12, 13, 97, 100, 118
Declaration of Ecological Intent, 112
Despeux, Catherine, 25, 26, 44, 46
diamond practice, 39, 40, 41
*Diamond Sūtra*, 6
Ding Changyun, 122
donations, 10, 70, 75, 79, 88, 103, 105
Dong Zhiguang, 97
dream, transmission in, 26, 28, 33, 35, 85
dual cultivation, 24, 41
Dunnett, Hooileng, 86
Dunnett, Paul, 86
dynasties: Ming, 7-9, 17, 52, 60, 69, 73, 142; Qin, 24, 51, 78; Qing, 6, 8, 43, 52-55, 71, 73; Republic, 5, 18, 64; Six, 45; Song, 7, 43, 45, 54, 60, 88, 100; Tang, 6, 9, 45, 56, 78, 133; Three Kingdoms, 2; Yuan, 7, 19, 24
Earth Official, 61
ecology, 10, 91, 103, 109-14, 119, 124, 135
education, religious, 14-16, 19, 91-92, 98, 105, 112, 128-129
Eight Immortals, 20, 38
elixir fields, 25, 31
emptiness, 24, 26, 34, 50
encounters, transmission through, 5, 27, 29, 33, 35, 102
*Encyclopedia of Taoism*, 44
environment, 10, 36, 93-94, 101, 103, 106-09, 111-15, 124
Esposito, Monica, 7, 9

Index / 171

essence, 25, 30, 44, 47, 48, 50, 51, 53, 92, 106, 119, 122, 138
ethics, 24, 46, 55, 91, 100
Europe-Asia Economic Forum, 103
family, of Daoists, 31, 38, 40, 55, 67, 77, 84, 87, 88
Fan Guangchun, 19, 96, 99, 106, 110
Faye Wong, 121
Feng Lihe, 97
Feng Xingzhao, 1-2, 10, 15-16, 55, 62-63, 65-66, 68, 70, 77, 84-87, 92-93, 97, 100, 106-07, 131, 135-37, 141-44; *see also* Master Feng
Feng Zhongkun, 65
Feng, Gia-Fu, 85
*Fengdao kejie*, 56, 58
Fengshui, 98
Fifth International Daoist Forum, 95
fire phasing, 30, 33
First International Daoist Forum, 39, 93, 113
Five Patriarchs, 49
foreigners, 14, 16, 17, 19, 85, 89, 118, 122, 127, 134, 136, 139
Fourth International Daoist Forum, 81, 109, 124
freedom, of religion, 9, 14, 16, 31, 32
Fu Jinquan, 52
Fu Yuantian, 20
Fungying Seenkoon, 19, 18, 19, 43, 79, 92, 104, 108
*Fuqi jingyi lun*, 45
*Ganshui xianyuan lu*, 32
Gansu, 103, 112, 130
*Ganying pian*, 88, 97, 100
garb, Daoist, 23, 133
Ge Hong, 45, 51
Gexinzi, 66
God of Fire, 71
God of Wealth, 70, 72
God of Wealth,, 70
Goddess of Mercy, 61, 70
gods, 10, 22, 23, 51, 55, 97, 100, 102
Goossaert, Vincent, 19, 3, 5, 7, 12, 23, 116
government, impact of, 1-3, 11-13, 17-21, 60, 69-74, 80, 82, 86, 92-93, 100, 103-06, 110, 113-19, 125-36, 139

government: officials, 1, 74, 100, 126
Graduate Science Institute, 53
Green Pilgrimage Network, 109
Gu Chenghua, 98
Guangchengzi, 102
Guangdong, 108, 113, 130
Guanyin, 61, 72, 81
Guanyin'ai, 70, 81-82
Guernavaca, 86
guidelines, official, 17, 88, 92, 114, 131, 139
Guo Yunjie, 108
Hainan, 38, 39
Han Chinese, 11, 125-26
Hangkou, 71
Hangu Pass, 6
Hanjiang, 58, 60, 68, 81, 82
Hanwang, 65
Hanzhong, 68, 70, 79, 80, 97, 143
Hao Datong, 49
*Hao Taigu zhenren yulu*, 49
Haoping, 73, 144
harassment, of religions, 127
harmony, as ideology, 13, 41, 49, 55, 92-95, 102, 115, 120, 129
Hassan, Tirana, 127
He Xinping, 111
healing exercises, 43, 44, 45, 46, 49, 50, 85, 107
*Heart Sūtra*, 6
Heaven of Grand Network, 6, 95
Heavenly Gate, 25, 26
Heilongjiang, 130
Henan, 86, 95
Hengkou, 66, 71, 72, 143, 144
hermits, 38, 39, 41, 136, 138
Herrou, Adeline,5
Hong Kong, 4, 7, 15, 19, 37, 43, 79, 92-94, 104, 108, 115-16, 128
Hu Jintao, 114
*Huainanzi*, 44
Huang Shizhen, 16, 10, 73, 77, 78, 84, 85, 86, 96, 130, 136, 137, 143
Huang Sishou, 65, 142
Huang Xinyang, 4, 36, 43, 49, 50, 51, 53, 55, 62, 112, 122, 123
Huang Zhijie, 122
*Huangdi neijing*, 123

172 / Index

*Huangting jing*, 51
Huaqing chi, 78
Huazhou, 38
Hunan, 19, 20, 45, 64
identity, Daoist, 5, 7, 29
ideology, Chinese, 10, 13, 19, 55, 125, 127
immortal embryo, 25, 31
immortality, 1, 25, 31-32, 43-45, 137
immortals, 7, 10, 25, 27, 29, 31, 33, 35, 56-57, 89, 92, 135
indoctrination, 127, 133
innate nature, 24, 41, 44, 49, 50
inner cultivation,41, 55, 60, 86, 137, 139
Institute of World Religions, 12, 94
internal alchemy, 2, 7, 9, 10, 24-27, 30, 35-36, 41-55, 60, 123, 137-38
internet, *see* websites
Islam,11- 12, 16, 125
Japan, 4, 118, 119
Jiang Jianyong, 118, 119
Jiang Weiqiao, 52
Jiang Yupu, 7
Jiangsu, 19, 109, 110
Jiangxi, 116, 118
*Jin'gang jing*, 6
Jinan, 4, 107
Jingyi, 2
*Jinlian zhengzong ji*, 24
journalists, 4, 108, 118
Jurong, 124
karma, 30, 36
Kerouac, Jack, 85
King of Medicines, 66, 70
Kohn, Livia, 6-9, 18, 26, 30, 43-46, 52, 55-57, 61
Komjathy, Louis, 5-8, 22-27, 29-32, 49-50, 55, 85
Lantian, 97
Lanzhou, 22, 103
Lao-Zhuang Academy, 98
Laomu dian, 78
Laozi, 6, 71, 86, 93, 116
learning, Daoist, 92, 97, 98
leaving the mountains, 38, 39
legal system, 2, 4, 5, 9, 14-16, 19-21, 78-79, 128

Leigutai, 15, 2, 55, 56, 58, 60, 61, 62, 63, 64, 65, 66, 67, 72, 74, 77, 78, 80, 84, 85, 97, 130, 135, 137, 142, 143, 144, 145, 146, Leishen, 75
Li Daoqian, 32
Li Guangfu, 138
Li Jingsong, 66
Li Xinjun, 54, 55
Li Xiyue, 52
Li Yangzheng, 5, 99
Li Yuhang, 19
life-destiny, 22, 24, 41, 49
Lin Anwu, 113
Lin Zhou, 2, 122
lineage, Daoist,3, 7, 10, 11, 15, 41, 55, 61-67, 76-78, 83-87, 91, 108, 116, 130, 135-37, 141
Lintong, 105
Lishan laomu, 78
Liu Chenghong, 64, 142
Liu Huaiyuan, 101
Liu Jinguang, 119
Liu Mingcang, 38, 40
Liu Shitian, 2, 4, 10, 16, 55, 66, 77-84, 90-94, 97-100, 103-08, 114-16, 135-37, 143-44
Liu Shouyuan, 7
Liu Xingdi, 66, 77, 78, 84, 136, 137, 142, 143
Liu Yandong, 118
Liu Yiming, 52, 54
Liu Zhikun, 80, 144
Liu Zhongyu, 113
longevity, 30, 39, 40, 41, 46, 52, 90, 92, 138
*Longmen xinfa*, 52
Longmen, 1, 18-20, 23-25, 29, 34-37, 52-55, 63-65, 84, 86, 142
Lord Lao, 102
Louchouarn, Hervé, 86
Louguantai, 6, 20, 35, 38, 62, 66, 95, 116
Lü Dongbin, 7, 27, 32, 35, 54
Lu Liqi, 97
Lu Xixing, 52
Luo Gaolian, 65, 142
Luoba, 79, 144
Luyi, 86

Index / 173

*Lüzu baogao*, 33
Ma Bin, 118
Ma Yu, 48, 50
Macao Daoist Festival, 103
Malaysia, 119
Mao Zedong, 129
Maomao, 75, 88
Marxism, 13, 128
Maslow, Abraham, 85
Master Feng, 1, 10, 55, 62, 64, 66-76,
    84-89, 106, 136-37
Master Yinshi, 52
masters, Daoist, 2-10, 19, 22-23, 26,
    30-36, 39-40, 45-50, 52-55, 64, 67,
    83, 87-89, 91, 93, 97, 102, 107, 122,
    134, 137-141
Mawangdui, 45
media, 10, 14, 42, 103, 107, 118, 121, 122,
    124, 126, 127, 129, 138
medicine, 44-45, 52, 54, 57, 98, 106,
    111, 122-23
meditation, 1, 2, 7, 24, 25, 29, 44, 45,
    51, 53, 55, 57, 85, 86, 106, 107, 123,
    132, 136
Mexico, 86, 119
Mi Jingzi, 39
Miaohe, 66
Min Zhiting, 20, 66, 76, 78, 136, 143
Mingsheng gong, 20, 67, 78, 79, 81,
    94, 98, 105, 107, 108, 114, 136, 143
Ministry of Rites, 17
minorities, 125, 126
*Miyu wupian*, 27
monasteries, Daoist, 1-3, 15, 21, 22,
    43, 55-58, 61-62, 91, 98-99, 116, 137
monastics, 1-11, 15, 19, 23, 36, 41, 55,
    103, 107-08, 115, 128, 130-35, 137-39
Montluçon, 87
Mount Baiyun, 63, 86, 97, 104
Mount Banjie, 38
Mount Daba, 58
Mount Fenghuang, 58, 80
Mount Hanyin, 60
Mount Hua, 105, 122
Mount Hua, 6, 22, 40, 63, 66, 95-96,
    100, 142
Mount Lao, 95

Mount Li, 20, 67, 78, 95, 98, 106, 114,
    136, 143
Mount Longhu: 10, 106, 115-17, 121,
    144; Declaration, 123; Tourism
    Group, 121
Mount Lu, 33
Mount Luofu, 113
Mount Mao, 19, 101, 104, 106, 109, 112,
    124, 134
Mount Nanyue, 2, 19, 113, 116, 144
Mount Panxi, 34
Mount Song, 22
Mount Tai, 95, 97, 100
Mount Taibai, 109-12
Mount Tiantai, 54
Mount Wenbi: 75, 81-82, 106, 109,
    136, 144, 146; Forest Park, 81
Mount Wudang, 6 v4, 67, 95, 104,
    107, 124, 130, 142
Mount Wutai, 128
Mount Yunwu, 64, 142
Mount Zhongnan, 6, 9, 38, 66
Mount Zibai, 79
music, Daoist, 10, 103-04, 114, 121, 135
musical, performance of, 91, 108, 121,
    135, 137
Nanjing, 19, 121, 124
National Competition of Scriptural
    Discussion, 100
National Conference on Religious
    Work, 125
National Conference on Work
    Related to Religious Affairs, 128
National Congress, 114, 119
National Ethnic Affairs Commission,
    126
National Youth Summer Camp on
    Daoist Culture, 107
Niwan Palace, 25
Nourishing Life and Culture Park,
    106
nourishing life, 10, 37-39, 41-54, 81-
    82, 98, 103, 106-07, 111, 114-17, 122-
    23, 135-38
nuns, Daoist, 1, 19, 130, 133, 137
Olympics. 121
orchestras, Daoist, 10, 103-04, 114, 137

174 / Index

organizations, charitable, 10, 35, 40, 9-94, 103, 105, 123, 135
Overseas Chinese Affairs Office, 126
Palmer, David, 5
Palmer, Martin, 110-13, 118
parallel verses, 33, 36
patriarchs, 5, 8, 33, 36, 37, 49, 51, 70, 138
People's Political Consultative Conference, 118
Perfect Warrior, 60, 61
Perfected Sun, 64, 142
permits, 16, 130, 134, 144
petitions, 23, 116, 120
precepts, 8, 21, 22, 23, 61, 63, 66, 88, 101, 143
precious invocations, 33, 36
priest of high merit, 22
priests, new generation of, 19, 90, 92, 100, 108, 135, 137
Prince Philip, 109, 118
public order, 14, 17
publications, 3-4, 15-17, 36, 43, 54-55, 86, 99, 100, 102, 128-29, 138
*qi*, 8, 25, 30, 32, 44-51, 56-57, 69, 106
Qianyuan guan, 101, 104
Qibao zhai, 73, 74, 75
Qin Zhi'an, 24
Qingcheng, 19, 20, 63, 66, 98, 143
Qingdao, 18
*Qinggui xuanmiao*, 9
Qinghai, 130
*Qinghe zhenren beiyou yulu*, 27
Qinghua gong, 86, 130
*Qingjing jing*, 6, 9
Qinglong guan, 80, 97
Qingsong guan, 4
Qingyang gong, 98, 104
Qinling, 2, 58, 78, 109, 112
Qiu Chuji, 1, 23, 24, 27, 34, 35, 54, 63, 64
*Quanzhen bidu*, 6, 52
*Quanzhen qinggui*, 7
Quanzhen, *passim*
Questions about Dao on Mount Li, 94, 98, 106, 137
rebuilding, 2, 10, 38, 41, 58, 62, 68, 86, 121, 143-44

reconstruction, 19, 55, 69, 73-74, 76-79, 81, 99, 130, 136, 139
Redman, Alan, 85, 86, 143
regional autonomy,, 14
Regulations of Religious Affairs, 5, 9, 14-17, 19, 58, 62, 80, 124-30, 133-34
religions, in China, 11-13, 16-17, 109, 114, 119, 125-30, 139
religious activities, 1, 9, 11, 13-19, 38, 58, 60, 64, 68-71, 74, 79-80, 129, 144
Religious Culture Press, 94
Ren Farong, 20, 80, 110
Ren Zongquan, 3, 108
Ren Zongzhe, 110
renovation, of temples, 1, 4, 55, 68, 79, 80, 81, 83, 90, 116, 127, 130, 143, 144
representatives, Daoist, 4, 13, 18, 19, 20, 97, 99, 110, 118, 122
restrictions, 5, 134
resurgence, 2, 19, 135
retribution, 30, 31, 87
revelation, 8, 29
rites: 3, 5, 20-23, 43, 66, 70, 75, 83, 88, 120-21; audience, 23; bowing to a master, 20; ceremonies, 4, 20-23, 61, 63, 70, 74-81, 86-87, 95, 105, 108, 116-22, 131, 136, 143-44; chanting, 68; Christmas, 126; festivals, 70, 72, 75, 104, 113, 126; funerals, 131; incense burning, 67, 70, 74, 76, 80, 87, 88, 89, 111, 144; initiation, 5, 20, 21, 22, 23, 78, 86, 89, 134; liturgy, 6, 33; morning and evening services, 32-33, 72, 88; Opening the Light, 87; ordination, 21, 22, 66, 76, 89, 136; Receiving the Registers, 22; refuge, 8, 22, 61, 89; worship, 7, 10, 11, 57, 61-62, 69, 71-74, 78, 87-90, 111, 121, 127, 128
robes, wearing of, 39, 127
Robinet, Isabelle, 46, 47
*Sacred Mountains*, 111
*San guiyi wujie*, 88
sanctuary, 35, 60, 70-75, 80-81, 87, 103

Sanqing dian, 60, 81
Sansheng miao, 71, 72, 86, 143, 144, 146
Santa Cruz,, 85
SARA, 4, 9, 10, 14, 15, 17, 100, 105, 109, 110, 115, 118, 119, 126
Schipper, 6, 7, 8
scriptures, 8, 9, 19, 22, 46, 50, 58, 88, 89, 90, 95, 96, 97, 101, 102, 107, 127
seclusion, 38, 41, 133
Second International Daoist Forum, 113
secrecy, 7, 24, 26-31, 33-42, 134, 137-39
self-cultivation, 5, 24, 29, 33, 34, 35, 53
Seven Perfected, 34, 35, 48, 49, 64
Shaanxi Academy of Social Sciences, 19, 94, 96, 99, 110
Shaanxi, 1-5, 15-20, 38, 53, 58, 62-68, 78-80, 84-86, 93-99, 105-06, 109-10, 131, 136, 142-43
Shandong, 4, 32, 95, 101, 107
Shanghai, 12, 18, 19, 85, 95, 101, 104
Shangluo, 97
Shannon, Bernard, 123
Shijing, 86
Shiqing, 86
Shiran, 86
Shitao, 86
Shizhi, 86
Shizi, 86
Sichuan, 19, 52, 58, 60, 63, 94, 95, 98, 99, 105
Sima Chengzhen, 45
sincerity, 32, 35, 41, 57, 76, 87, 89, 90, 97, 123
Singapore, 37, 39, 101, 104, 119
sinicization, 11, 125, 128, 129, 130, 139
Siwang miao, 75, 130, 144
Sixth National Competition, 100
Smith, Peter, 85, 86, 143
socialism, 12-13, 16, 119, 127-29
society, and religion, 5, 12, 13, 93, 99, 103, 106, 114, 120, 138
soft power, 119, 120, 124
Southern School, 54, 60, 69, 70

Specification of Daoist Professionals, 21
spirit-writing, 7, 9, 52
spread, of teachings, 39, 42, 55, 77
Standing Committee of the People's Congress, 118
State Council Information Office, 14, 126
statues, 65, 70, 73, 75, 81, 87, 144
stillness, 24, 25, 45, 51
Stillpoint (Daoist Center), 85
Sui, 45
Summer Camp on Daoist Culture, 107
Sun Media Group, 121
Sun Simiao, 45
superstition, 12, 13
surveillance, 129
Symposium on Traditional Culture and Eco-Civilization, 112
Taibai miao, 68, 143
taijiquan, 52, 53, 85, 107, 122, 123, 138
Taipei, 52, 78, 104
Taiqing gong, 18, 86
*Taishang xuanmen gongke jing*, 34
Taizipo, 64
Taizu, 17
taking the cap, 20, 61
Tan Zhenren, 64, 142
Tao Guanjing, 97
temple: cave, 68, 86; charity, 92; closure, 1, 9, 11, 65, 130-32, 139; eco, 111; functions, 10, 54-58, 67, 83, 87-90, 103-04, 134, 135; fate, 27; hereditary, 3, 10, 20-21, 54, 91, 107-08; leaders, 92; life in, 106; location of, 145-46; management, 1, 75-76, 78, 84, 86, 97, 107-08; network, 82; numbers of, 2, 19, 62, 109, 116; opening, 4, 66; paintings, 33; and politics, 128, 130-31; public, 55, 63, 79; rebuilding, 2, 10, 19, 37, 40, 55-76, 78, 80, 90, 98, 121, 136-37; regulation, 5, 15, 79; rites at, 22, 60-61, 66, 75-76, 79, 97, 101; tourism, 78-79, 90, 111-12; websites, 131; *see also* Leigutai

## 176 / Index

Ten Charitable Personalities, 105
Tencent, 108
*Tengxun daoxue,* 108
Terracotta Warriors, 78, 79
tests, and transmission, 24, 32, 76
Third International Daoist Forum,
  18, 2, 10, 113, 115
Three Officials, 23
Three Passes, 30, 31
Three Treasures, 22
Thunder Drum, 13, 2, 3, 4, 9, 10, 64,
  76, 77, 83, 84, 86, 87, 91, 93, 96,
  97, 98, 108, 115, 116, 130, 136, 141
Tianshi dong, 63
Tianshi, 18
Tiantai guan, 64, 142
*Tianxian dajie,* 9
Tibet, 11, 125-26
tomb, 45, 78, 132, 133
topknot, 21, 23, 133
tourism, 69, 79, 80, 82, 87, 90, 106,
  109, 116, 121, 136, 143
training, Daoist, 3, 8-9, 19-21, 24, 29,
  34, 41-42, 46, 55, 58, 76, 78, 84,
  86, 91-92, 97, 99, 101, 106, 126-29,
  133, 137-38, 143
transmission, 2, 7-10, 21, 24-29, 35-37,
  40-43, 64, 76, 87, 92, 95, 108, 137,
  143
trials, for transmission, 27, 33, 35, 36,
  42, 90
TV, 113, 117, 118, 124, 138
UNESCO, 103, 104, 118
United Front Work Department, 14,
  126, 128, 134
United States., 119
University: Arizona State, 118;
  Chinese of Hong Kong, 104;
  Fudan, 12; Huadong Normal, 113;
  Huazhong Normal, 4, 98;
  Nanjing, 101; National Taiwan,
  118; Northwest, 110; Peking, 4;
  People's (Renmin) 92, 107;
  Shandong Normal, 4; Taiwan
  Ciji, 113; Xiamen, 94
Uyghurs, 125-26

villages: Hanyin Puxi, 58, Hengkou,
  66, Huangjin, 73, 75, Lianhua, 68,
  Luya, 65, Miaohe, 66
Wang Changyue, 8, 63
Wang Chi, 101, 102
Wang Chongyang, 1, 6, 7, 27, 28, 32,
  55, 64, 137
Wang Lingguan, 81
Wang Linguan, 23
Wang Xiping, 53
Wang Zhiyi, 122
Wang Zhyi, 122
Wang Zuoan, 118
Watts, Alan, 85
websites: 3, 4, 10, 36, 39-42, 98-99,
  101-03, 105, 107-08, 127, 131, 138;
  Baidu, 78, 127; Bing, 127;
  Facebook, 37; WeChat, 108, 127;
  Youku, 98, 108, 138; YouTube, 39
Wei Boyang, 51
Wei Huacun, 51
*Weisheng shengli xue mingzhi,* 25
Wenchang dijun, 75, 95
Windsor Castle, 112
World Daoist Federation, 134
World Religions and Ecology
  Meeting, 112
Wu Shouyang, 52
Wu Siliang, 65, 142
*Wudao lu,* 52
Wuhan, 3, 4, 22, 98, 104, 107, 108
*Wuliang duren miaojin,* 6
Wuzhen guan, 75, 81, 82, 109, 130,
  144, 146
*Wuzhen pian,* 54, 60, 109
Xi Jinping: 11, 13, 114, 115, 119, 125;
  Thought, 125-34
Xi'an Bureau of Religious Affairs, 79
Xi'an, 20, 38, 39, 58, 66, 67, 77, 78,
  79, 84, 85, 86, 93, 97, 105, 108,
  109, 111, 115, 116, 130, 131, 136, 142,
  143, 144, 145
Xianren dong, 68, 69
Xianyue si, 73, 144
Xianyuesi, 131
Xiao Tianshi, 52, 53
Xie Xincheng, 64, 142
Xie Yangju, 110

Xie Yingdeng, 78
*Xingming fajue mingzhi*, 26
*Xingming guizhi*, 26
Xinjiang, 11
*Xinjing*, 6
*Xiudao yangsheng jue*, 43
*Xiudao yangsheng zhenjue*, 36
Xu Jialu, 118
Xuanmiao guan, 104
Xuantian guan, 60
*xunjiang tuan*, 96
Yan Wuxiong, 78
Yang Chongyi, 64, 142
Yang Faxiang, 65, 66, 67, 77, 84, 85, 142, 143
Yang Lan, 121
Yang Shihua, 110
yang spirit, 24, 26, 27
Yangsheng gu, 81, 106
*yangsheng*, 36, 37, 39, 43, 44, 54, 106; *see also* nourishing life
Yangtze, 58
*Yansheng yaoji*, 45
Yaowang dian, 66
Yaowang miao, 66, 146
Yellow Emperor, 40, 102
*Yijing*, 46, 51, 98
Yin Xi, 6
Yin Xingshu, 63, 66, 142, 143
Yin Zhiping, 27
*Yinfu jing*, 6, 95, 123
Yingtan, 116, 117, 122
Yu Zhengsheng, 118
Yuan Zhihong, 110, 111
Yuchan gong, 38
Yue Chongdai, 18
Yuhuang, 75
Yuquan yuan, 22, 62, 63, 66
*Zangwai daoshu*, 9, 26
Zhang Boduan, 54, 60, 68, 69, 75
Zhang Daoling, 102, 116
Zhang Jiyu, 98, 113, 123
Zhang Liang miao, 79, 80
Zhang Minggui, 86
Zhang Sanfeng, 52
Zhang Xianhou, 68
Zhang Xingde, 66, 93, 97, 143
Zhang Xingfa, 122

Zhang Yimou, 121
Zhang Yuanxu, 18
Zhang Zhishun, 37, 38, 39, 42, 43, 138
Zhangliang miao, 62, 79, 80
Zhao Bichen, 25, 26
Zhao Daojian, 64
Zhao Jianzheng, 110
Zhao Yizhen, 8
Zhejiang, 54, 60, 102
Zhengyi, 18, 19, 22, 98, 103, 116
Zhenren gong, 71, 75, 81, 82, 86, 88, 143, 146
Zhenwu dian, 60
Zhenwu, 60, 65, 72, 75-76, 80, 88, 97, 130, 144
Zhidao, 108
*Zhong-Lü erxian biandan yi*, 32
Zhong-Lü, 7, 24, 30, 123
*Zhongguo daojiao*, 3, 17, 36, 99, 133
*Zhonghua daoxue baiwen*, 54
*Zhongji jie*, 9
Zhongli Quan, 7, 33, 34
Zhongyue miao, 95
*Zhuangzi*, 44, 98, 113
Zhuge Liang, 2
Zhuo Xinping, 12
Zixiao gong, 104
Ziyang: county, 1-2, 15, 54, 58, 60, 64-71, 75-76, 81-86, 99, 106, 109-10, 114, 130, 136, 143-44; Culture Park, 81; Declaration, 109; zhenren, 60, 68-70, 76, 81, 143-44
Zou Tongxuan, 110